# Superconducting- and Graphene-Based Devices

# Superconducting- and Graphene-Based Devices

Editor

**Filippo Giubileo**

MDPI • Basel • Beijing • Wuhan • Barcelona • Belgrade • Manchester • Tokyo • Cluj • Tianjin

*Editor*
Filippo Giubileo
CNR-SPIN Salerno via Giovanni Paolo II 132
Italy

*Editorial Office*
MDPI
St. Alban-Anlage 66
4052 Basel, Switzerland

This is a reprint of articles from the Special Issue published online in the open access journal *Nanomaterials* (ISSN 2079-4991) (available at: https://www.mdpi.com/journal/nanomaterials/special_issues/graphene_nano).

For citation purposes, cite each article independently as indicated on the article page online and as indicated below:

LastName, A.A.; LastName, B.B.; LastName, C.C. Article Title. *Journal Name* **Year**, *Volume Number*, Page Range.

**ISBN 978-3-0365-4761-9 (Hbk)**
**ISBN 978-3-0365-4762-6 (PDF)**

© 2022 by the authors. Articles in this book are Open Access and distributed under the Creative Commons Attribution (CC BY) license, which allows users to download, copy and build upon published articles, as long as the author and publisher are properly credited, which ensures maximum dissemination and a wider impact of our publications.

The book as a whole is distributed by MDPI under the terms and conditions of the Creative Commons license CC BY-NC-ND.

# Contents

**About the Editor** .................................................... vii

**Filippo Giubileo**
Superconducting- and Graphene-Based Devices
Reprinted from: *Nanomaterials* **2022**, *12*, 2055, doi:10.3390/nano12122055 .............. 1

**Wei Qin, Wen-Cai Lu, Xu-Yan Xue, Kai-Ming Ho and Cai-Zhuang Wang**
Lithium Diffusion in Silicon Encapsulated with Graphene
Reprinted from: *Nanomaterials* **2021**, *11*, 3397, doi:10.3390/nano11123397 .............. 3

**Abid, Poonam Sehrawat, Christian M. Julien and Saikh S. Islam**
Interface Kinetics Assisted Barrier Removal in Large Area 2D-$WS_2$ Growth to Facilitate Mass Scale Device Production
Reprinted from: *Nanomaterials* **2021**, *11*, 220, doi:10.3390/nano11010220 .............. 21

**Alejandro Toral-Lopez, Enrique G. Marin, Francisco Pasadas, Jose Maria Gonzalez-Medina, Francisco G.Ruiz, David Jiménez and Andres Godoy**
GFET Asymmetric Transfer Response Analysis through Access Region Resistances
Reprinted from: *Nanomaterials* **2019**, *9*, 1027, doi:10.3390/nano9071027 .............. 39

**Jose C. Verde, Alberto S. Viz, Martín M. Botana, Carlos Montero-Orille and Manuel V. Ramallo**
Calculations of Some Doping Nanostructurations and Patterns Improving the Functionality of High-Temperature Superconductors for Bolometer Device Applications
Reprinted from: *Nanomaterials* **2020**, *10*, 97, doi:10.3390/nano10010097 .............. 51

**Paola Romano, Francesco Avitabile, Angela Nigro, Gaia Grimaldi, Antonio Leo, Lei Shu, Jian Zhang, Antonio Di Bartolomeo and Filippo Giubileo**
Transport and Point Contact Measurements on $Pr_{1-x}Ce_xPt_4Ge_{12}$ Superconducting Polycrystals
Reprinted from: *Nanomaterials* **2020**, *10*, 1810, doi:10.3390/nano10091810 .............. 71

**Carlo Barone, Hannes Rotzinger, Jan Nicolas Voss, Costantino Mauro, Yannick Schön, Alexey V. Ustinov and Sergio Pagano**
Current-Resistance Effects Inducing Nonlinear Fluctuation Mechanisms in Granular Aluminum Oxide Nanowires
Reprinted from: *Nanomaterials* **2020**, *10*, 524, doi:10.3390/nano10030524 .............. 87

**Sergio Pagano, Nadia Martucciello, Emanuele Enrico, Eugenio Monticone, Kazumasa Iida and Carlo Barone**
Iron-Based Superconducting Nanowires: Electric Transport and Voltage-Noise Properties
Reprinted from: *Nanomaterials* **2020**, *10*, 862, doi:10.3390/nano10050862 .............. 99

# About the Editor

**Filippo Giubileo**

Filippo Giubileo is a Senior Researcher working at the Institute for Superconductors, Innovative Materials and Devices (SPIN) of the Italian National Research Council (CNR) since 2004. He has a National Scientific Qualification as Full Professor in Experimental Condensed Matter Physics. He has been a member of the scientific evaluation panel for the Flag-Era Joint Transnational call on graphene basic research. His research activity deals with electrical properties of 1D and 2D materials and their application as field effect transistors, photodetectors, chemical sensors, and field emitters. His expertise includes advanced surface analysis on the nanometer scale via scanning probe microscopy/spectroscopy in high magnetic fields and variable temperatures, fabrication and characterization of superconducting heterostructures, and pairing symmetry and electronic properties in superconductors. FG is listed in the World Top 2% Scientist classification released by PlosBiology in 2021. He has published more than 100 papers in peer-reviewed journals, and he was Chair-Organizer of 6 international conferences (ISMN08, SM-2010, S4E-2014, GM-2016, TTN-2018, NANO M&D-2019). He also serves as a member of editorial board for several international journals (Nanomaterials, Nano Express, Journal of Nanomaterials, Chemosensors).

*Editorial*

# Superconducting- and Graphene-Based Devices

Filippo Giubileo

CNR-SPIN Salerno, 84084 Fisciano, Italy; filippo.giubileo@spin.cnr.it

**Citation:** Giubileo, F. Superconducting- and Graphene-Based Devices. *Nanomaterials* **2022**, *12*, 2055. https://doi.org/10.3390/nano12122055

Received: 7 June 2022
Accepted: 10 June 2022
Published: 15 June 2022

**Publisher's Note:** MDPI stays neutral with regard to jurisdictional claims in published maps and institutional affiliations.

**Copyright:** © 2022 by the author. Licensee MDPI, Basel, Switzerland. This article is an open access article distributed under the terms and conditions of the Creative Commons Attribution (CC BY) license (https://creativecommons.org/licenses/by/4.0/).

This Special Issue has been organized to collect new or improved ideas regarding the exploitation of superconducting materials, as well as graphene, aiming to develop innovative devices. For instance, several graphene applications can be enhanced by modifying their surface to introduce a non-zero bandgap, tune adhesion and/or hydrophobicity/hydrophilicity, etc. Similarly, contact resistance in graphene-based field effect transistors can be improved by irradiation [1], leading to an improved device performance. Wei Qin et al. [2] conducted a detailed theoretical investigation using first-principles calculations of "Lithium Diffusion in Silicon Encapsulated with Graphene". They considered monolayer graphene on silicon substrate to simulate the Si microparticles that were encapsulated in a graphene cage, which can be exploited as anodes in lithium-ion batteries. They demonstrated that defective graphene strongly reduces the energy barriers for Li diffusion in Gr or Gr/Si. Abid et al.'s [3] report, entitled "Interface Kinetics Assisted Barrier Removal in Large Area 2D-$WS_2$ Growth to Facilitate Mass Scale Device Production", employed chemical vapor deposition technique to synthesize mono- and few-layer $WS_2$ with areas up to $cm^2$ on graphene-oxide-coated $Si/SiO_2$ substrates. They show that as-developed $WS_2$ layers are polycrystalline (mono- and few-layer), with single-crystal domains that are triangular and hexagonal in shape. Alejandro Toral-Lopez et al.'s [4] report, on "GFET Asymmetric Transfer Response Analysis through Access Region Resistances", aimed to exploit graphene-based devices to increase the functionality of Si-technology in the field of radio-frequency electronics. They conducted an in-depth investigation of the role of access regions on the performance of graphene-based field effect transistors (GFETs). They demonstrated that the access region conductivity can be tuned by the back-gate bias, improving the RF performance. Graphene represents a prototype of 2D materials and is still widely investigated. Many layered materials, such as the transition metal dichalcogenides, are largely studied for their use as a conducting channel in nanometric field effect transistors, including $MoS_2$ [5–7], $ReSe_2$ [8], $WSe_2$ [9], etc. Regarding superconducting-based devices, Jose C. Verde et al.'s [10] report is entitled "Calculations of Some Doping Nanostructurations and Patterns Improving the Functionality of High-Temperature Superconductors for Bolometer Device Applications". They propose that high-temperature superconductors (HTS) can be nanostructured (and patterned) to obtain an increased functionality as sensing materials for resistive transition-edge bolometer devices (TES). Calculations have been performed to consider the spatial variations in carrier doping into the $CuO_2$ planes of the YBaCuO perovskite superconductor, demonstrating an improvement in the bolometric parameters with respect to conventional, nonstructured HTS materials. Paola Romano et al. [11] report, "Transport and Point Contact Measurements on $Pr_{1-x}Ce_xPt_4Ge_{12}$ Superconducting Polycrystals" demonstrated that the material has a collective pinning regime with a quasi-2D character for a Ce-doping of about x = 0.07. Moreover, while investigating the properties of metal/superconductor nano-junctions, they showed that the observed conductance features are explained in terms of a superconducting-order parameter with nodal directions, as well as a sign change in the momentum space. Indeed, numerical simulations reported in the framework of Blonder–Tinkham–Klapwijk model show that s-wave pairing and anisotropic s-wave are unsuitable for the reproduction of experimental data obtained at a low temperature. Carlo Barone et al.'s [12] report is entitled "Current-Resistance Effects

Inducing Nonlinear Fluctuation Mechanisms in Granular Aluminum Oxide Nanowires". They measured electric transport and voltage fluctuations in the normal state and in the temperature range of 8–300 K, observing both nonlinear resistivity and two-level tunneling fluctuators. This study helps to improve the fabrication process, therefore reducing the possible sources of decoherence in the superconducting state. This is crucial in quantum technology applications. Sergio Pagano et al.'s [13] report is entitled "Iron-Based Superconducting Nanowires: Electric Transport and Voltage-Noise Properties". In this work, they fabricated ultra-thin Co-doped $BaFe_2As_2$ nanowires and characterized their transport and intrinsic noise properties. They also investigated the ageing effect on device degradation by means of noise spectroscopy. Interestingly, iron-based superconducting nanowire detectors have several advantages, due to their high operating temperature, when used as innovative single-photon detectors working in the visible and infrared spectral region.

**Funding:** This research received no external funding.

**Conflicts of Interest:** The authors declare no conflict of interest.

## References

1. Giubileo, F.; Di Bartolomeo, A.; Martucciello, N.; Romeo, F.; Iemmo, L.; Romano, P.; Passacantando, M. Contact Resistance and Channel Conductance of Graphene Field-Effect Transistors under Low-Energy Electron Irradiation. *Nanomaterials* **2016**, *6*, 206. [CrossRef] [PubMed]
2. Qin, W.; Lu, W.-C.; Xue, X.-Y.; Ho, K.-M.; Wang, C.-Z. Lithium Diffusion in Silicon Encapsulated with Graphene. *Nanomaterials* **2021**, *11*, 3397. [CrossRef] [PubMed]
3. Abid; Sehrawat, P.; Julien, C.M.; Islam, S.S. Interface Kinetics Assisted Barrier Removal in Large Area 2D-WS2 Growth to Facilitate Mass Scale Device Production. *Nanomaterials* **2021**, *11*, 220. [CrossRef] [PubMed]
4. Toral-Lopez, A.; Marin, E.G.; Pasadas, F.; Gonzalez-Medina, J.M.; Ruiz, F.G.; Jiménez, D.; Godoy, A. GFET Asymmetric Transfer Response Analysis through Access Region Resistances. *Nanomaterials* **2019**, *9*, 1027. [CrossRef] [PubMed]
5. Urban, F.; Passacantando, M.; Giubileo, F.; Iemmo, L.; Di Bartolomeo, A. Transport and Field Emission Properties of $MoS_2$ Bilayers. *Nanomaterials* **2018**, *8*, 151. [CrossRef] [PubMed]
6. Iemmo, L.; Urban, F.; Giubileo, F.; Passacantando, M.; Di Bartolomeo, A. Nanotip Contacts for Electric Transport and Field Emission Characterization of Ultrathin $MoS_2$ Flakes. *Nanomaterials* **2020**, *10*, 106. [CrossRef] [PubMed]
7. Giubileo, F.; Grillo, A.; Passacantando, M.; Urban, F.; Iemmo, L.; Luongo, G.; Pelella, A.; Loveridge, M.; Lozzi, L.; Di Bartolomeo, A. Field Emission Characterization of $MoS_2$ Nanoflowers. *Nanomaterials* **2019**, *9*, 717. [CrossRef] [PubMed]
8. Faella, E.; Intonti, K.; Viscardi, L.; Giubileo, F.; Kumar, A.; Lam, H.T.; Anastasiou, K.; Craciun, M.F.; Russo, S.; Di Bartolomeo, A. Electric Transport in Few-Layer $ReSe_2$ Transistors Modulated by Air Pressure and Light. *Nanomaterials* **2022**, *12*, 1886. [CrossRef] [PubMed]
9. Urban, F.; Martucciello, N.; Peters, L.; McEvoy, N.; Di Bartolomeo, A. Environmental Effects on the Electrical Characteristics of Back-Gated $WSe_2$ Field-Effect Transistors. *Nanomaterials* **2018**, *8*, 901. [CrossRef] [PubMed]
10. Verde, J.C.; Viz, A.S.; Botana, M.M.; Montero-Orille, C.; Ramallo, M.V. Calculations of Some Doping Nanostructurations and Patterns Improving the Functionality of High-Temperature Superconductors for Bolometer Device Applications. *Nanomaterials* **2020**, *10*, 97. [CrossRef] [PubMed]
11. Romano, P.; Avitabile, F.; Nigro, A.; Grimaldi, G.; Leo, A.; Shu, L.; Zhang, J.; Di Bartolomeo, A.; Giubileo, F. Transport and Point Contact Measurements on $Pr_{1-x}Ce_xPt_4Ge_{12}$ Superconducting Polycrystals. *Nanomaterials* **2020**, *10*, 1810. [CrossRef] [PubMed]
12. Barone, C.; Rotzinger, H.; Voss, J.N.; Mauro, C.; Schön, Y.; Ustinov, A.V.; Pagano, S. Current-Resistance Effects Inducing Nonlinear Fluctuation Mechanisms in Granular Aluminum Oxide Nanowires. *Nanomaterials* **2020**, *10*, 524. [CrossRef] [PubMed]
13. Pagano, S.; Martucciello, N.; Enrico, E.; Monticone, E.; Iida, K.; Barone, C. Iron-Based Superconducting Nanowires: Electric Transport and Voltage-Noise Properties. *Nanomaterials* **2020**, *10*, 862. [CrossRef] [PubMed]

Article

# Lithium Diffusion in Silicon Encapsulated with Graphene

Wei Qin [1,2,*], Wen-Cai Lu [1,2,3,*], Xu-Yan Xue [1,2], Kai-Ming Ho [4] and Cai-Zhuang Wang [4,*]

1. College of Physics, Qingdao University, Qingdao 266071, China; xuexy@qdu.edu.cn
2. State Key Laboratory of Bio-Fibers and Eco-Textiles, Qingdao University, Qingdao 266071, China
3. Institute of Theoretical Chemistry, Jilin University, Changchun 130021, China
4. Ames Laboratory-U.S. DOE and Department of Physics and Astronomy, Iowa State University, Ames, IA 50011, USA; kmh@iastate.edu
* Correspondence: qinw@qdu.edu.cn (W.Q.); wencailu@jlu.edu.cn (W.-C.L.); wangcz@ameslab.gov (C.-Z.W.)

**Abstract:** The model of a graphene (Gr) sheet putting on a silicon (Si) substrate is used to simulate the structures of Si microparticles wrapped up in a graphene cage, which may be the anode of lithium-ion batteries (LIBS) to improve the high-volume expansion of Si anode materials. The common low-energy defective graphene (d–Gr) structures of DV5–8–5, DV555–777 and SV are studied and compared with perfect graphene (p–Gr). First-principles calculations are performed to confirm the stable structures before and after Li penetrating through the Gr sheet or graphene/Si-substrate (Gr/Si) slab. The climbing image nudged elastic band (CI-NEB) method is performed to evaluate the diffusion barrier and seek the saddle point. The calculation results reveal that the d–Gr greatly reduces the energy barriers for Li diffusion in Gr or Gr/Si. The energy stability, structural configuration, bond length between the atoms and layer distances of these structures are also discussed in detail.

**Keywords:** perfect graphene (p–Gr); defective graphene (d–Gr); Gr/Si slab; diffusion barrier; CI-NEB calculation

## 1. Introduction

Facing the ever-growing demands for electrical vehicles and portable electronic devices [1–3], rechargeable lithium-ion batteries (LIBS) with high energy density, long cycle life and fast charge rate have become the focus of intense research. Silicon is an attractive and promising anode material for LIBS due to its high theoretical capacity (~4200 mAh/g) [4], over ten times higher than conventional graphite, and abundance on Earth. However, the large-volume expansion of silicon as an anode material upon lithiation (~300%) [5,6] in practical applications leads to fracture and loss of inter-particle electrical contact, consequently causing early capacity fading, thus blocking the further improvement of LIBS. Attempting to avoid the mechanical fracture via decreasing the material size, the use of nanostructure silicon (nano–Si) has been shown to be fruitful, such as in silicon crystalline amorphous core-shell nanowires [7], interconnected Si hollow nanosphere [8], Si nanotubes [9], and so on. In particular, Si–C nanostructure materials combining Si with carbonaceous materials [10–24] can retain capacity well, further enhancing the cycling stability and charging rate [10,25] due to the buffering effect and high electrical conductivity of carbon. On the other hand, a large number of theoretical calculations have been focused on the interactions between Li and Si crystals or between Li and graphite separately [26–34], or on the influence of Si–C composites on lithiation [35]. Despite the impressive improvement of the stability of Si anodes after adopting nano-Si, the Coulombic efficiency is still far lower than conventional graphite due to the large surface area. In addition, the complex synthesis process makes nano-Si costly. These are the major obstacles to the further development and mass production of LIBS technology. Subsequently, Si microparticles were explored to replace nano-Si as an anode material due to the lower cost in manufacture, but the cycling performance is far poorer than that of nano-Si. After the first few cycles, Si microparticles are pulverized into smaller sizes, turn into amorphous particles from Si crystalline, and then lose electrical contact [36–39].

In recent years, a strategy of Si microparticles surrounded by a porous carbon matrix was used to counteract these inadequacies. The combination maintains both Li absorption capacity and electrical conductivity well for many battery-charging cycles. For example, a conformal growth of the conductive graphene cage, which can wrap up Si microparticles, was reported as a promising encapsulation material [40]. The similar surface chemistry to graphite allows graphene cage to form a stable solid electrolyte interphase [41,42]. Being mechanically strong and flexible, graphene cages remain undamaged with Si microparticles fracturing and confine all the fractured Si pieces within the cages, thus maintaining the essential electrical contact between broken Si particles within [40]. Graphene-encapsulated Si microparticles thus provide a new architecture of materials for the development of LIBS technology. A theoretical understanding of Li diffusion in such materials could therefore provide information and guidance for the design and development of LIBS, but the relevant calculated studies are scarce. Odbadrakh et al. reported that cavities along the reconstructed Si surface provide diffusion paths for Li [43]. Chou and Hwang investigated the role of the interface in lithiation of silicon/graphene (Si/Gr) [44] composites and demonstrated the charge transfer from Li to both silicon and graphene. They also showed that Li cations exhibit substantially higher mobility along the Si/Gr interface than that of bulk Si [44]. For Li diffusion, most studies focused on diffusion paths of Li on the graphene surface [45–47]. However, the difficulty of Li intercalating through the graphene sheet to bind to Si particles, i.e., the diffusion barrier during lithiation, is deeply influenced by the surface characterics of graphene for such a combination. It is well known that many defects will inevitably occur in the process of graphene producing. Can these defects be used to facilitate the diffusion of Li? If so, which common defects are easier for Li to intercalate through to reduce the diffusion barrier of Li? Do Si particles affect the diffusion? Does the diffusion barrier increase or decrease in the presence of Si particles? Studying these issues could assist in exploring more suitable encapsulation materials.

Usually, single–vacancy (SV), Stone–Wales (SW) and divacancy (DV) defects are typical point defects in graphene and the subjects of intense research [48–54]. SV and SW defects are created by removing a C atom and rotating a C–C bond by 90° in the plane, respectively. The DV defect is formed by removing a C–C dimer; when the dimer is removed from graphene, a series of reconstructions around the DV defect take place upon annealing. In this work, the Gr/Si (a monolayer graphene is put on the silicon substrate) is used to simulate the Si microparticles encapsulated with the graphene cage. The Si substrate and defective graphene ($d$–Gr) are adopted to simulate Si particles and porous graphene, respectively. The perfect graphene ($p$–Gr) is also studied as a comparison. The energy stability of these models (both Gr and Gr/Si, Gr = $p$–Gr, DV5-8-5, DV555-777 and SV) are investigated by first-principles calculations. Their energy barriers of Li diffusion through them are also determined.

## 2. Computational Methods

Considering both the calculation cost and accuracy, a $6 \times 6$ hexagonal supercell of $d$–Gr is employed to model the porous graphene cage. Three common defects [55], including the SV defect, DV5-8-5 defect (containing two pentagons and one octagon) and DV555-777 defect (three heptagons in the center surrounded by three pentagons) are considered. A $4 \times 4$ supercell of the Si (111) surface containing two double atomic layers are employed as the Si substrate. The silicon dangling bonds on the bottom are passivated by hydrogen atoms, and these hydrogen atoms and silicon atoms on the bottom are fixed. The Si–Si bond lengths in Si substrate are adjusted by about 4% to fit the $6 \times 6$ Gr sheet to minimize the effect of the lattice mismatch on graphene when the in-plane periodic boundary conditions are used. To eliminate the interaction between Gr (or Gr/Si) and their periodic replicas, the vacuum layers of 20 Å and 18 Å are adopted in the perpendicular direction to the Gr surface for monolayers Gr and Gr/Si, respectively. The structures of Gr and Gr/Si are displayed in Figure 1. All calculations are performed using the projector-augmented wave (PAW) with Perdew, Burke, and Ernzerh of (PBE) GGA functional for the exchange-correlation energy [56,57], as implemented in the Vienna ab initio simulation package (VASP) [58]. We also consider the Van der Waal's force followed by the well-established Grimme's DFT-D2 formula [59,60] in the VASP calculation for all the Gr/Si. The Brillouin zone (BZ) integration is approximated by using the Gamma centered k-grid. For structural relaxation and energy evaluation, the $8 \times 8 \times 1$ k-grid and $4 \times 4 \times 1$ k-grid are adopted for the monolayer Gr and Gr/Si slab, respectively. We also calculate the energy barriers of Li diffusion in Gr and Gr/Si, and the climbing image nudged elastic band (CI-NEB) method implemented in the VASP code is used to seek the saddle points and the minimum energy path. As a reference, we study the adsorption sites about Li on the surfaces of perfect graphene (p–Gr) and p–Gr/Si. Three typical adsorption sites are considered: the top (T) site (Li is above a C atom), the bridge (B) site (Li is above the midpoint of a C–C bond) and the hollow (H) site (Li is above the center of a hexagon ring). The results show that the H site is the most stable adsorption site. Similarly, in d–Gr and d–Gr/Si (Gr = DV5–8–5, DV555–777 and SV), the structures are more stable when Li is above the center of the polygon rings. These lowest-energy structures are shown in Figures 2–4 as the initial configurations of the CI-NEB calculations. We call them Li/Gr and Li/Gr/Si (Gr = p–Gr, DV5–8–5, DV555–777 and SV), respectively. When Li penetrates through the Gr sheet, Li is basically on the symmetric sites of the other surface of the graphene due to the planar structures of the monolayer Gr sheet. Their configurations are similar to the initial points from the top view, while for Gr/Si, Li is between the Gr sheet and Si substrate after passing through the Gr layer. We consider various relative sites between Li and Si atoms, such as Li above a Si atom, Li above a Si–Si bond, Li above a folded Si hexagon ring, and so on. All of the candidates are relaxed to find the lowest-energy structures. These lowest-energy structures after Li intercalates into Gr or Gr/Si are adopted as the end points and called Gr/Li and Gr/Li/Si (Gr = p–Gr, DV5–8–5, DV555–777 and SV), respectively. In the CI-NEB calculation, four images are employed in addition to the initial and end points. The structures of the saddle points are found and called Li@Gr and Li@Gr/Si (Gr = p–Gr, DV5–8–5, DV555–777 and SV), respectively. They are also displayed in Figures 2–4.

In order to evaluate the energetic stability of different d–Gr and d–Gr/Si (Gr = DV5–8–5, DV555–777 and SV), we firstly calculate their formation energies ($E_f$). For monolayer Gr sheets, their $E_f$ is defined as

$$E_f = E_d - N \mu_C \qquad (1)$$

and for d–Gr/Si slab, the $E_f$ is defined as

$$E_f = E_d - E_{sub} - N \mu_C \qquad (2)$$

where $E_d$ and $E_{sub}$ are the total energy of d–Gr (or d–Gr/Si) and Si substrate in the given supercells, respectively; N is the number of C atoms in the supercell, and $\mu_C$ is the chemical potential of carbon, which is leveled from perfect graphene with the same unit cell size. Our calculation results showed that the formation energies ($E_f$) of DV5–8–5, DV555–777 and SV are 7.645, 6.386 and 7.579 eV, respectively, which is in agreement with previous studies [51,59]. The formation energies ($E_f$) of DV5–8–5/Si, DV555–777/Si and SV/Si are 2.621, 1.254 and 1.906 eV, respectively. The order of $E_f$ does not alter with the existence of the Si substrate.

To examine the stability of the structures upon Li adsorption, we also calculate the adsorption energies ($E_{ads}$) of Li/Gr and Li/Gr/Si (Gr = p–Gr, DV5–8–5, DV555–777 and SV) which are defined as

$$E_{ads} = E_t (\text{Li-S}) - E_t (\text{S}) - E_{Li} \qquad (3)$$

where $E_t$ (Li-S) and $E_t$ (S) are the total energies of Gr (or Gr/Si) with and without a Li atom adsorbing on their surfaces, respectively. $E_{Li}$ is the energy of putting one Li atom into the same unit cell size. The results of the Li adsorption energies ($E_{ads}$) are listed in the second column of Table 1. The lower the $E_{ads}$, the more stable the adsorption structure (Li/Gr and Li/Gr/Si). From Table 1, we can see that for monolayer Gr (Gr = $p$–Gr, DV5–8–5, DV555–777 and SV), Li prefers to adsorb on the $d$–Gr (Gr = DV5–8–5, DV555–777 and SV), compared with $p$–Gr. The $E_{ads}$ of $d$–Gr is more than 1 eV lower than that of $p$–Gr. In particular, Li/SV is the most stable adsorption structure among the four sheets, whose $E_{ads}$ is nearly 1.8 eV lower than that of $p$–Gr. For Li/Gr/Si, the order of their $E_{ads}$ is consistent with that of Li/Gr, except Li/SV/Si. Comparing with $p$–Gr/Si, Li prefers to adsorb on DV5–8–5/Si and DV555–777/Si. The differences of their $E_{ads}$ are not as large as that between monolayer $p$–Gr and $d$–Gr, about 0.5 eV. It indicates that the differences of $E_{ads}$ are reduced between $p$–Gr/Si and $d$–Gr/Si ($d$–Gr = DV5–8–5 and DV555–777) due to the Si substrate. However, it is difficult to adsorb on SV/Si for Li. The $E_{ads}$ of Li/SV/Si is even higher, about 1 eV, than that of Li/$p$–Gr/Si. It may be related to the structural deformation of SV/Si when Li adsorbs on it (detailed in Results and Discussion).

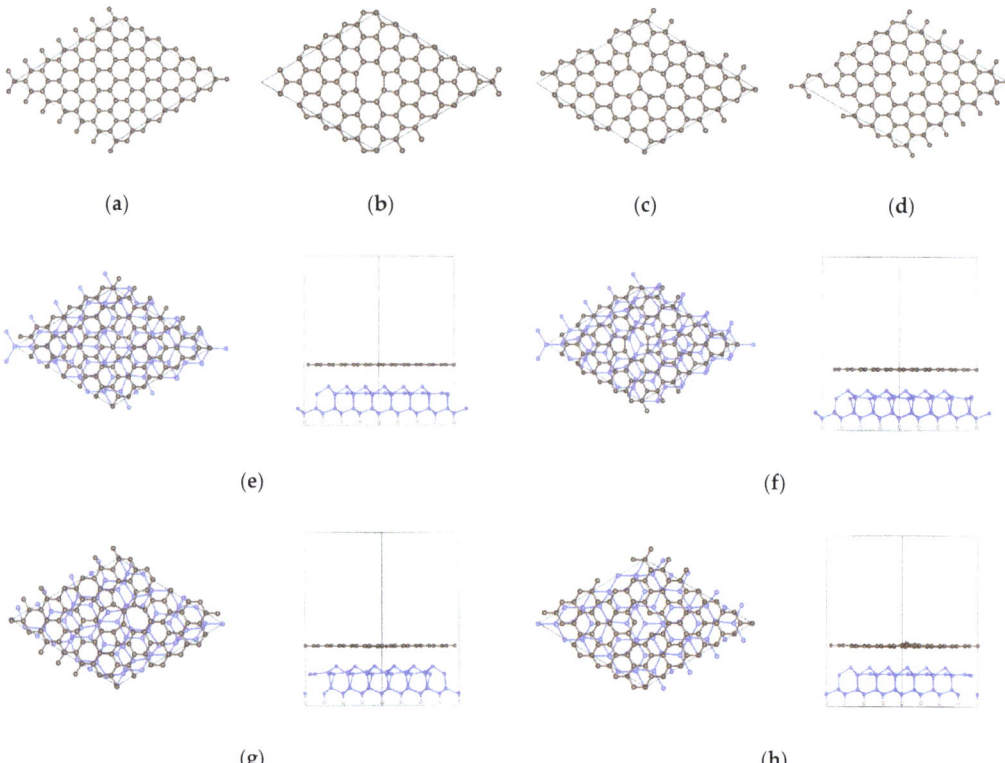

**Figure 1.** Structures of (a) $p$–Gr, (b) DV5–8–5, (c) DV555–777, (d) SV, (e) $p$–Gr/Si, (f) DV5–8–5/Si, (g) DV555–777/Si and (h) SV/Si; the left and right configurations (e–h) are the top and side views of Gr/Si, respectively.

The formation energies ($E_f$) of Gr/Li/Si (Gr = $p$–Gr, DV5–8–5, DV555–777 and SV) are also calculated when Li intercalates the Gr sheet and is located between Gr and the Si substrate, which is defined as

$$E_f = E_t\,(Gr/Li/Si) - E_t\,(Gr) - E_t\,(Si) - E_{Li} \tag{4}$$

where $E_t$ (Gr/Li/Si) is the total energies of the Gr/Li/Si (Gr = $p$–Gr, DV5–8–5, DV555–777 and SV) intercalated structures; $E_t$ (Gr) and $E_t$ (Si) are the total energies of the Gr sheet and Si substrate, respectively. In order to measure the energy stability of the structures before and after Li intercalation, we also calculate their energy differences ($E_{diff}$), which are defined as

$$E_{diff} = E_f (Li/Gr/Si) - E_f (Gr/Li/Si) \quad (5)$$

where $E_f$ (Li/Gr/Si) and $E_f$ (Gr/Li/Si) are the formation energies of Li/Gr/Si and Gr/Li/Si (Gr = $p$–Gr, DV5–8–5, DV555–777 and SV) calculated in the same method (Formula (4)). The values of $E_f$ of Gr/Li/Si and $E_{diff}$ are shown in the third and fourth columns of Table 1, respectively. The results show that the structures after Li passes through the Gr sheet are more stable than those of the adsorption on the Gr surface. It may be because Li combines with both C atoms in the Gr and Si atoms on the surface of the Si substrate when Li passes through the Gr sheet, which make the structure more stable. The difference value of $p$–Gr/Si is the largest. It indicates that the stability of the intercalated structure ($p$–Gr/Li/Si) after Li passes through $p$–Gr is much higher than that of the adsorption on the Gr surface (Li/$p$–Gr/Si). By comparison, the $E_{diff}$ value for $d$–Gr/Si is relatively low.

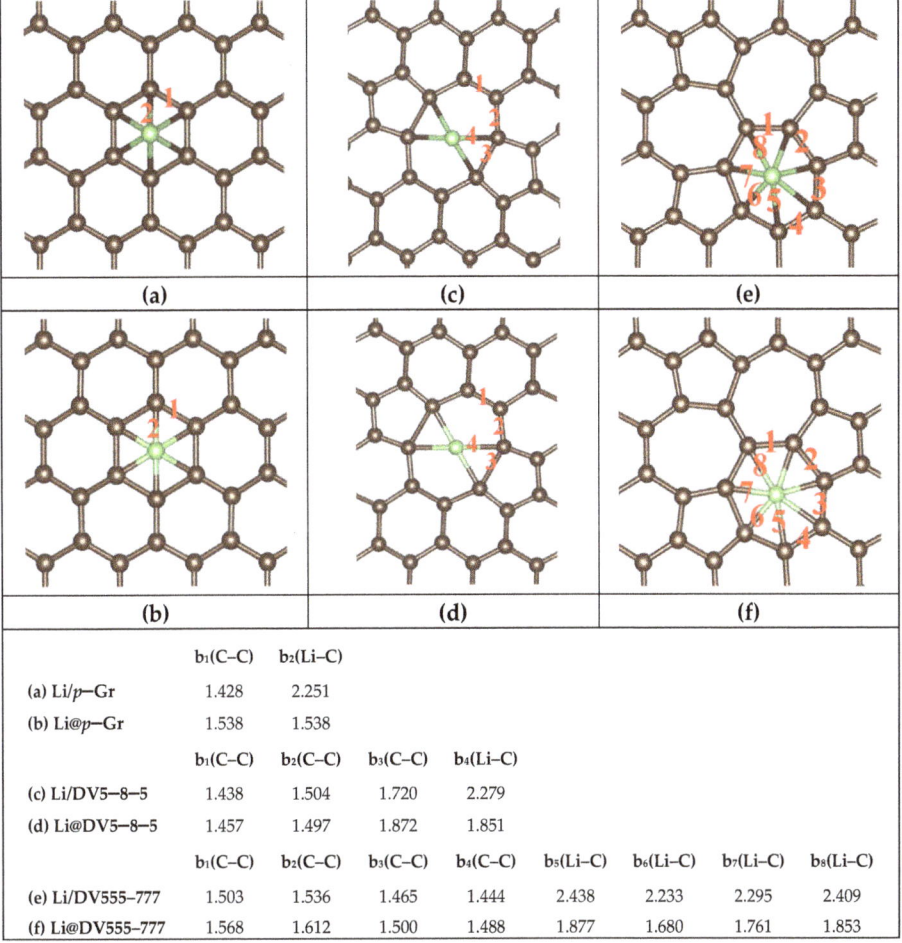

|  | $b_1$(C–C) | $b_2$(Li–C) |  |  |  |  |  |  |
|---|---|---|---|---|---|---|---|---|
| (a) Li/$p$–Gr | 1.428 | 2.251 |  |  |  |  |  |  |
| (b) Li@$p$–Gr | 1.538 | 1.538 |  |  |  |  |  |  |
|  | $b_1$(C–C) | $b_2$(C–C) | $b_3$(C–C) | $b_4$(Li–C) |  |  |  |  |
| (c) Li/DV5–8–5 | 1.438 | 1.504 | 1.720 | 2.279 |  |  |  |  |
| (d) Li@DV5–8–5 | 1.457 | 1.497 | 1.872 | 1.851 |  |  |  |  |
|  | $b_1$(C–C) | $b_2$(C–C) | $b_3$(C–C) | $b_4$(C–C) | $b_5$(Li–C) | $b_6$(Li–C) | $b_7$(Li–C) | $b_8$(Li–C) |
| (e) Li/DV555–777 | 1.503 | 1.536 | 1.465 | 1.444 | 2.438 | 2.233 | 2.295 | 2.409 |
| (f) Li@DV555–777 | 1.568 | 1.612 | 1.500 | 1.488 | 1.877 | 1.680 | 1.761 | 1.853 |

**Figure 2.** Structures of (**a**) Li/$p$–Gr (**b**) Li@$p$–Gr (**c**) Li/DV5–8–5 (**d**) Li@DV5–8–5 (**e**) Li/DV555–777 and (**f**) Li@DV555–777; their main bond lengths (abbreviated "b" in the list, Å) are shown in the list at the bottom of the figure. The red numbers in these figures correspond to the subscripts in the list.

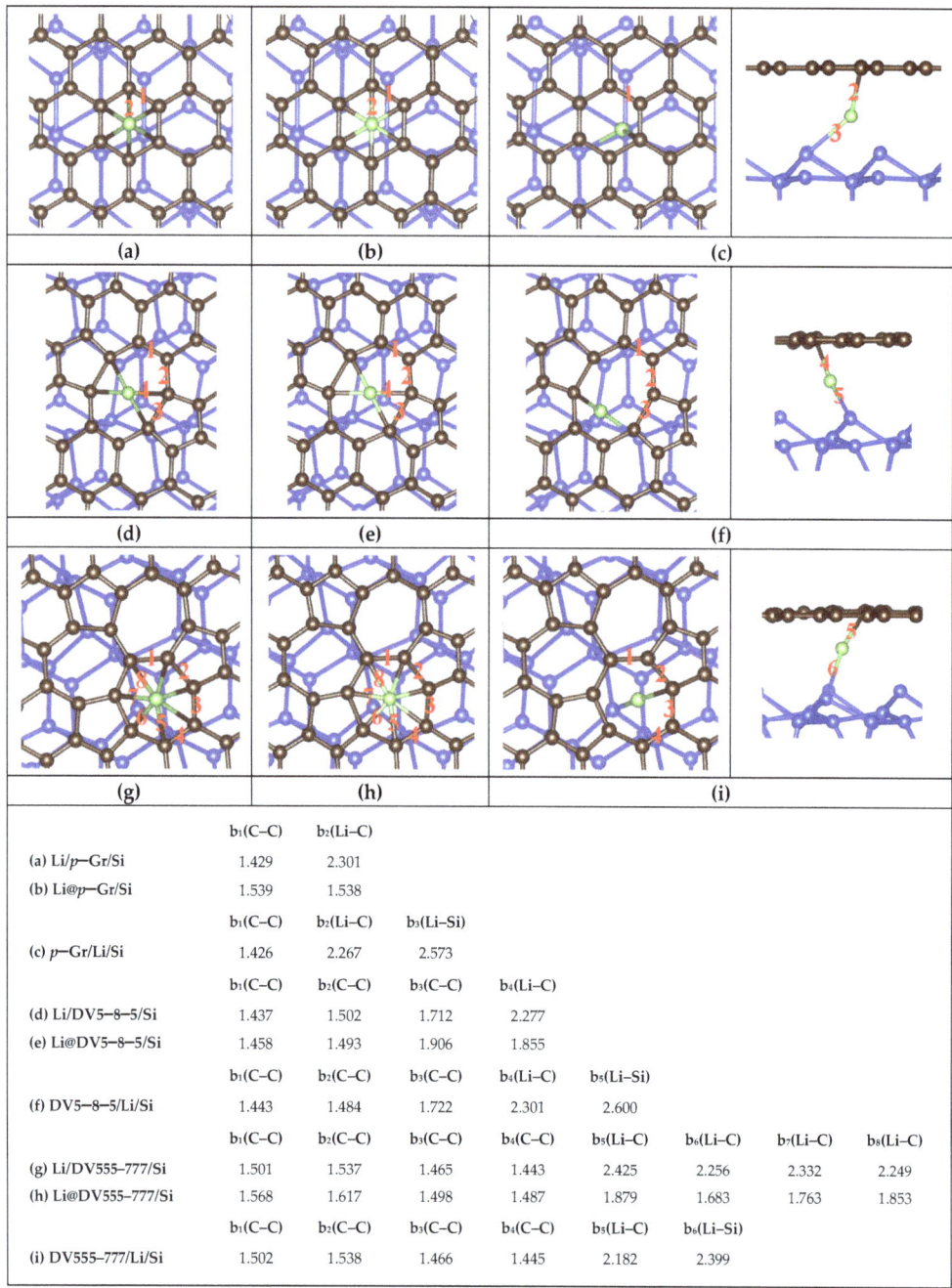

**Figure 3.** Structures of (**a**) Li/p−Gr/Si (**b**) Li@p−Gr/Si (**c**) p−Gr/Li/Si (**d**) Li/DV5−8−5/Si (**e**) Li@DV5−8−5/Si (**f**) DV5−8−5/Li/Si (**g**) Li/DV555−777/Si (**h**) Li@DV555−777/Si and (**i**) DV555−777/Li/Si. The left and right configurations (**c,f,i**) are the top and side views of the end structures in the CI-NEB calculation, respectively. The main bond lengths (abbreviated as "b" in the list, Å) are shown in the list at the bottom of the figure. The red numbers in these figures correspond to the subscripts.

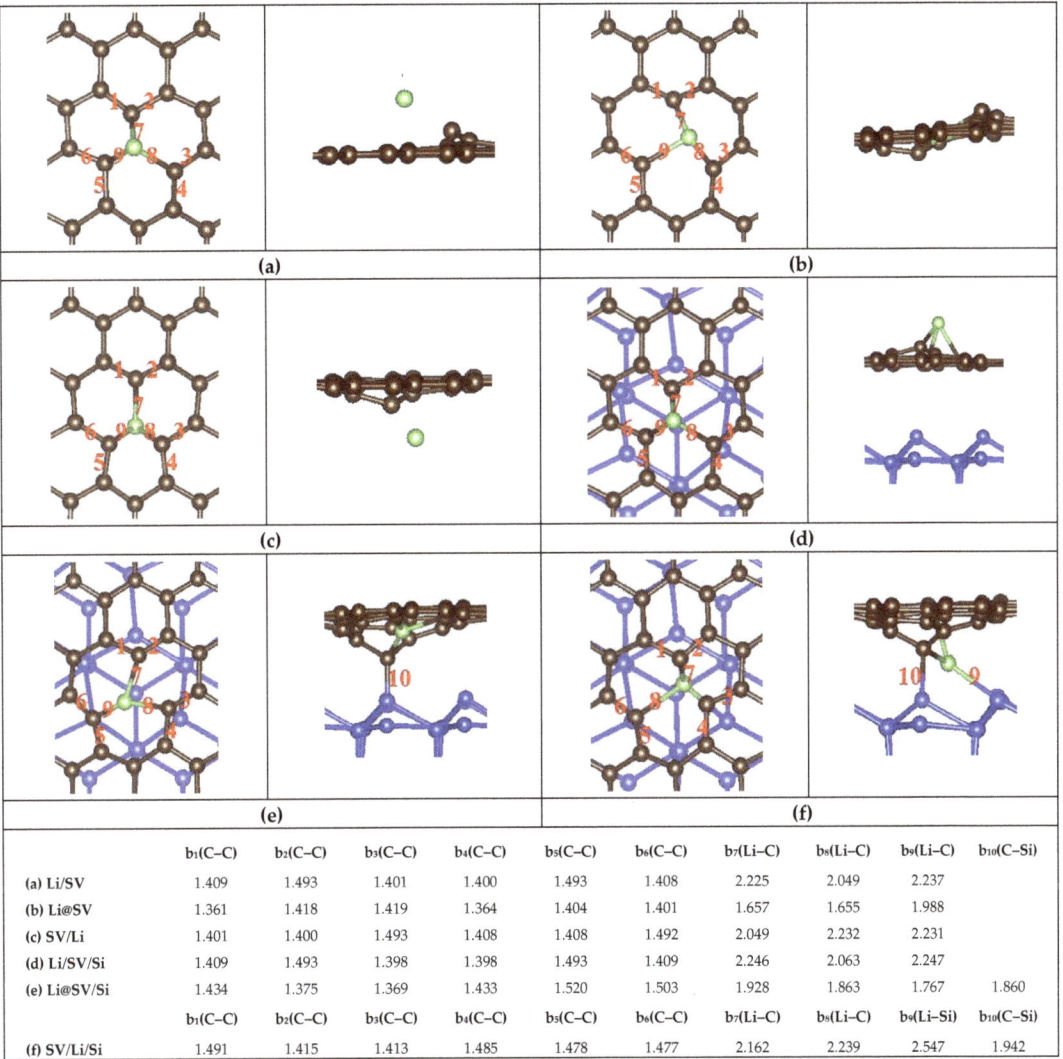

**Figure 4.** Structures of (**a**) Li/SV (**b**) Li@SV (**c**) SV/Li (**d**) Li/SV/Si (**e**) Li@SV/Si and (**f**) SV/Li/Si. The left and right configurations are the top and side views of the six structures in the CI-NEB calculation, respectively. The main bond lengths (abbreviated as "b" in the list, Å) are shown in the list at the bottom of the figure. The red numbers in these figures correspond to the subscripts.

**Table 1.** Adsorption energies ($E_{ads}$, eV) of the initial structures and the formation energies ($E_f$, eV) of the end structures with Li diffusion in Gr and Gr/Si (Gr = p–Gr, DV5–8–5, DV555–777 and SV); the energy differences ($E_{diff}$, eV) between the initial and end structures with Li diffusion in Gr/Si (Gr = p–Gr, DV5–8–5, DV555–777 and SV).

| Structures | $E_{ads}$ (eV) | $E_f$ (eV) | $E_{diff}$ (eV) |
|---|---|---|---|
| Li/p-Gr | −1.308 | | |
| Li/DV5–8–5 | −2.340 | | |
| Li/DV555–777 | −2.505 | | |
| Li/SV | −3.065 | | |
| Li/p–Gr/Si | −4.135 | | |
| Li/DV5–8–5/Si | −4.552 | | |
| Li/DV555–777/Si | −4.693 | | |
| Li/SV/Si | −3.154 | | |
| p–Gr/Li/Si | | −9.322 | 1.254 |
| DV5–8–5/Li/Si | | −10.189 | 0.610 |
| DV555–777/Li/Si | | −10.170 | 0.334 |
| SV/Li/Si | | −9.601 | 0.374 |

## 3. Results and Discussion

### 3.1. Energetic Stability

Figures 2–4 show the most stable structures of Li adsorbed on different Gr and Gr/Si (Gr = p–Gr, DV5–8–5, DV555–777 and SV) surfaces. From the figures, we can see that Li prefers to absorb above the center of the polygon ring with the most sides so that it can have more carbon neighbors. For instance, the adsorption energies ($E_{ads}$) are lower when Li absorbs above the hexagon ring center on the p–Gr and p–Gr/Si surfaces. Similarly, the lowest-energy adsorption sites are above the centers of the heptagon and octagon rings for DV555–777 (or DV555–777/Si) and DV5–8–5 (or DV5–8–5/Si) structures, respectively. For SV (or SV/Si), the most stable adsorption site is just above the C atom, removed from the SV defect. When Li is diffused into the Gr (or Gr/Si), Li is in the plane of Gr for the saddle-point structures. After penetrating through the Gr sheet, Li is basically on the symmetric sites of the other surface of the Gr sheet, and in Gr/Si, the positions of Li are slightly shifted from the top view. The Gr (Gr = p–Gr, DV5–8–5 and DV555–777) layer maintains a planar structure throughout, whether there is the Si substrate or not (see Figures 2 and 3). The SV defect is a little special. When Li is adsorbed on the surface of SV, the C atoms in the SV are no longer in the same plane. One of the C atoms is obviously deviated from the SV plane and approaches the Li atom, whether in Li/SV or Li/SV/Si. After Li penetrates through SV, the SV layer is also non-planar, whether for SV/Li or SV/Li/Si. In SV/Li, one C atom is close to the Li atom; more C atoms deviate from the SV plane and approach the Li atom and Si surface in SV/Li/Si. For the saddle-point structures, the Li atom is basically in the initial plane of SV, but the C atoms around Li are almost deviated from the original plane. In Li@SV, these C atoms are distributed on both sides of the plane, while in Li@SV/Si, they are all close to the side of the Si surface (see Figure 4).

In the bottom of Figures 2–4, the relevant bond lengths, including b(C–C), b(Li–C) and b(Li–Si) are also listed. The C–C bond length ($b_1$(C–C) in Figure 2a) of the hexagon ring absorbed by Li in Li/p–Gr is 1.428 Å. The corresponding value is 1.429 Å ($b_1$(C–C) in Figure 3a) when there is the Si substrate, which is basically unchanged. Similar behavior is seen in DV5–8–5 and DV555–777 (see Figures 2 and 3). We also find the similar regular pattern in their saddle-point structures Li@Gr/Si (Gr = p–Gr, DV5–8–5 and DV555–777). The maximum variation of the C–C bond length is about 0.03 Å when there is the Si substrate. It indicates that the Si substrate has negligible effects on the C–C bond lengths. Furthermore, the C–C bond lengths in the saddle-point structures are larger than the ones of the corresponding initial structures Li/Gr or Li/Gr/Si (Gr = p–Gr, DV5–8–5 and DV555–777). When Li penetration is complete, the C–C bond lengths are basically restored to the values of the initial structures. It may be due to Li being in the plane of Gr in the saddle-point structures, while Li leaves the plane of Gr in Gr/Li or Gr/Li/Si (Gr = p–Gr, DV5–8–5 and DV555–777). Similarly, the Li–C bond lengths also vary very little when there is the Si substrate. Among the three Gr sheets (Gr = p–Gr, DV5–8–5 and DV555–777), the Li–C bond lengths' value of DV555–777 changes most. Despite all this, its average Li–C bond length changes less than 0.03 Å when there is the Si substrate, compared with the values $b_{5-8}$(Li–C) in Li/DV555–777 (from 2.233 Å to 2.438 Å in Figure 2e) and Li/DV555–777/Si (from 2.249 Å to 2.425 Å in Figure 3g). Comparing with the three Gr (or Gr/Si) above, there are some different results due to the C atoms around Li deviating from the SV plane when Li diffuses in the SV (or SV/Si). The average bond lengths of C–C and Li–C in the saddle-point structure Li@SV do not increase although the Li atom is in the SV plane but decrease. After Li penetrates the SV plane, both C–C and Li–C bond lengths completely return to the initial values. For SV/Si, the results are slightly complicated due to the existence of Si substrate. The average bond length of C–C in the saddle-point structure Li@SV/Si increases slightly (~0.006 Å) compared to the value of the initial structure (Li/SV/Si), while the average bond length of Li–C decreases over 0.3 Å compared to the initial structure. After Li penetrates the SV plane, the positions of the C atoms around Li change greatly, and the average bond length of C–C does not return to the initial value, but is increased by about 0.03 Å. Similar to the other three Gr/Si, both the C and Si atoms bond with the Li atom at this time. In addition, the shortest bond length of Li–C in Li/SV ($b_8$(Li–C) in Figure 4a) is 2.049 Å, which is lower than the values in other Li/Gr ($b_2$(Li–C) in Figure 2a, $b_4$(Li–C) in Figure 2c and $b_6$(Li–C) in Figure 2e). The closer combination between Li and C in Li/SV can reduce $E_{ads}$. The order of $E_{ads}$ does not change when putting these Gr sheets on the Si substrate, except SV/Si. It is the most difficult to adsorb on the surface of SV/Si for the Li atom in these four slabs, which may be due to the structural deformation of SV/Si when Li adsorbs on it.

As a reference, we also calculate the layer distances of each structure, displayed in Table 2. We first calculate the average coordinates of all the C atoms in the Gr (Gr = p–Gr, DV5–8–5, DV555–777 and SV) sheet and Si atoms on the surface of the Si substrate as the positions of the Gr sheet and Si surface, respectively. Then the distances between the Li atoms, Gr sheet and Si surface are calculated and labeled as $d_{C-Si}$, $d_{Li-C}$ and $d_{Li-Si}$ in Table 2. The distances between the Gr sheet and the surface of Si substrate ($d_{C-Si}$) in most Gr/Si slabs change little upon Li adsorption. Especially for DV555–777/Si, its $d_{C-Si}$ value is almost unchanged before and after Li adsorption. However, the $d_{C-Si}$ value of SV/Si decrease by about 0.1 Å upon Li adsorption, which is about 10 times that of other structural variation. It indicates that the adsorption of Li has the greatest effect on the bonding between SV and the surface of the Si substrate among the four Gr above, while the effect is the smallest in DV555–777/Si. In Gr/Li/Si (Gr = p–Gr, DV5–8–5, DV555–777 and SV), Li is located between the Gr and the surface of the Si substrate as Li diffuses into the Gr. Although there is one more Li atom between them, compared with Gr/Si, most $d_{C-Si}$ values of Gr/Li/Si do not increase but decrease, except Li/DV555–777/Si. In sum, the adsorption of Li has a slight effect on the $d_{C-Si}$ values in p–Gr/Si and DV5–8–5/Si, and the effect disappears after Li diffuses into p–Gr/Si (or DV5–8–5/Si). For DV555–777/Si, when Li is adsorbed on the DV555–777 surface, the $d_{C-Si}$ value is almost unchanged. However, when Li diffuses into DV555–777, the distance between DV555–777 and the surface of Si substrate is widened. Nevertheless, its $d_{C-Si}$ value is still the smallest of the corresponding four slabs, whether in Gr/Si, Li/Gr/Si, or Gr/Li/Si (Gr = p–Gr, DV5–8–5, DV555–777 and SV). In these Gr/Si slabs, the adsorption of Li has the greatest influence on the $d_{C-Si}$ value of SV/Si. The $d_{C-Si}$ value decreases when Li is adsorbed on the SV/Si surface; its value further decreases when Li passes through the SV. The total reduction is more than 0.2 Å. It may be due to the larger change of the C positions in SV during Li diffusion to SV/Si. The existence of the Si substrate also slightly affects the distances ($d_{Li-C}$) from the Li to Gr sheet. With the Si substrate, the values of $d_{Li-C}$ increase for Li/p–Gr/Si but decrease for Li/d–Gr/Si (Gr = DV5–8–5, DV555–777 and SV). The value of $d_{Li-C}$ in Li/SV/Si reduces most, about 0.1 Å. For monolayer Gr (Gr = p–Gr, DV5–8–5, DV555–777 and SV), the $d_{Li-C}$ values are basically unchanged due to Li being in the symmetrical position of Li/Gr after Li passes through the Gr sheet. Nevertheless, the $d_{Li-C}$ values in Gr/Li/Si increase, except DV555–777/Li/Si, when there is the Si substrate. The $d_{Li-C}$ value in DV5–8–5/Li/Si increase the most, over 0.4 Å. Considering the distance between Gr and the surface of the Si substrate ($d_{C-Si}$), Li is generally closer to the Si surface, except DV555–777/Li/Si. In proportion, the distance from Li to Gr is SV > $p$–Gr > DV5–8–5 > DV555–777. Comparing with the other three Gr/Si slabs, Li in DV555–777/Li/Si is closer to DV555–777. From this point of view, Li seems to prefer to bond to DV555–777, or it may be less easily bonded to the Si substrate in DV555–777/Si. For $d_{Li-Si}$ in Gr/Li/Si (Gr = $p$–Gr, DV5–8–5, DV555–777 and SV), in proportion, the order is the opposite of $d_{Li-C}$ mentioned above, i.e., SV < $p$–Gr < DV5–8–5 < DV555–777. The layer distances indirectly show the bonding between Li and Gr (or Si substrate) in the four Gr/Si slabs above, which can help us better understand the energy stability of these structures.

**Table 2.** The layer distances (Å) of Gr and Si surface of Si substrate ($d_{C-Si}$) and the distances (Å) between Li atom and Gr ($d_{Li-C}$) or Si surface ($d_{Li-Si}$) during Li diffusion in Gr and Gr/Si (Gr = $p$–Gr, DV5–8–5, DV555–777 and SV).

| Structures | Distances (Å) | | |
| --- | --- | --- | --- |
| | $d_{C-Si}$ | $d_{Li-C}$ | $d_{Li-Si}$ |
| $p$–Gr/Si | 3.567 | | |
| DV5–8–5/Si | 3.400 | | |
| DV555–777/Si | 3.233 | | |
| SV/Si | 3.555 | | |
| Li/$p$–Gr | | 1.755 | |
| Li/DV5–8–5 | | 1.427 | |
| Li/DV555–777 | | 1.565 | |
| Li/SV | | 1.930 | |
| Li/$p$–Gr/Si | 3.577 | 1.778 | |
| Li/DV5–8–5/Si | 3.384 | 1.416 | |
| Li/DV555–777/Si | 3.236 | 1.546 | |
| Li/SV/Si | 3.426 | 1.833 | |
| $p$–Gr/Li/Si | 3.565 | 2.045 | 1.520 |
| DV5–8–5/Li/Si | 3.397 | 1.862 | 1.534 |
| DV555–777/Li/Si | 3.267 | 1.471 | 1.796 |
| SV/Li/Si | 3.337 | 2.014 | 1.323 |

From the bond lengths and layer distances analysis above, we can see that the SV defect is special. Although the structural stability of Li/SV is high, the adsorption and diffusion of Li have a great impact on the planar structure of SV when the Si substrate exists. In the process of Li diffusion, the position of the C atom around the defect, structural configuration, bond lengths and layer distances in SV/Si changes greatly. In other words, the structure of SV/Si changes greatly, and its structural stability is low during Li diffusion in it. For the other three Gr/Si slabs, the structural configurations, bond lengths and layer distances are relatively stable during Li diffusion in them, that is, the influence of the Si substrate on them can be basically ignored.

### 3.2. Li Diffusion in Gr and Gr/Si (Gr = $p$–Gr, DV5–8–5, DV555–777 and SV)

In order to better illustrate the difficulty of Li diffusion in Gr and Gr/Si (Gr = $p$–Gr, DV5–8–5, DV555–777 and SV), we calculate their diffusion barrier as shown in Figure 5. As a reference, we firstly study Li diffusion in $p$–Gr and $p$–Gr/Si. It is the most stable structure when Li is adsorbed on the H site of $p$–Gr and the $d_{Li-C}$ is about 1.755 Å as shown in Table 2, which is chosen as the initial point (Li/$p$–Gr) in the CI-NEB calculations. The end point ($p$–Gr/Li) is the symmetric adsorption position on the other side of the $p$–Gr plane. The calculation results show that the energy barrier of the Li diffusion in $p$–Gr is as high as 7.559 eV, shown in Figure 5a, which indicates that it is quite difficult for Li to penetrate through the $p$–Gr sheet. For $p$–Gr/Si, the most stable structure when Li is adsorbed on it (Li/$p$–Gr/Si shown in Figure 3a) is still chosen as the initial point, and $p$–Gr/Li/Si in Figure 3c is the end point in the CI-NEB calculation after Li intercalates $p$–Gr. From Figure 5, we can see that the energy barrier for Li diffusion in $p$–Gr/Si is higher (0.176 eV) than in the case of the $p$–Gr sheet. That is, the presence of the Si substrate increases the energy barrier for Li penetration through $p$–Gr. These calculation results suggest that in the model (Si microparticles encapsulated with graphene cage), it is very difficult for Li to diffuse into the $p$–Gr layer when Si particles are encapsulated with $p$–Gr. Furthermore, it is even more difficult for Li to diffuse out once it is intercalated between $p$–Gr and the Si substrate since the energy barrier of diffusion is higher, shown in Figure 5b. It can be seen that it does not seem to be a good choice to encapsulate Si particles by $p$–Gr. In that way, what about the common defective graphene ($d$–Gr)?

Defects will inevitably occur in the process of graphene producing, and DV5–8–5, DV555–777 and SV are the common low-energy defect structures on graphene. Therefore, we also study the diffusion behavior of Li diffusion in $d$–Gr and $d$–Gr/Si (Gr = DV5–8–5, DV555–777 and SV), which is shown in Figure 5c–h. In the CI-NEB calculations, the lowest-energy structures of Li adsorbed on $d$–Gr (or $d$–Gr/Si) are used as the initial point structures. Similar to $p$–Gr, for $d$–Gr, their end points are the symmetric adsorption position on the other side of the plane, and for $d$–Gr/Si, they are the $d$–Gr/Li/Si structures shown in Figures 3 and 4. The calculation results show that the defective graphenes greatly reduce the energy barriers when Li diffusion in graphene. Comparing with the energy barrier of Li diffusion in $p$–Gr, the corresponding values of DV555–777 and SV are significantly lower by ~4.723 eV and ~4.92 eV, respectively. The value of DV5–8–5 decreases the most, and its diffusion barrier is only 1.406 eV, which is lower (~6.153 eV) than the value of $p$–Gr. How about encapsulating Si particles using these defective graphenes since defects can reduce the energy barrier of Li diffusion into graphene? $d$–Gr/Si is used to simulate the encapsulating structures. When Li diffuses in DV555-777/Si and DV5–8–5/Si, the energy barriers are slightly increased compared with the case of monolayer DV555-777 and DV5–8–5. Nevertheless, their diffusion barriers decrease by 4.705 eV and 6.276 eV than the value in $p$–Gr/Si, respectively. For SV/Si, the energy barrier of Li diffusion to it is unexpectedly decreased to 0.587 eV. It is probably because the position of the C atom around the SV defect changes greatly during Li diffusion, and SV no longer maintains planar configuration. In addition, the structures of Gr/Li/Si are more stable after Li penetrating in the Gr sheet than adsorption on the surface of Gr/Si, whether for $p$–Gr/Si or $d$–Gr/Si. It indicated that it is more difficult for Li to diffuse out from Gr/Si. However, it is much easier for Li to diffuse out from $d$–Gr/Si than from $p$–Gr/Si, shown in Figure 5. From the perspective of the diffusion barrier, the SV defective graphene seems to be a good material for encapsulating Si particles. However, our calculation results suggest that the C atoms and surface Si atoms around SV defects in SV/Si greatly shift during Li diffusion. The times of charge and discharge are reduced and the battery life is shortened if Si particles are encapsulated with SV. On the other hand, the energy barrier of Li diffusion from SV/Si is not low; it is even slightly higher than the value of DV5–8–5/Si. In brief, the probability of Li penetration through graphene would be greatly enhanced if Si particles are encapsulated with defective graphene instead of perfect graphene. Considering the energy barriers of Li diffusion into and out from Gr/Si and the stability of the structures of Gr/Si during Li diffusion, DV5–8–5 defective graphene may be a good choice as the material for encapsulated Si particles.

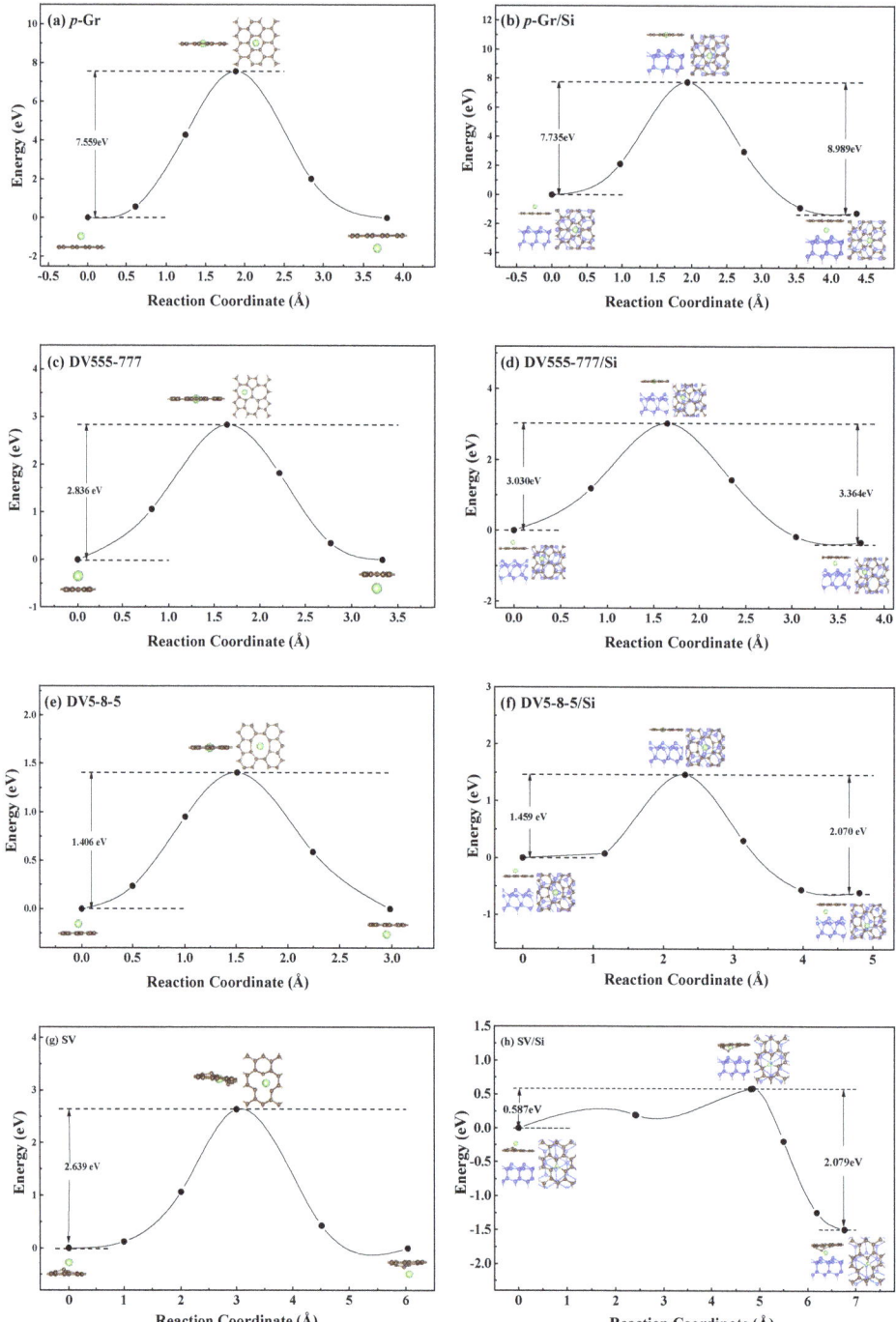

**Figure 5.** Energy barrier of Li diffusion.

In order to better understanding the electronic structures of DV5–8–5, we also calculate the Bader charge, band structures and PDOS of these structures during Li diffusion in DV5–8–5 and DV5–8–5/Si. As a reference, the electronic structures of corresponding p–Gr are also calculated, which are shown in the supplementary material. The DV5–8–5 defect exhibits a Dirac-like cone band structure, but a gap opens between the Dirac-like cones as shown in Figure S2a. There is a nearly flat band above the $E_F$ level and within the gap between the Dirac-like cones. When the Li atom adsorbs on it (i.e., Li/DV5–8–5), the band in the gap becomes more dispersive and partially occupied as shown in Figure S2b. Meanwhile, the gap between the Dirac-like cones reduces. With the diffusion of the Li atom (Li@DV5–8–5), the gap between the Dirac-like cones becomes wider as shown in Figure S2c. After Li penetration is completed, the band structure is recovered as shown in Figure S2b. During Li diffusion, the Li atom maintains the $Li^+$ ion. When the Si substrate is included, the DV5–8–5 still exhibits a Dirac-like cone structure. The gap between the cones becomes wider. There are three flat bands in the gap due to the influence of the Si substrate, and these bands are all above $E_F$ as shown in Figure S2d. During Li diffusion in DV5–8–5/Si, the system remains as p–type doping; the Li atom maintains the $Li^+$ ion; the bands in the gap become more complex; and some of the bands become more dispersive and partially occupied. Similar to the case of DV5–8–5, the gap between the Dirac-like cones experiences a process of first reducing (Li/DV5–8–5/Si), then increasing (Li@DV5–8–5/Si), and finally basically recovering (DV5–8–5/Li/Si).

## 4. Conclusions

During Li diffusion in the Gr sheet and Gr/Si slab (Gr = p–Gr, DV5–8–5, DV555–777 and SV), the initial points, saddle points and end structures are studied by first-principles calculation. Firstly, the initial and end points of different structures are screened, and their energetic stability is also discussed. Then the CI-NEB calculations are employed to evaluate the diffusion barrier by seeking the saddle point and the minimum energy path. For monolayer Gr, Li prefers to adsorb on d–Gr (Gr = DV5–8–5, DV555–777 and SV), comparing with p–Gr. The $E_{ads}$ of Li/DV5–8–5 and Li/DV555–777 is more than 1 eV lower than that of Li/p–Gr; the $E_{ads}$ of the most stable adsorption structure Li/SV is nearly 1.8 eV lower than that of Li/p–Gr. The $E_{ads}$ order of Li/Gr/Si is consistent with that of Li/Gr, except Li/SV/Si. It is difficult to adsorb on SV/Si for Li, as its $E_{ads}$ is even higher about 1 eV than that of Li/p–Gr/Si. It may be related to the structural deformation of SV/Si. During Li diffusion in Gr, the Gr sheets basically maintain the planar whether for Gr or Gr/Si, except for SV. When Li diffuses in SV, one of the C atoms is obviously deviated from the SV plane and approaches the Li atom whether in the initial point Li/SV or the end point SV/Li. More C atoms deviate from the SV plane and approach the Li atom when Li diffuses in SV/Si. Even in the saddle point Li@SV and Li@SV/Si, the C atoms around Li are almost deviated from the original plane, i.e., during Li diffusion in SV and SV/Si, the SV plane structure is seriously deformed; moreover, several Si atoms on the surface of Si substrate deviate from their original positions in SV/Li/Si. It may be the reason why many properties of Li diffusing in SV or SV/Si are different from those of the other Gr, including the order of $E_{ads}$, bond lengths between atoms, layer distance and even the diffusion barrier. For monolayer Gr (Gr = p–Gr, DV5–8–5 and DV555–777), the average bond lengths of C–C and Li–C in the saddle-point structures (Li@Gr) are larger than the ones of the corresponding initial structures (Li/Gr) due to Li being in the plane of Gr. When Li penetration is complete, the bond lengths are basically restored to the values of the initial structures. In Gr/Si, the Si substrate has negligible effects on these bond lengths. Comparing with the three defects above, the average C–C and Li–C bond lengths of the saddle-point structure Li@SV are not increased but decreased, although the Li atom is also in the SV plane. In Li@SV/Si, the average C–C bond length increases slightly, while its Li–C average bond length decreases over 0.3 Å compared to the initial structure. After Li penetrates the SV plane, the C–C average bond length does not return to the initial value but is increased. The distances between the Gr sheet and the surface of the Si substrate ($d_{C-Si}$) in Gr/Si (Gr = p–Gr, DV5–8–5 and DV555–777) change little during Li diffusion in them. However, the $d_{C-Si}$ value of SV/Si decreases about 0.1 Å upon Li adsorption, which is about 10 times that of other structural variation. When Li passes through the SV, its $d_{C-Si}$ value further decreases, and the total reduction is more than 0.2 Å. The existence of the Si substrate also slightly affects the distances ($d_{Li-C}$) from Li to the Gr sheet. Comparing with Li/Gr (Gr = p–Gr, DV5–8–5, DV555–777 and SV), the $d_{Li-C}$ in Li/p–Gr/Si increases, while decreasing in Li/d–Gr/Si. The $d_{Li-C}$ in Li/SV/Si decreases most, about 0.1 Å. After passing through Gr, Li is generally closer to the Si surface, except for DV555–777/Li/Si. Considering the distance between Gr and the Si surface ($d_{C-Si}$), the distance from Li to Gr is SV > p–Gr > DV5–8–5 > DV555–777 in proportion. Accordingly, the order of $d_{Li-Si}$ is opposite to that above. It indirectly provides evidence that Li binds more closely to the Si surface in SV/Li/Si while bonding more tightly to the DV555–777 layer in DV555–777/Li/Si. The CI-NEB calculation results show that d–Gr greatly reduces the energy barriers whether Li diffuses into Gr or Gr/Si. The energy barrier of Li diffusion in DV5–8–5 is just 1.406 eV, which is lower by ~6.153 eV than the value of p–Gr. When Li diffuses into Gr/Si, the energy barriers are slightly increased comparing with the case of monolayer Gr. Nevertheless, the diffusion barriers of d–Gr/Si are still much lower than the value in p–Gr/Si. The energy barrier of Li diffusion to SV/Si is unexpectedly decreased to 0.587 eV. In addition, the structures of Gr/Li/Si are more stable than Li/Gr/Si whether for p–Gr or d–Gr, which indicates that it is more difficult for Li to diffuse out from Gr/Si. However, it is much easier for Li to diffuse out from d–Gr/Si than from p–Gr/Si. Our results suggest that the Si particles encapsulated by defective graphene may be a candidate for anode materials of LIBS. From the perspective of the diffusion barrier, both SV and DV5–8–5 defective graphenes seem to be good materials for encapsulated Si particles, and SV is better. However, the SV/Si structure is deformed greatly during Li diffusion, which reduces the times of charge and discharge and shortens the battery life. Moreover, the energy barrier of Li diffusion out from SV/Si is not low and is even slightly higher than the value of DV5–8–5/Si. In contrast, DV5–8–5/Si remains a relatively stable structure during Li diffusion within it. Therefore, DV5–8–5 defective graphene may be a good choice as the material of encapsulated Si particles.

**Supplementary Materials:** The following are available online at https://www.mdpi.com/article/10.3390/nano11123397/s1: Table S1: The bader charges of Li atom, Gr (Gr = p–Gr and DV5–8–5) sheet and Si substrate of the initial, saddle and end structures during Li diffusion in Gr and Gr/Si. Figure S1: Band structures of (a) p–Gr (b) Li/p–Gr (c) Li@p–Gr (d) Si Substrate (e) p–Gr/Si (f) Li/p–Gr/Si (g) Li@p–Gr/Si (h) p–Gr/Li/Si. Figure S2: Band structures of (a) DV5–8–5 (b) Li/DV5–8–5 (c) Li@DV5–8–5 (d) DV5–8–5/Si (e) Li/DV5–8–5/Si (f) Li@DV5–8–5/Si and (g) Li/DV5–8–5/Si. Figure S3: The line configurations of the initial, saddle and end structures during Li diffusion in Gr and Gr/Si (Gr = p–Gr and DV5–8–5); and the typical C atoms discussed in Figures S4–S11 are labeled. The green ball represents Li atom; and the brown and blue lines represent C atoms and Si atoms and their bonding, respectively. Figure S4: PDOS of the typical C atoms (labeled in Figure S3) of p–Gr and all Si atoms of Si substrate. Figure S5: PDOS of Li atom and the typical C atoms (labeled in Figure S3) in (a) Li/p–Gr and (b) Li@p–Gr. Figure S6: PDOS of the typical C atoms (labeled in Figure S3) and all Si atoms in p–Gr/Si. Figure S7: PDOS of Li atom, all Si atoms and the typical C atoms (labeled in Figure S3) in (a) Li/p–Gr/Si (b) Li@p–Gr/Si and (c) p–Gr/Li/Si. Figure S8: PDOS of the typical C atoms in DV5–8–5 labeled in Figure S3. Figure S9: PDOS of Li atom and the typical C atoms (labeled in Figure S3) in (a) Li/DV5–8–5 and (b) Li@DV5–8–5. Figure S10: PDOS of all Si atoms of the typical C atoms (labeled in Figure S3) in DV5–8–5/Si. Figure S11: PDOS of Li atom, all Si atoms and the typical C atoms (labeled in Figure S3) in (a) Li/DV5–8–5/Si (b) Li@DV5–8–5/Si and (c) DV5–8–5/Li/Si.

**Author Contributions:** Data curation, investigation, writing—original draft preparation, reviewing and editing, W.Q.; supervision, W.-C.L.; investigation, X.-Y.X.; reviewing and editing, K.-M.H.; reviewing and editing, supervision, C.-Z.W. All authors have read and agreed to the published version of the manuscript.

**Funding:** This research was funded by the National Natural Science Foundation of China (Grant Nos. 21603114 and 21773132) and US DOE-BES: DE-AC02-07CH11358.

**Institutional Review Board Statement:** Not applicable.

**Informed Consent Statement:** Not applicable.

**Data Availability Statement:** Not applicable.

**Acknowledgments:** Work at Ames Laboratory was supported by Department of Energy, Office of Science, Basic Energy Sciences, Division of Materials Science and Engineering including a grant of computer time at the National Energy Research Scientific Computing Center (NERSC) in Berkeley. Ames Laboratory is operated for the U.S. Department of Energy by Iowa State University under Contract No. DE-AC02-07CH11358.

**Conflicts of Interest:** The authors declare no conflict of interest.

## References

1. Bruce, P.G.; Freunberger, S.A.; Hardwick, L.J.; Tarascon, J.M. Li-$O_2$ and Li-S batteries with high energy storage. *Nat. Mater.* **2011**, *11*, 19–29. [CrossRef]
2. Armand, M.; Tarascon, J.M. Building better batteries. *Nature* **2008**, *451*, 652–657. [CrossRef]
3. Arico, A.S.; Bruce, P.; Scrosati, B.; Tarascon, J.M.; Van Schalkwijk, W. Nanostructured materials for advanced energy conversion and storage devices. *Nat. Mater.* **2005**, *4*, 366–377. [CrossRef]
4. Kasavajjula, U.; Wang, C.; Appleby, A.J. Nano- and bulk-silicon-based insertion anodes for lithium-ion secondary cells. *J. Power Sources* **2007**, *163*, 1003–1039. [CrossRef]
5. Beaulieu, L.Y.; Hatchard, T.D.; Bonakdarpour, A.; Fleischauer, M.D.; Dahn, J.R. Reaction of Li with Alloy Thin Films Studied by In Situ AFM. *J. Electrochem. Soc.* **2003**, *150*, A1457–A1464. [CrossRef]
6. Huang, S.; Zhu, T. Atomistic mechanisms of lithium insertion in amorphous silicon. *J. Power Sources* **2011**, *196*, 3664–3668. [CrossRef]
7. Cui, L.F.; Ruffo, R.; Chan, C.K.; Peng, H.L.; Cui, Y. Crystalline-Amorphous Core-Shell Silicon Nanowires for High Capacity and High Current Battery Electrodes. *Nano Lett.* **2009**, *9*, 491–495. [CrossRef] [PubMed]
8. Yao, Y.; McDowell, M.T.; Ryu, I.; Wu, H.; Liu, N.; Hu, L.; Nix, W.D.; Cui, Y. Interconnected silicon hollow nanospheres for lithium-ion battery anodes with long cycle life. *Nano Lett.* **2011**, *11*, 2949–2954. [CrossRef] [PubMed]
9. Park, M.H.; Kim, M.G.; Joo, J.; Kim, K.; Kim, J.; Ahn, S.; Cui, Y.; Cho, J. Silicon Nanotube Battery Anodes. *Nano Lett.* **2009**, *9*, 3844–3847. [CrossRef] [PubMed]
10. Magasinski, A.; Dixon, P.; Hertzberg, B.; Kvit, A.; Ayala, J.; Yushin, G. High-performance lithium-ion anodes using a hierarchical bottom-up approach. *Nat. Mater.* **2010**, *9*, 353–358. [CrossRef] [PubMed]
11. Son, I.H.; Hwan Park, J.; Kwon, S.; Park, S.; Rummeli, M.H.; Bachmatiuk, A.; Song, H.J.; Ku, J.; Choi, J.W.; Choi, J.M.; et al. Silicon carbide-free graphene growth on silicon for lithium-ion battery with high volumetric energy density. *Nat. Commun.* **2015**, *6*, 7393. [CrossRef]
12. Evanoff, K.; Magasinski, A.; Yang, J.; Yushin, G. Nanosilicon-Coated Graphene Granules as Anodes for Li-Ion Batteries. *Adv. Energy Mater.* **2011**, *1*, 495–498. [CrossRef]
13. Yi, R.; Dai, F.; Gordin, M.L.; Chen, S.; Wang, D. Micro-sized Si-C Composite with Interconnected Nanoscale Building Blocks as High-Performance Anodes for Practical Application in Lithium-Ion Batteries. *Adv. Energy Mater.* **2013**, *3*, 295–300. [CrossRef]
14. Wang, J.W.; Liu, X.H.; Zhao, K.J.; Palmer, A.; Patten, E.; Burton, D.; Mao, S.X.; Suo, Z.G.; Huang, J.Y. Sandwich-Lithiation and Longitudinal Crack in Amorphous Silicon Coated on Carbon Nanofibers. *ACS Nano* **2012**, *6*, 9158–9167. [CrossRef]
15. Lu, Z.D.; Liu, N.; Lee, H.W.; Zhao, J.; Li, W.Y.; Li, Y.Z.; Cui, Y. Nonfilling Carbon Coating of Porous Silicon Micrometer-Sized Particles for High-Performance Lithium Battery Anodes. *ACS Nano* **2015**, *9*, 2540–2547. [CrossRef]
16. Wang, C.M.; Li, X.; Wang, Z.; Xu, W.; Liu, J.; Gao, F.; Kovarik, L.; Zhang, J.G.; Howe, J.; Burton, D.J.; et al. In situ TEM investigation of congruent phase transition and structural evolution of nanostructured silicon/carbon anode for lithium ion batteries. *Nano Lett.* **2012**, *12*, 1624–1632. [CrossRef]
17. Ge, M.; Rong, J.; Fang, X.; Zhou, C. Porous doped silicon nanowires for lithium ion battery anode with long cycle life. *Nano Lett.* **2012**, *12*, 2318–2323. [CrossRef]
18. Klankowski, S.A.; Rojeski, R.A.; Cruden, B.A.; Liu, J.; Wu, J.; Li, J. A high-performance lithium-ion battery anode based on the core–shell heterostructure of silicon-coated vertically aligned carbon nanofibers. *J. Mater. Chem. A* **2013**, *1*, 1055–1064. [CrossRef]
19. Ji, L.; Zheng, H.; Ismach, A.; Tan, Z.; Xun, S.; Lin, E.; Battaglia, V.; Srinivasan, V.; Zhang, Y. Graphene/Si multilayer structure anodes for advanced half and full lithium-ion cells. *Nano Energy* **2012**, *1*, 164–171. [CrossRef]
20. Luo, J.; Zhao, X.; Wu, J.; Jang, H.D.; Kung, H.H.; Huang, J. Crumpled Graphene-Encapsulated Si Nanoparticles for Lithium Ion Battery Anodes. *J. Phys. Chem. Lett.* **2012**, *3*, 1824–1829. [CrossRef]

21. Li, Y.; Guo, B.; Ji, L.; Lin, Z.; Xu, G.; Liang, Y.; Zhang, S.; Toprakci, O.; Hu, Y.; Alcoutlabi, M.; et al. Structure control and performance improvement of carbon nanofibers containing a dispersion of silicon nanoparticles for energy storage. *Carbon* **2013**, *51*, 185–194. [CrossRef]
22. Song, T.; Lee, D.H.; Kwon, M.S.; Choi, J.M.; Han, H.; Doo, S.G.; Chang, H.; Park, W.I.; Sigmund, W.; Kim, H.; et al. Silicon nanowires with a carbon nanofiber branch as lithium-ion anode material. *J. Mater. Chem.* **2011**, *21*, 12619–12621. [CrossRef]
23. Ren, J.-G.; Wu, Q.-H.; Hong, G.; Zhang, W.-J.; Wu, H.; Amine, K.; Yang, J.; Lee, S.-T. Silicon-Graphene Composite Anodes for High-Energy Lithium Batteries. *Energy Technol.* **2013**, *1*, 77–84. [CrossRef]
24. He, Y.S.; Gao, P.F.; Chen, J.; Yang, X.W.; Liao, X.Z.; Yang, J.; Ma, Z.F. A novel bath lily-like graphene sheet-wrapped nano-Si composite as a high performance anode material for Li-ion batteries. *RSC Adv.* **2011**, *1*, 958–960. [CrossRef]
25. Gohier, A.; Laik, B.; Kim, K.H.; Maurice, J.L.; Pereira-Ramos, J.P.; Cojocaru, C.S.; Van Tran, P. High-rate capability silicon decorated vertically aligned carbon nanotubes for Li-ion batteries. *Adv. Mater.* **2012**, *24*, 2592–2597. [CrossRef]
26. Chan, M.K.; Wolverton, C.; Greeley, J.P. First principles simulations of the electrochemical lithiation and delithiation of faceted crystalline silicon. *J. Am. Chem. Soc.* **2012**, *134*, 14362–14374. [CrossRef]
27. Tritsaris, G.A.; Kaxiras, E.; Meng, S.; Wang, E. Adsorption and diffusion of lithium on layered silicon for Li-ion storage. *Nano Lett.* **2013**, *13*, 2258–2263. [CrossRef]
28. Jung, S.C.; Choi, J.W.; Han, Y.K. Anisotropic volume expansion of crystalline silicon during electrochemical lithium insertion: An atomic level rationale. *Nano Lett.* **2012**, *12*, 5342–5347. [CrossRef]
29. Zhao, K.; Wang, W.L.; Gregoire, J.; Pharr, M.; Suo, Z.; Vlassak, J.J.; Kaxiras, E. Lithium-assisted plastic deformation of silicon electrodes in lithium-ion batteries: A first-principles theoretical study. *Nano Lett.* **2011**, *11*, 2962–2967. [CrossRef]
30. Kaghazchi, P. Mechanism of Li intercalation into Si. *Appl. Phys. Lett.* **2013**, *102*, 093901. [CrossRef]
31. Jung, S.C.; Han, Y.K. Facet-dependent lithium intercalation into Si crystals: Si (100) vs. Si (111). *Phys. Chem. Chem. Phys.* **2011**, *13*, 21282–21287. [CrossRef]
32. Johari, P.; Qi, Y.; Shenoy, V.B. The mixing mechanism during lithiation of Si negative electrode in Li-ion batteries: An ab initio molecular dynamics study. *Nano Lett.* **2011**, *11*, 5494–5500. [CrossRef]
33. Zhang, Q.; Cui, Y.; Wang, E. Anisotropic Lithium Insertion Behavior in Silicon Nanowires: Binding Energy, Diffusion Barrier, and Strain Effect. *J. Phys. Chem. C* **2011**, *115*, 9376–9381. [CrossRef]
34. Khantha, M.; Cordero, N.A.; Molina, L.M.; Alonso, J.A.; Girifalco, L.A. Interaction of lithium with graphene: An ab initio study. *Phys. Rev. B* **2004**, *70*, 125422. [CrossRef]
35. Wang, J.; Liew, K.M. Density Functional Study of Interaction of Lithium with Pristine and Stone-Wales-Defective Single-Walled Silicon Carbide Nanotubes. *J. Phys. Chem. C* **2012**, *116*, 26888–26897. [CrossRef]
36. Wang, C.; Wu, H.; Chen, Z.; McDowell, M.T.; Cui, Y.; Bao, Z. Self-healing chemistry enables the stable operation of silicon microparticle anodes for high-energy lithium-ion batteries. *Nat. Chem.* **2013**, *5*, 1042–1048. [CrossRef]
37. Saint, J.; Morcrette, M.; Larcher, D.; Laffont, L.; Beattie, S.; Pérès, J.P.; Talaga, D.; Couzi, M.; Tarascon, J.M. Towards a Fundamental Understanding of the Improved Electrochemical Performance of Silicon–Carbon Composites. *Adv. Funct. Mater.* **2007**, *17*, 1765–1774. [CrossRef]
38. Liu, X.H.; Zheng, H.; Zhong, L.; Huang, S.; Karki, K.; Zhang, L.Q.; Liu, Y.; Kushima, A.; Liang, W.T.; Wang, J.W.; et al. Anisotropic swelling and fracture of silicon nanowires during lithiation. *Nano Lett.* **2011**, *11*, 3312–3318. [CrossRef] [PubMed]
39. Lee, S.W.; McDowell, M.T.; Choi, J.W.; Cui, Y. Anomalous shape changes of silicon nanopillars by electrochemical lithiation. *Nano Lett.* **2011**, *11*, 3034–3039. [CrossRef]
40. Li, Y.; Yan, K.; Lee, H.-W.; Lu, Z.; Liu, N.; Cui, Y. Growth of conformal graphene cages on micrometre-sized silicon particles as stable battery anodes. *Nat. Energy* **2016**, *1*, 15029. [CrossRef]
41. Jeong, S.K.; Inaba, M.; Mogi, R.; Iriyama, Y.; Abe, T.; Ogumi, Z. Surface film formation on a graphite negative electrode in lithium-ion batteries: Atomic force microscopy study on the effects of film-forming additives in propylene carbonate solutions. *Langmuir* **2001**, *17*, 8281–8286. [CrossRef]
42. Profatilova, I.A.; Kim, S.-S.; Choi, N.-S. Enhanced thermal properties of the solid electrolyte interphase formed on graphite in an electrolyte with fluoroethylene carbonate. *Electrochim. Acta* **2009**, *54*, 4445–4450. [CrossRef]
43. Odbadrakh, K.; McNutt, N.W.; Nicholson, D.M.; Rios, O.; Keffer, D.J. Lithium diffusion at Si-C interfaces in silicon-graphene composites. *Appl. Phys. Lett.* **2014**, *105*, 053906. [CrossRef]
44. Chou, C.-Y.; Hwang, G.S. Role of Interface in the Lithiation of Silicon-Graphene Composites: A First Principles Study. *J. Phys. Chem. C* **2013**, *117*, 9598–9604. [CrossRef]
45. Uthaisar, C.; Barone, V. Edge effects on the characteristics of Li diffusion in graphene. *Nano Lett.* **2010**, *10*, 2838–2842. [CrossRef]
46. Zhou, L.-J.; Hou, Z.F.; Wu, L.-M. First-Principles Study of Lithium Adsorption and Diffusion on Graphene with Point Defects. *J. Phys. Chem. C* **2012**, *116*, 21780–21787. [CrossRef]
47. Fan, X.; Zheng, W.T.; Kuo, J.L. Adsorption and diffusion of Li on pristine and defective graphene. *ACS Appl. Mater. Interfaces* **2012**, *4*, 2432–2438. [CrossRef] [PubMed]
48. Stone, A.J.; Wales, D.J. Theoretical Studies of Icosahedral $C_{60}$ and Some Related Species. *Chem. Phys. Lett.* **1986**, *128*, 501–503. [CrossRef]
49. Banhart, F.; Kotakoski, J.; Krasheninnikov, A.V. Structural Defects in Graphene. *ACS Nano* **2011**, *5*, 26–41. [CrossRef]

50. Jiang, H.R.; Wu, M.C.; Ren, Y.X.; Shyy, W.; Zhao, T.S. Towards a uniform distribution of zinc in the negative electrode for zinc bromine flow batteries. *Appl. Energy* **2018**, *213*, 366–374. [CrossRef]
51. Jiang, H.R.; Tan, P.; Liu, M.; Zeng, Y.K.; Zhao, T.S. Unraveling the Positive Roles of Point Defects on Carbon Surfaces in Nonaqueous Lithium–Oxygen Batteries. *J. Phys. Chem. C* **2016**, *120*, 18394–18402. [CrossRef]
52. Jiang, H.R.; Wu, M.C.; Zhou, X.L.; Yan, X.H.; Zhao, T.S. Computational insights into the effect of carbon structures at the atomic level for non-aqueous sodium-oxygen batteries. *J. Power Sources* **2016**, *325*, 91–97. [CrossRef]
53. Zhang, W.; Lu, W.C.; Zhang, H.X.; Ho, K.M.; Wang, C.Z. Tight-binding calculation studies of vacancy and adatom defects in graphene. *J. Phys. Condens. Matter* **2016**, *28*, 115001. [CrossRef]
54. Ugeda, M.M.; Brihuega, I.; Hiebel, F.; Mallet, P.; Veuillen, J.-Y.; Gómez-Rodríguez, J.M.; Ynduráin, F. Electronic and structural characterization of divacancies in irradiated graphene. *Phys. Rev. B* **2012**, *85*, 121402. [CrossRef]
55. Lee, G.D.; Wang, C.Z.; Yoon, E.; Hwang, N.M.; Kim, D.Y.; Ho, K.M. Diffusion, coalescence, and reconstruction of vacancy defects in graphene layers. *Phys. Rev. Lett.* **2005**, *95*, 205501. [CrossRef]
56. Kresse, G.; Joubert, D. From ultrasoft pseudopotentials to the projector augmented-wave method. *Phys. Rev. B* **1999**, *59*, 1758–1775. [CrossRef]
57. Perdew, J.P.; Burke, K.; Ernzerhof, M. Generalized gradient approximation made simple. *Phys. Rev. Lett.* **1996**, *77*, 3865–3868. [CrossRef]
58. Kresse, G.; Furthmuller, J. Efficient iterative schemes for ab initio total-energy calculations using a plane-wave basis set. *Phys. Rev. B* **1996**, *54*, 11169–11186. [CrossRef]
59. Harl, J.; Kresse, G. Accurate bulk properties from approximate many-body techniques. *Phys. Rev. Lett.* **2009**, *103*, 056401. [CrossRef]
60. Harl, J.; Schimka, L.; Kresse, G. Assessing the quality of the random phase approximation for lattice constants and atomization energies of solids. *Phys. Rev. B* **2010**, *81*, 115126. [CrossRef]

Article

# Interface Kinetics Assisted Barrier Removal in Large Area 2D-WS$_2$ Growth to Facilitate Mass Scale Device Production

Abid [1], Poonam Sehrawat [1], Christian M. Julien [2,*] and Saikh S. Islam [1,*]

[1] Centre for Nanoscience and Nanotechnology, Jamia Millia Islamia (A Central University), New Delhi 110025, India; abid.zak@gmail.com (A.); sehrawatpoonam@gmail.com (P.S.)
[2] Institut de Minéralogie, de Physique des Matériaux et de Cosmologie (IMPMC), Sorbonne Université, CNRS-UMR 7590, 4 Place Jussieu, 75252 Paris, France
* Correspondence: christian.julien@sorbonne-universite.fr (C.M.J.); sislam@jmi.ac.in (S.S.I.)

**Abstract:** Growth of monolayer WS$_2$ of domain size beyond few microns is a challenge even today; and it is still restricted to traditional exfoliation techniques, with no control over the dimension. Here, we present the synthesis of mono- to few layer WS$_2$ film of centimeter$^2$ size on graphene-oxide (GO) coated Si/SiO$_2$ substrate using the chemical vapor deposition CVD technique. Although the individual size of WS$_2$ crystallites is found smaller, the joining of grain boundaries due to $sp^2$-bonded carbon nanostructures (~3–6 nm) in GO to reduced graphene-oxide (RGO) transformed film, facilitates the expansion of domain size in continuous fashion resulting in full coverage of the substrate. Another factor, equally important for expanding the domain boundary, is surface roughness of RGO film. This is confirmed by conducting WS$_2$ growth on Si wafer marked with few scratches on polished surface. Interestingly, WS$_2$ growth was observed in and around the rough surface irrespective of whether polished or unpolished. More the roughness is, better the yield in crystalline WS$_2$ flakes. Raman mapping ascertains the uniform mono-to-few layer growth over the entire substrate, and it is reaffirmed by photoluminescence, AFM and HRTEM. This study may open up a new approach for growth of large area WS$_2$ film for device application. We have also demonstrated the potential of the developed film for photodetector application, where the cycling response of the detector is highly repetitive with negligible drift.

**Keywords:** chemical; vapor deposition; graphene oxide; transition-metal dichalcogenides; WS$_2$

## 1. Introduction

Lamellar two-dimensional (2D) WS$_2$ has immense potential for electronic applications because of its remarkable properties such as tunable direct bandgap [1–3], high photoluminescence intensity [4,5], high emission quantum field [6], attractive spin-orbit coupling [6], substantial exciton/trion binding energies [7–9], etc., which give WS$_2$ superior leverage over other transition-metal dichalcogenides (TMDCs). Unfortunately, the research on WS$_2$ is not matured yet, especially large-scale production of single-crystal monolayers [10–12]. Challenges lie in reliable synthesis of atomically thick 2D layers and controlled manipulation of electronic properties [13]. Though mechanical cleaving still remains a relatively facile technique to prepare high quality single to few layered WS$_2$, problems such as absence of control over thickness, relatively small lateral size and low yield limit its applications and commercialization [14,15]. The most popular techniques to produce few-layered WS$_2$ include intercalation driven exfoliation [16], liquid phase exfoliation [17], physical vapor deposition [18], hydrothermal reaction [19], and heat treatment of W and S containing precursors [20]. However, the domain size of developed WS$_2$ via aforementioned methods is generally restricted to a few microns (μm), and the production of WS$_2$ monolayer films with desired domain size remains a distant dream. To achieve this, several strategies (e.g., atomic layer deposition [21], pulsed-laser deposition [22,23], metal/metal oxide thin films [24], suitable metal substrates [25], etc.), have been suggested to achieve uniform dispersion of precursors over substrates. Presently, large scale continuous growth of TMDCs is highly complex and expensive, and results in poor quality films [9].

Chemical vapor deposition (CVD) remains a challenge for a long time for growing two-dimensional TMDC materials with high crystallinity, desired thickness, and sufficient domain size [10,12,26–28]. For $WS_2$ growth, typical synthesis approach involves sulfidation of $WO_3$ powders at sufficiently high temperature. The growth conditions such as precursor type, process step, and their manipulations during growth, are found to greatly affect the product quality. Most of the reports on CVD grown $WS_2$ solely bank on vapor phase reaction between S and W precursors at suitably high temperatures, where a single furnace is used for both precursors. In such systems, there is no control over the temperature of individual precursor, thereby limiting the parameter space of growth reaction [28]; leading to poor uniformity and repeatability. High melting point of $WO_3$ powders and sulfurization rate are found to influence the growth process. Achieving large triangle shaped growth is challenging, because of lower vapor pressure of $WO_3$ due to its high melting temperature (1473 °C) [29]. This is a serious problem and severely lowers the partial pressure of $WO_3$ vapors [29]. Further, the low vapor pressure of $WO_3$ also hampers the availability of W atoms on substrate surface. Thus, enhancing the partial pressure of $WO_3$ vapors is a natural approach to obtain large sized $WS_2$ flakes [12]. This can be accomplished by reducing the pressure of the furnace. However, this increases the S vapor transfer speed, thereby increasing the sulfurization rate [10]. Fast sulfurization is not desirable for the transport and diffusion of precursor vapors on a substrate and may result in aggregation of precursors at certain locations on the substrate, thereby limiting the growth of large sized $WS_2$ crystals [10,30,31]. An efficient way involves a trade-off between the increase in partial pressure of $WO_3$ vapors and lower the transfer speed of S vapors.

Recently, many researchers have focused on developing monolayer $WS_2$ via CVD. Zhang et al. employed low-pressure chemical vapor deposition (LPCVD) technique to synthesize atomically thin triangle shaped $WS_2$ crystals on sapphire substrate having single domain size ~50 μm [32]. An improvement was introduced in the CVD process by Cong et al. to effectively increase the concentration of precursors and furnace pressure [33]. They achieved single-domain growths of ~178 μm [33]. Li et al. introduced further changes in the CVD reaction by employing alkali metal halides as growth promoters [34]. The groups of Zhang [32] and Li [34] reported that due to strong reducing nature, the mixing of suitable amount of $H_2$ enhances the sublimation and sulfurization of $WO_3$ precursor. Fu et al. [35] investigated the influence of CVD reaction temperature and gas flow rate (comprising a mixture of 97% Ar and 3% $H_2$) on the growth size and morphology of $WS_2$ films. The optimized growth conditions yielded a domain size of ~52 μm. Rong's group [28] achieved precise control over S introduction time by utilizing a two-zone furnace and obtained very large area $WS_2$ films of 370 μm domain size. Recently, Liu et al. [36] reported sequential synthesis of several one-, and two-dimensional nanomaterials by intentionally creating initial low sulfur conditions, to divide the growth process in two stages: the first stage is a partial reduction and the second one is sulfurization. By this, they could exploit a $WO_{3-x}$ intermediate route, and were able to grow large size $WS_2$ (150 μm).

TMDCs growth is very susceptible to substrate treatment prior to formation [37]. To assist the nucleation by seeding the substrate with various aromatic molecules, such as -3,4,9,10-tetracarboxylic acid tetrapotassium salt (PTAS), perylene-3,4,9,10-tetracarboxylic dianhydride (PTCDA), and reduced graphene oxide (RGO), perylene encourages the lateral growth of TMDCs. However, this seeding technique helps to grow the large area mono-to few layer TMDCs but continuous film from the abovementioned technique is still limited. Although the CVD method has many advantages, the coordination among various growth parameters is highly complex and requires further elucidation.

In this work, we present a novel approach for large area synthesis of $WS_2$ on graphene oxide (GO) surface via CVD under high temperature conditions of 1070 °C. Upon transformation to RGO during growth process, GO becomes a mixed $sp^3$-$sp^2$ bonded network, where nano-sized $sp^2$-patches of size ~3–6 nm, are randomly distributed with more than 60–70% coverage [38–40]. The $sp^2$-patches are six-fold aromatic carbon atoms with C=C bonds, whereas major percentage of $sp^3$ bonds constitutes epoxides (C–O) and hydroxyl (−OH) groups in the basal plane and somewhat lesser amount of carboxyl (−COOH) and carbonyl (−C=O) functionalities in the edges [38–40]. These $sp^2$-chemical bonds act as a seed to promote the growth of large area $WS_2$ film. The as-developed $WS_2$ layers are polycrystalline comprising mainly mono- to few layers. The single-crystal domains are triangular and hexagonal in shape, with sizes up to 60 μm on Si/SiO$_2$ and ~15 μm on the GO coated Si/SiO$_2$, respectively. The domain size of $WS_2$ film on GO coated Si/SiO$_2$ is much smaller than that on non-GO substrate, but the development of large continuous surface makes a great footprint in $WS_2$ growth, attributed to C=C assisted coalescence of high-density polycrystalline grain boundaries into large domain area. Suitable explanation is given how $sp^2$-patches comprised of C=C bonds are pivotal in the expansion of domain size of $WS_2$ film. Surface roughness of the top layer of substrate is a well-recognized technique for nucleation of nanostructure growth and is cross-checked with intentionally created rough surface on silicon wafer. The proposed device fabrication technique is well suited for mass production of identical devices, and therefore bids for commercial scale development. Moreover, this technique can be extended to the fabrication of other TMDCs. We have further demonstrated the use of the developed film for photodetector applications.

## 2. Materials and Methods

$WO_3$ powders (≥99.995% trace metals basis), sulfur (≥99.998% trace metals basis), natural graphite powders (flakes size: 45 μm, ≥99.99% trace metals basis), and sodium nitrate ($NaNO_3$, ≥99.995% trace metals basis) were commercially secured from Sigma Aldrich, India. Sulfuric acid ($H_2SO_4$) and potassium permagnate ($KMnO_4$) have been supplied by Thermo Fisher Scientific, India and DI water was obtained from Merck (Darmstadt, Germany). For experimental purposes, only analytical grade materials/chemicals were procured and used as received.

The morphology, size and structure of as-synthesized $WS_2$ were examined via a transmission electron microscope (TEM) (JEOL JEM F-200, Tokyo, Japan) working at 200 kV. The samples for TEM investigations were kept on the conventional holey carbon Cu grid. High-resolution transmission electron microscopy (HRTEM, JEOL, Tokyo, Japan) studies reveal the uniformity and high quality of $WS_2$ samples grown on both Si/SiO$_2$ and GO coated Si/SiO$_2$ substrates. Basic studies of $WS_2$ growth and the domain size were performed on an optical microscope (Leica DM4 P, Wetzlar, Germany). Raman spectrophotometers (WITec Alpha 300RA, Ulm, Germany and LabRAM HR800 HORIBA JY, Kyoto, Japan) fitted with a Peltier cooled CCD detector and confocal microscope were operated for verifying the crystallinity, defects and number of layers. A diode laser of excitation wavelength 532 nm was used to excite the samples. A 100X objective lens with spot size of 1 μm was used to focus the excitation onto the samples. The thickness of grown sample was analyzed by atomic force microscopy (AFM) fitted with the Raman system. Surface morphology of the CVD grown $WS_2$ on Si/SiO$_2$ and GO coated Si/SiO$_2$ was studied on a scanning electron microscope (SEM) (Nova Nano SEM 450, FEI, Oregon, USA). The photoluminescence (PL) measurements were performed by fluorescence spectrometer (Agilent Technologies, Carry Eclipse fluorescence spectrometer, California, USA). For PL investigations, the prepared samples were dispersed in ethanol by simply ultrasonicating the growth substrate for few minutes and isolating the upper one-third solution into a quartz cuvette.

## 3. Results and Discussion

Two approaches have been adopted to synthesize monolayer $WS_2$ of large domain size, where CVD is employed to grow $WS_2$ on two substrates, i.e., Si/SiO$_2$ and GO-coated Si/SiO$_2$ (Si/SiO$_2$/GO), with the aim to extend the domain size of $WS_2$ and uniform coverage of the entire substrate area (see Sections 3.1 and 3.2).

## 3.1. First Approach: Mono- to Few-Layered $WS_2$ Growth on $Si/SiO_2$

$WS_2$ growth was carried out inside a two-zone tube furnace having separate high- and low-temperature zones, denoted as HT and LT, respectively, as shown in Figure 1a. Ultrahigh purity argon at flow rate of 100 sccm under atmospheric pressure was used as carrier gas to transport sulfur vapors to the HT zone. In a typical experiment, $WO_3$ powders (200 mg of pure grade 99.9%) was placed in an alumina crucible at the center of HT-zone of the furnace. $Si/SiO_2$ substrate (10 mm × 10 mm) was placed on the alumina crucible in inverted position so as to allow $WO_3$ vapor to hits the substrate and deposit on it. The sulfur powder (400 mg of pure grade 99.5%) was loaded upstream, and heated in LT-zone of the furnace. The HT- and LT-zone temperatures were controlled in such a way that the temperature in both the zones simultaneously reach at 1070 °C and 220 °C, respectively [28]. Monolayer $WS_2$ grains were grown on $Si/SiO_2$ substrate having small domain size and the growth remained scattered. The reaction occurring at the surface of the substrate can be summarized as:

$$2WO_3 + 7S \rightarrow 2WS_2 + 3SO_2. \tag{1}$$

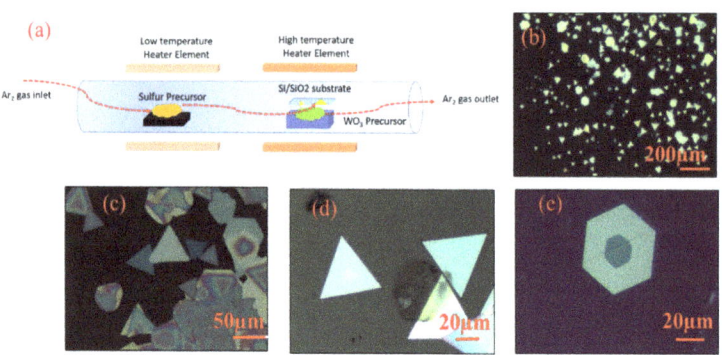

**Figure 1.** (a) Experimental setup. (b–e) Optical images of synthesized $WS_2$ film showing the presence of mono-to-few layered $WS_2$ on $Si/SiO_2$ substrate.

Thus, the vapor phase reaction between tungsten oxide and sulfur, produces tungsten disulfide and sulfur dioxide as end products. The optimized time duration for $WS_2$ growth is found to be 45 min, once the temperature of HT zone reaches 1070 °C. After completing the growth process, the CVD system was allowed to cool naturally to the room temperature.

Figure 1b–e shows the optical images of the $WS_2$ sample grown on $Si/SiO_2$ substrate. Two types of crystallites are visible: (a) equilateral triangles, and (b) hexagons; both are characteristic of $WS_2$ single crystal formation. Most of the crystals include monolayers. However, bi- and tri-layered regions are also visible at the center of large monolayer crystals, which is supposed to be the nucleation site, even for further growth of multi-layers [41].

Formation of hexagons in case of multilayer grains originates from the random orientation of individual $WS_2$ layers and differences in crystal orientation, where each orientation acts as nucleation site [41–43]. The side length of the crystals in case of equilateral triangles is found to be ~60 μm, which is reasonably large. The CVD growth of TMDCs is generally believed to be a self-limiting process [44]. The lateral size of $WS_2$ increases with the partial pressure of chalcogen precursors [45], while its thickness is determined by the partial pressure of transition metal precursors [46]. We have kept the weight of sulfur powders to be the twice of the weight $WO_3$ (chalcogen precursor). Thus, the lateral growth dominates in our case and could explain the growth of large size single crystals [46]. Furthermore, we could find $WS_2$ single crystals in variable sizes, ranging from 100 nm to 60 μm on the same $Si/SiO_2$ substrate. The growth duration is found to directly influence the area of grown crystals, before the crystal growth reaches its limit. Therefore, large sized WS$_2$ crystals can be formed if the growth time is kept sufficiently long.

- Electron Microscope Analysis

Figure 2a–c shows the FESEM images of WS$_2$ samples deposited on Si/SiO$_2$ substrate, corroborating the findings of optical microscopy, indicating both equilateral triangles and hexagons. In case of WS$_2$, the growth of equilateral triangles suggests single crystallinity; whereas the hexagonal or star-like structures result from several rotationally symmetric grains [4,9,26,46,47]. The size distribution histogram of hexagonal and triangle flakes of WS$_2$ is shown in Figure 2d–e. Where the average size of the hexagonal and triangular flake is found to be 71.5 µm and 44.5 µm, respectively. The ratio of the hexagon to the triangular flakes over the substrate is 2:1. Notably, the growth products, though consisting of monolayers, are scattered over the substrate and do not cover the entire substrate surface.

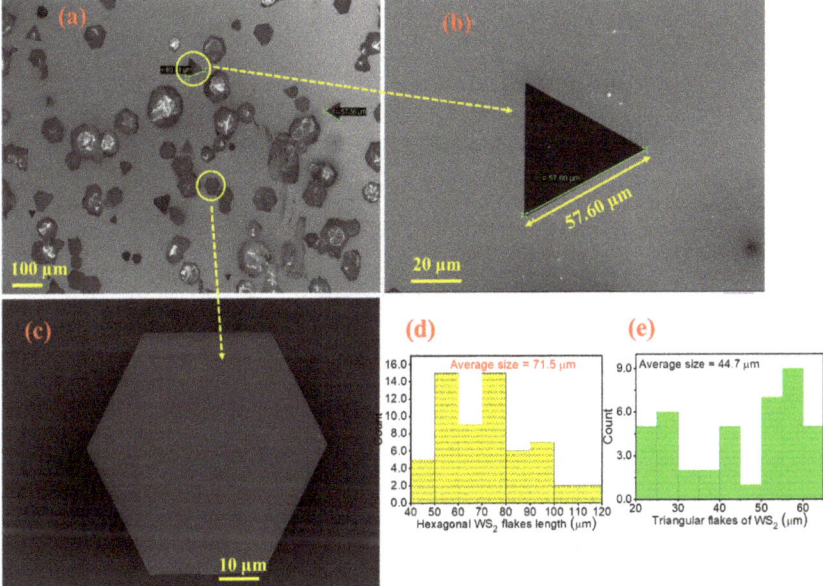

**Figure 2.** (a–c) FESEM micrographs of the WS$_2$ layers grown on Si/SiO$_2$ substrate at various magnification levels and (d,e) Size distribution histogram of hexagonal and triangle WS$_2$ flakes.

Figure 3a–c shows a low magnification bright field TEM imaging of WS$_2$ crystals suspended on a holey carbon Cu grid. For TEM imaging, first the WS$_2$ grown onto the Si/SiO$_2$ substrate was ultrasonicated in ethanol for 20 min to get the WS$_2$ flakes. After this, the suspension was centrifuged at a speed of 3000 rpm for 15 min to remove unwanted contamination or to allow settling down of heavy particles. Finally, top one-third supernatant was used for TEM analysis. We used HRTEM and selected area electron diffraction (SAED) to characterize the WS$_2$ domains. Figure 3a shows the hexagonal flakes with lateral dimension of about ~2.5 µm. In Figure 3b, the distorted cum truncated WS$_2$ triangle is clearly observable. At higher resolutions (Figure 3c,d), the crystalline nature of the flakes is clearly displayed. In Figure 3e, the selected area electron diffraction (SAED) pattern is indicated, which further confirms the highly crystalline morphology of as-grown WS$_2$.

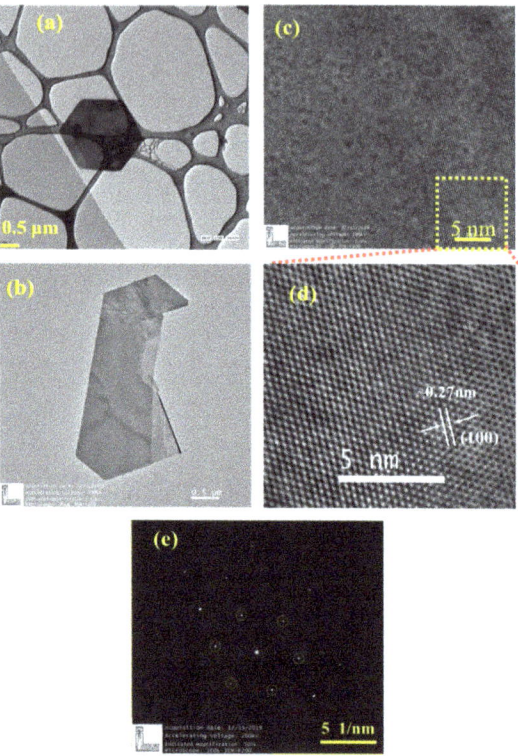

**Figure 3.** The TEM images of WS$_2$ flakes shown in (**a,b**) both at low magnification, (**c**) at high magnification. (**d**) zoomed view of (**c**), and (**e**) SAED pattern of the zoomed area.

- Raman Analysis

The E-k diagram and the phonon dispersion in Brillouin zone for WS$_2$ are shown in Figure 4a–c. Raman spectroscopy was employed to detect both the in-plane ($E_{2g}^1$) and out-of-plane ($A_{1g}$) phonon modes. Figure 4d shows Raman spectrum of the WS$_2$ flakes deposited over the Si/SiO$_2$ substrate, indicating a strong peak at 354 cm$^{-1}$ (2LA(M)), signifying a longitudinal acoustic mode at M point. This signals the monolayer growth of WS$_2$ [9,26]. The peak at 421 cm$^{-1}$ corresponding to the $A_{1g}$ mode, although weak, is also observed. As is widely reported, the separation between these two peaks increases from 67 to 72 cm$^{-1}$ with increasing the number of layers from single- to tri-layer due to a red-shifting of 2LA(M) mode [26,48–51]. However, the observed peak separation of ~67 cm$^{-1}$ is the fingerprint of WS$_2$ monolayer growth. Its topography, revealing a triangular shape probed via Atomic Force Microscopy (AFM), is shown in Figure 4e,f. The whole crystal is almost atomically flat and clean. The height profile in Figure 4f indicates the as-grown WS$_2$ on Si/SiO$_2$ having a step size of 0.89 nm; reaffirming the growth of a WS$_2$ monolayer. To verify the uniformity in the flakes, Raman mapping studies were performed from one edge to the other (Figure 5a,b). The synthesized WS$_2$ flakes were further analyzed by recording multiple Raman spectra across the area of post WS$_2$ grown substrate. Typically, seven measurement sites were selected on the top surface, and it can be concluded that we have achieved the monolayered WS$_2$ flakes. As seen in Figure 5a,b, the spots 1 and 7 only show the Raman-active LO mode of Si, while spots 2, 3, 4, 5, and 6 express the Raman features of WS$_2$ monolayers, and interestingly, the Raman result is also found supplemented by AFM studies.

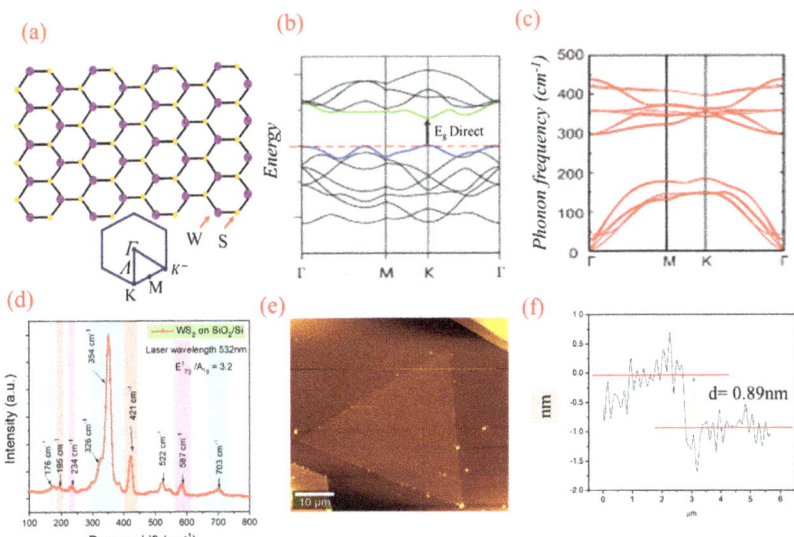

**Figure 4.** (a) Real space lattice structure and Brillouin zone in reciprocal space, (b) electronic band structure (E-K diagram), (c) phonon dispersion, (d) Raman spectrum, (e) AFM image of WS$_2$ monolayer crystal grown on Si/SiO$_2$ substrate and (f) AFM cross-section height profile for the deposited sample revealing a thickness of the grown film to be ~0.89 nm.

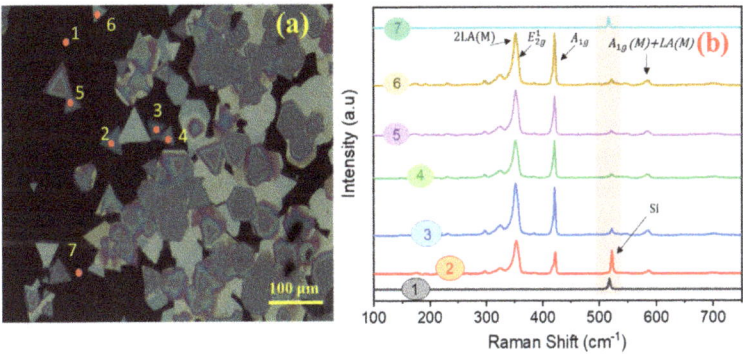

**Figure 5.** (a) Optical microscope image of WS$_2$ deposited over Si/SiO$_2$, indicating the selected measurement spots, and (b) Raman spectra of the spots identified in (a) where peak at 520 cm$^{-1}$ in all the spectra is the LO mode of the silicon wafer.

- Photoluminescence (PL) Analysis

The PL properties of 2D-TMDCs are mainly governed by their excitonic features [1,7–9,52]. In the limiting case of 2D materials, as shown in Figure 6a, the lines of electric field between the hole and electron start extending beyond the material, thereby reducing the dielectric screening and enhancing coulomb interactions [36,38,39]. A strong coulombic force is the main reason behind strong photoemission efficiency. This enhanced coulomb interaction suggests formation of bound e-h pairs or "excitons", having greater binding energies making them stable even at room temperature [7,52–54]. In case of monolayer 2D material, significant deviation is expected from the hydrogenic model, prevalent to describe Wannier-excitons in inorganic semiconducting materials [7,51]. Therefore, the calculation of binding energy of excitons in case of single-layered WS$_2$ needs to consider modified potential [54]. High intense peak is observed at 630 nm (1.968 eV) in the as-synthesized monolayer WS$_2$, which mainly originates from neutral-exciton (X$_A$) emission due to direct transition between the lowest conduction band (CB) and the highest valence band (VB) at the same K-point in the Brillouin zone [7,49,55–58], and schematically represented in Figure 4c. The fundamental bandgap of a single layer WS$_2$ is ~2.1 eV, but the large excitonic binding energy of 0.032 eV renders the optical bandgap measured at 1.968 eV [8,50–52] as shown schematically in Figure 6a,c shows the PL spectra of WS$_2$ flakes on the Si/SiO$_2$ substrate. Figure 6b represents the Neutral A-excitonic transition (XA) in the energy level diagram. The FWHM values of the PL spectra lie between 25 to 35 meV for both the approaches which is in accordance with the literature and further establish the fact of monolayer formation [59,60]. The presence of enhanced coulombic interaction at higher distant points suggests more likelihood of formation of higher-order excitons, i.e., trions and bi-excitons [51].

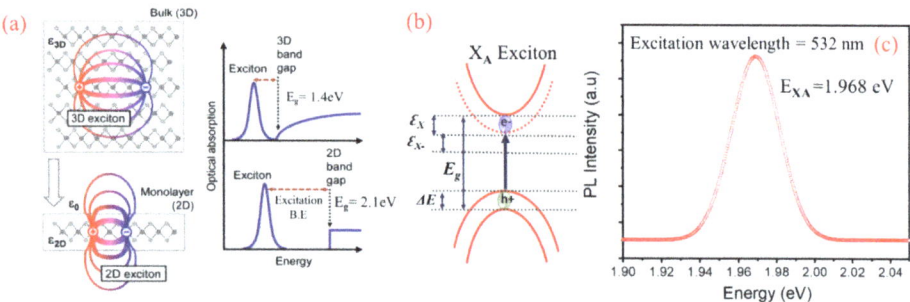

**Figure 6.** (**a**) Schematic diagram showing the reduced dielectric screening on the e-h pair bonding in a typical 2D material [38–40]. (**b**) Neutral A-excitonic transition (X$_A$) in the energy level diagram, and (**c**) PL spectra of WS$_2$ grown over Si/SiO$_2$ substrate.

*3.2. Second Approach: Uniform Growth of WS$_2$ Flakes on Spin-Coated GO*

In this approach, we have spin coated pre-synthesized graphene oxide (GO) solution over the Si/SiO$_2$ substrate prior to CVD growth. Hummers' method [38–40] has emerged as a well-established technique to prepare graphite oxide which can then be ultrasonicated to yield graphene oxide (GO). Briefly, natural graphite powders (5.0 g), H$_2$SO$_4$ (120 mL) and NaNO$_3$ (2.5 g) were mixed via continuous stirring. During stirring, the temperature was kept below 10 °C in order to check overheating of the mixture. After obtaining a uniform mixing, KMnO$_4$ (15.0 g) was added to this mixture by stirring for 24 h at room temperature. A condensed light brown colored slurry was obtained, which was diluted with deionized water (150 mL) and stirring for 2 h at 98 °C. The resulting mixture was vigorously washed with HCl and deionized water, to yield graphite oxide. Subsequently, graphite oxide was ultrasonicated (37 kHz, 500 W) for 3 h. The resulting suspension was centrifuged at 5000 rpm and GO was obtained by collecting the top one-third supernatant from the centrifugation product. A suspension of GO was prepared by mixing 5 mg GO in deionized water via ultrasonication. The substrate for WS$_2$ growth was prepared by spin coating (2500 rpm) 100 µL GO suspension on a Si/SiO$_2$ wafer. Figure 7a includes the SEM micrograph of the GO film coated over Si/SiO$_2$ substrate. The GO flakes appear uniformly dispersed over the surface of the substrate, and are expected to act as a seed layer for the growth of WS$_2$ film. In Figure 7b, the Raman spectrum of the GO film is displayed in 500–3500 cm$^{-1}$ range, in which the D-, G- and 2D-band are clearly defined at 1354, 1592, and 2712 cm$^{-1}$, respectively. Further, XRD analysis was performed to confirm the quality of prepared GO. The XRD pattern in Figure 7c shows the peak at 2θ ≈ 11°, which validates the high quality of the GO flakes.

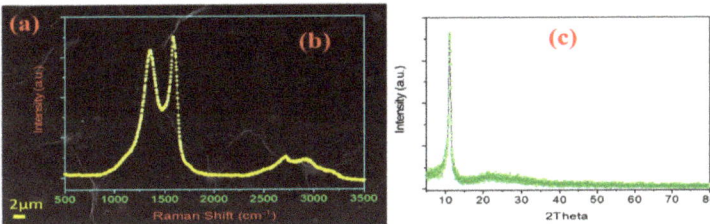

**Figure 7.** (a) FESEM micrograph, (b) Raman spectrum, and (c) XRD pattern of the GO film deposited on Si/SiO$_2$ substrate before the growth of the WS$_2$ layer.

The WS$_2$ growth was performed similar to that described in Section 3.1 (i.e., WS$_2$ grown at Si/SiO$_2$ substrate). The only difference is the coating of Si/SiO$_2$ substrate with GO, which is expected to get converted into RGO due to in-situ heating encountered in the HT-zone during the growth process. The synthesis process is schematically illustrated in Figure 8a–c. Figure 8d–g shows the Optical images of the WS$_2$ grown on the GO coated Si/SiO$_2$, where in Figure 8d clear interface is shown between WS$_2$ film and the Si substrate. Figure 8h–k shows the FESEM micrographs at different magnification. In this approach, sufficient amount of sulfur vapor is taken into consideration for the reaction, similar to the first approach. Here, it is noteworthy to say that the $sp^2$-carbon nanostructures in the RGO matrix fulfill three-pronged objectives: (i) they improve the surface adhesion, thereby enhancing local adsorption of WO$_3$ molecules; (ii) they reduce WO$_3$ to yield WO$_{3-x}$; and finally, (iii) they also act as active sites for heterogeneous nucleation, as demonstrated in Figure 9.

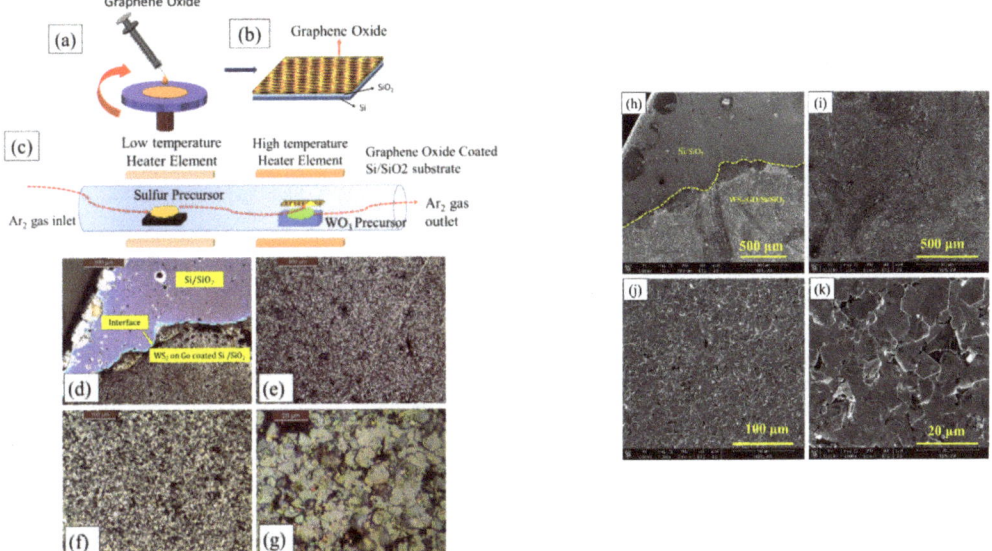

**Figure 8.** (a) Spin coating GO solution over Si/SiO$_2$ substrate, (b) GO coated Si/SiO$_2$ substrate, (c) CVD experimental setup used for WS$_2$ growth, and (d–g) optical microscope images of WS$_2$ grown on GO coated Si/SiO$_2$ substrate, and (h–k) FESEM micrographs of WS$_2$ grown over GO coated Si/SiO$_2$ substrate.

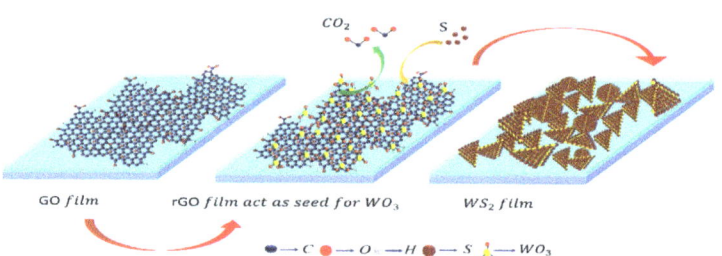

**Figure 9.** Schematic diagram to represent WS$_2$ growth mechanism on GO coated Si/SiO$_2$ substrate.

Upon heating, WO$_3$ vapors reach the surface of the substrate. A portion of these vapors diffuses and reacts with $sp^2$-bonded carbon patches of RGO, resulting in the formation of an intermediate phase, WO$_{3-x}$, along with the release of CO$_2$. Thus, an increase in the concentration of WO$_3$ vapors, results in simultaneous increase in the CO$_2$ and a corresponding decrease in the size of $sp^2$-carbon patches. Further, at elevated temperatures, WO$_{3-x}$ molecules gain the tendency to migrate and aggregate around the $sp^2$-bonded carbon patches. These carbon patches or 'carbon nanostructures' are expected to act as heterogeneous nucleation sites; where nucleation takes place via sulfurization of adjoining WO$_{3-x}$ molecules. The synthesis kinetics involve heterogeneous and homogeneous nucleation reactions, occurring simultaneously and competing with each other, as the main growth processes [61,62]. Initially, due to a lower surface free-energy barrier, heterogeneous nucleation outpaces the homogeneous nucleation [59]. In addition, the local high concentration of WO$_{3-x}$ facilitates the formation of bilayer nuclei. In case of perfectly overlapping bilayer formation, the nucleation shifts from the bottom layer to the second layer almost instantly. If growth does not stop at this point, few-or multi-layer WS$_2$ flakes are formed. Nonetheless, a complete understanding of growth mechanics warrants further investigations. The growth process can be summarized in the following chemical reactions [61,62]:

$$WO_3 + (x/2)C \rightarrow WO_{3-x} + (x/2)CO_2, \quad (2)$$

$$WO_3 + (x/2)S \rightarrow WO_{3-x} + (x/2)SO_2, \quad (3)$$

$$WO_{3-x} + (7-x)/2S \rightarrow WS_2 + (3-x)/2SO_2. \quad (4)$$

The use of GO produces substantially different growth characteristics than the isolated islands observed during the first approach. The WS$_2$ islands now coalesce to form nearly continuous films on centimeter scale as is evident in the optical images and SEM micrograph (Figure 8). Apart from the monolayers, multilayered growth is also visible. The multilayered growth is more favored at either the nucleation sites or grain boundaries (the locations shown by pointing arrows). Continuous monoto-few layer growths on centimeter scale are representative of the samples grown via the second approach, where the Si/SiO$_2$ substrate is coated with GO. We have found the size of the individual WS$_2$ crystals less than 15 µm, which is much larger than those reported for h-BN substrates, where a domain size of less than 1 µm is observed [63–65]. Although it is smaller than the WS$_2$ grown on pristine Si/SiO$_2$ substrate, its continuous expansion on the entire substrate has strong merits and fulfils the objectives of this work, as well as the requisite need for device applications.

Figure 10a shows the Raman spectrum of a WS$_2$ film grown on GO coated substrate. The peaks present at 351.2 and 421.4 cm$^{-1}$ is relatable with the $E^1_{2g}$ and $A_{1g}$ Raman modes. Besides, the $E^1_{2g}$ and $A_{1g}$ modes are found to be slightly red- and blue-shifted, respectively. Our concern is to study the shift in $E^1_{2g}$ and $A_{1g}$ peaks due to thickness variation in a mixed multi-layered WS$_2$ flake. The increase in number of layers strongly enhances the out-of-plane vibrations, while coulomb interactions tend to decrease the frequency of in-plane vibrations, thereby causing monotonous increase in frequency separation between $E^1_{2g}$ and $A_{1g}$ peaks [58]. While there is little variation in peak positions, small modifications in the relative intensities between $E_{2g}^1$ and $A_{1g}$ modes are clearly observed. Samples synthesized via first approach have a slightly higher $E_{2g}{}^1$ intensity, with the ratio $E_{2g}^1/A_{1g}$ of ~3.2. Conversely, the $A_{1g}$ intensity is higher for the second approach, where $E_{2g}^1/A_{1g}$ ratio is of ~1.25. Moderate changes in the Raman intensity ratio are believed to indicate changes in the number of layers for exfoliated WS$_2$ [46,66]. We have performed Raman mapping analysis at multiple spots of the same sample to confirm the uniformity of WS$_2$ across the substrate area as shown in Figure 10b,c. It is evident that there is slight variation in the separation as well as intensity ratio of in-plane and out-plane vibrational peaks as a function of sample spot location; and a summary of the peak position, difference in Raman peak frequency and intensity ratio of the peaks is tabulated in Table 1. The shift in the frequency of 2LA (M) and $A_{1g}$ modes has been employed as a measure of the number of layers. However, this approach to determine the number of layers is erroneous due to the close proximity of 2LA (M) and $E_{2g}^1$ phonon modes. It has been found that with increasing the number of layers, the intensity ratio $(I_{2LA(M)}/I_{A1g})$ decreases from 2.2 (for single layer) to 0.47 (for bulk) [64]. At the first instance, it looks the possible growth of mono- to few-layered WS$_2$. However, in case of monolayer MoS$_2$, such small intensity variations in $E_{2g}{}^1$ and $A_{1g}$ peaks were correlated to the differences in electronic doping levels or strain as WS$_2$ and RGO effectively combine to form heterostructures [67]. Generally, TMDCs are highly prone to significant number of chalcogenide vacancies [59,64,65]. Sulphur vacancies exist in WS$_2$, thus introducing localized donor states deep inside the bandgap, which can be subsequently filled by environmental impurities to make it doped. As of now, various competitive approaches exist to find out the origin of anomaly in the interpretation of peak intensity ratio and shift in peak position of Raman modes. Nonetheless, the contribution to the intensity changes due to sulfur content in WS$_2$ films as a dopant, and local strain in between WS$_2$ and RGO, cannot be ignored [66].

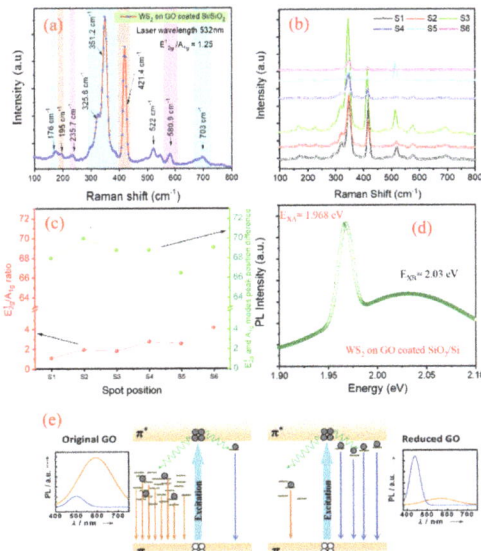

Figure 10. (a) Raman spectrum and (b) Raman spectra as a function of spot on different positions (c) Intensity ratio and difference of the peak as function of spot (d) Photoluminescence (PL) of WS$_2$ grown on GO coated Si/SiO$_2$ substrate, and (e) Evolution of PL spectra due to the transformation of $sp^3$- to $sp^2$-bonded region during the reduction of GO to RGO. Reproduced with permission from [67]. Copyright 2012 Wiley.

Table 1. Summary of Raman studies of WS$_2$ nanoflakes deposited on different spot of GO coated substrate.

| Sample | Spot | Raman Peak Frequency (cm$^{-1}$) | | Frequency Difference | Intensity Ratio |
|---|---|---|---|---|---|
| | | $E_{2g}$ | $A_{1g}$ | | |
| WS$_2$/SiO$_2$/Si | 1 | 354.3 | 421.1 | 66.7 | 1.75 |
| | 2 | 349.7 | 418.7 | 69 | 1.15 |
| | 3 | 350.1 | 419.2 | 69.1 | 0.96 |
| | 4 | 350.1 | 419.4 | 69.3 | 0.99 |
| | 5 | 352.4 | 419.3 | 66.9 | 1.2 |
| | 6 | - | - | - | - |
| WS$_2$/GO/SiO$_2$/Si | S1 | 350.8 | 418.8 | 68.0 | 1.10 |
| | S2 | 351.0 | 421.2 | 70.2 | 1.93 |
| | S3 | 349.7 | 418.25 | 68.5 | 1.80 |
| | S4 | 350.1 | 419.0 | 68.9 | 2.75 |
| | S5 | 352.9 | 419.6 | 66.5 | 2.55 |
| | S6 | 351.0 | ~420.1 | 69.1 | 4.19 |

The PL spectra, shown in Figure 10d, comprise with neutral A-exciton ($X_A$) at 1.968 eV as also observed in case of WS$_2$ growth on Si/SiO$_2$ substrate. A striking difference observed in WS$_2$ growth on GO-coated Si/SiO$_2$ substrate, is the appearance of a low intensity peak at 2.03 eV (611 nm), attributable to the weak transition of carriers from disorder induced states within $\pi$-$\pi^*$ band structure of RGO [67] (schematically shown in Figure 10e). Our laser excitation visible wavelength does not cover the intense emission peak around 440 nm. A comparative study in terms of PL spectral positions, FWHM and shift in peak positions are put in Table 2. Surface roughness, in particular, the sharp edges, is reported to help in catalyst-free CNT growth [68]. To ascertain the role of surface roughness on the continuous growth of WS$_2$, we conducted CVD growth in identical conditions: first, on polished surface, marked with scratches on polished side of silicon wafer; and second, on backside, the unpolished surface of the same wafer. In the polished wafer side, WS$_2$ debris having no shape and sizes of flakes, are observed on and around the scratch marks. SEM images (Figure 11a–d) show few vertically aligned and flower petal shaped flakes with some horizontal flakes on the scratch marked region having negligible presence of triangular as well as hexagonal WS$_2$ crystallites.

Table 2. Summary of Photoluminescence (PL) studies of WS$_2$ nanoflakes deposited on different substrates.

| Sample | Energy (eV) | FWHM (meV) | |
|---|---|---|---|
| | $E_{XA}$ | $E_{XA}$ | $E_{XB}$ |
| WS$_2$/Si/SiO$_2$ | 1.968 | 25.3 | - |
| WS$_2$/GO/SiO$_2$/Si | 1.968 | 35.5 | 35.6 |

In contrast, we have achieved horizontally grown WS$_2$ crystallites, majority in hexagonal shape on the unpolished surface (Figure 11e–g). In both cases, thickness of WS$_2$ flake(s) is multilayered. It may be inferred that surface roughness does also play an important role in the WS$_2$ growth. The optical profilometer image (surface microscopy) of the GO coated sample surface before WS$_2$ deposition is shown in Figure 11h. It is to be noted that surface of RGO film is highly rough in nature; and this may be one of the sources of nucleation sites too, in addition to the major contribution from high density $sp^2$-bonded patches, to enhance the joining of grain boundaries, resulting in continuous WS$_2$ film growth over GO coated Si/SiO$_2$ substrate. Therefore, it may be understood that continuous growth is possible in GO coated substrate, in which $sp^2$-patches of carbon purely act as a seed or catalyst that enhance growth origins.

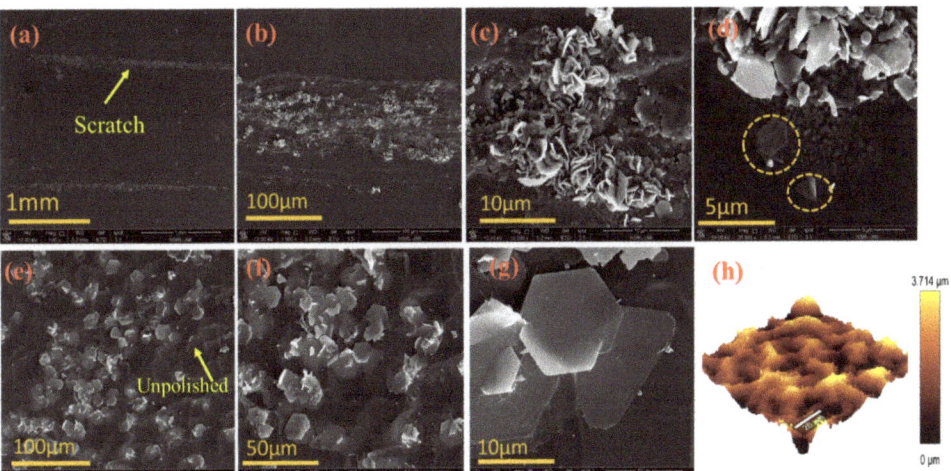

**Figure 11.** FESEM micrographs of WS$_2$ grown on scratch marks made on polished surface of Si wafer (**a**–**d**) and WS$_2$ grown on unpolished Si wafer (**e**–**g**). In both cases, other CVD growth parameters were constant. (**h**) The optical profilometer image (surface microscopy) of the GO coated sample surface before WS$_2$ deposition. The scale bar indicates the surface roughness of the sample close to 3.72 µm.

The present work has shown the successful growth of mono to few layer WS$_2$ film of square-centimeter size and triangular shape on graphene-oxide-coated Si/SiO$_2$ substrate using CVD technique. The real issue addressed in this work is the large area coverage of the WS$_2$ continuous film; however, many of the researchers have also tried to resolve this issue by using various approaches such as atomic layer deposition, pulse laser deposition, and metal/metal oxide thin film or noble metal substrates, etc. Although these strategies yield large area continuous TMDCs, these techniques also suffer from high costs, increased complexity, and sometimes poor quality. Further, to be useful, WS$_2$ grown over inert metal needs etching via acidic or basic (e.g., concentrated HF, KOH and NaOH) solutions, before transferring to Si or flexible substrates. Usually, the transfer processes not only end up in damaging the grown material (WS$_2$), but produce substrate residues and negative environment impact, as well. We successfully grew the continuous WS$_2$ film at very low cost by simply coating the Si/SiO$_2$ substrate with graphene oxide (GO) and this technique is highly reproducible. Table 3 enlists the optical properties of WS$_2$ nanoflakes deposited on different substrates. However, HRTEM and Raman spectroscopy confirm the high crystallinity and quality of the grown WS$_2$ flakes. Note that the Raman peak frequencies difference (66–72 cm$^{-1}$) and the PL peak position (2.00–1.92 eV) as well as intensity fluctuates over the WS$_2$ triangles as enlisted in Table 2. The change of frequency and/or width of Raman modes of 2H-type transition-metal dichalcogenides can be used to evaluate the sample quality because they are strongly sensitive to external electrostatic doping ($A_{1g}$ mode) and lattice strain ($E_{2g}^1$ mode) [69,70]. Wang et al. found that $E_{2g}^1$ mode exhibits obvious red-shift when increasing strain [70]. In contrast, Chakraborty demonstrated that a softening and broadening of the $A_{1g}$ mode occur with electron doping, whereas the $E_{2g}^1$ mode remains essentially inert [69].

**Table 3.** Summary of optical properties of WS$_2$ nanoflakes deposited on different substrates.

| Sample | Raman Peak Frequency (cm$^{-1}$) | | A-Exciton Energy (eV) | Ref. |
|---|---|---|---|---|
| | $E_{2g}$ | $A_{1g}$ | | |
| WS$_2$/Al$_2$O$_3$ | 352.7 | 421.2 | 2.000 | [10] |
| WS$_2$/SiO$_2$/Si | 353.0 | 418.3 | 1.920 | [18] |
| WS$_2$/Au | 356.2 | 420.9 | 1.935 | [25] |
| WS$_2$/SiO$_2$/Si | 352.5 | 419.0 | 1.977 | [12] |
| WS$_2$/sapphire | 354.0 | 412.0 | 2.000 | [26] |
| WS$_2$/SiO$_2$/Si | ~350 | ~416 | 1.949 | [28] |
| WS$_2$/SiO$_2$/Si | 354.0 | 421.0 | 1.968 | this work |
| WS$_2$/GO/SiO$_2$/Si | 351.2 | 421.4 | 1.968 | this work |

- Photoconductive response of sensor prepared with GO coated Si/SiO$_2$

To check the continuity of the grown film, I-V characteristics were monitored in the voltage range of −12 V to +12 V using Keithley SCS 4200 for variable channel length (from 0.5 to 5.0 mm). The inset of Figure 12a shows the digital photographs of the samples, where the electrical probes are set at different channel lengths. The observed I-V curves indicate that flakes grown over the GO modified substrate are interconnecting and form a continuous network. Figure 12b demonstrates the possible use of developed film as photodetector where the change in photocurrent under illumination of laser wavelength of 635 nm, keeping the laser power constant at 40 mW, is shown. The cyclic response is highly reproducible with negligible drift. The photoresponsivity and specific detectivity are found to be 0.9 µA W$^{-1}$ and 0.15 × 10$^5$ jones.

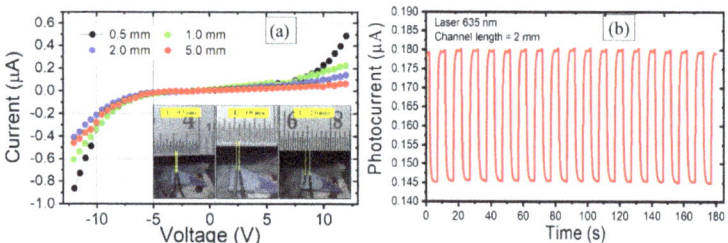

**Figure 12.** (a) Current vs. voltage characteristics at variable channel length and (b) photoconductive response under laser wavelength 635 nm.

## 4. Conclusions

Efforts have been made to understand the growth mechanics of large domain size of mono-to-few layer growth of WS$_2$. Nature of substrate is utilized to understand the intricate mechanism behind continuous film growth. Large area (domain size of around 60 µm), mono-to-few layer WS$_2$ crystals of triangular shape, were grown on pristine Si/SiO$_2$ and GO-coated Si/SiO$_2$ substrates, using CVD technique with a two-zone furnace. For GO coated Si/SiO$_2$ substrate, uniform mono-to-few layer growth of WS$_2$ crystals is achieved, although the size of WS$_2$ crystals is smaller than those grown on pristine Si/SiO$_2$ substrate. In case of growth on Si/SiO$_2$ substrate, monolayer WS$_2$ grain boundaries are in isolation, and highly scattered on the substrate surface. Further tests were conducted to examine the role of surface roughness, as reported in the past for catalyst-free CNT growth on pristine silicon surface. We conducted CVD growth in identical conditions, one on polished surface, marked with scratches; and the other one, on the unpolished surface of the same wafer. Strikingly, WS$_2$ growth exclusively on rough surface in both the cases, confirmed that surface roughness does play an important role. In addition, high density

$sp^2$-bonded patches enhance the joining of grain boundaries, to enable continuous $WS_2$ film growth over GO coated $Si/SiO_2$ substrate. It is concluded that the combination of high-temperature CVD with reduced graphene oxide surface is supposed to be a favorable condition for TMDCs growth with full coverage of the substrate. The idea of GO coated $Si/SiO_2$ substrate may be employed for mass production of identical devices, and therefore bids for commercial scale development and can be extended to other TMDCs.

**Author Contributions:** Conceptualization and Supervision, S.S.I.; formal analysis, A. and P.S.; investigation, A. and P.S.; writing—original draft preparation, S.S.I.; writing—review and editing, C.M.J. All authors have read and agreed to the published version of the manuscript.

**Funding:** This research received no external funding.

**Institutional Review Board Statement:** Not applicable.

**Informed Consent Statement:** Not applicable.

**Data Availability Statement:** The data presented in this study are available on request from the corresponding author.

**Acknowledgments:** The authors acknowledge the Inter-University Accelerator Centre (IUAC), New Delhi, India for providing the TEM facility. We are thankful to Debdulal Kabiraj and Ambuj Mishra for the TEM measurements. The author would also like to acknowledge Central Instrumentation Facility (CIF), Jamia Millia Islamia, New Delhi, India for Photoluminescence spectroscopic studies.

**Conflicts of Interest:** The authors declare no conflict of interest.

## Appendix A

*Photoresponsivity ($R_\lambda$)*

The ratio of photocurrent to the incident intensity of the laser wavelength $\lambda$ is defined as photoresponsivity of the photodetector and it can be calculated as [71]:

$$R_\lambda = \frac{\Delta I_{ph}}{P \cdot A}. \tag{A1}$$

*Photosensitivity (S)*

It is defined as the ratio of change in current under illumination and dark current [72]:

$$S\,(\%) = \frac{I_{photo} - I_{Dark}}{I_{Dark}} \times 100. \tag{A2}$$

*Specific Detectivity*

It represents the ability of the detector to capture the weakest signal, which can be mathematically expressed as [71]:

$$D = \frac{R_\lambda \sqrt{A}}{\sqrt{2eI_{Dark}}}, \tag{A3}$$

where $A$ represents the effective area of photodetector, and $e$ is the electronic charge.

## References

1. Cong, C.; Shang, J.; Wang, Y.; Yu, T. Optical properties of 2D semiconductor $WS_2$. *Adv. Opt. Mater.* **2018**, *6*, 1700767. [CrossRef]
2. Park, J.; Kim, M.S.; Cha, E.; Kim, J.; Choi, W. Synthesis of uniform single layer $WS_2$ for tunable photoluminescence. *Sci. Rep.* **2017**, *7*, 1–8. [CrossRef] [PubMed]
3. Rafiq, M.K.S.B.; Amin, N.; Alharbi, H.F.; Luqman, M.; Ayob, A.; Alharthi, Y.S.; Alharthi, N.H.; Bais, B.; Akhtaruzzaman, M. $WS_2$: A New Window Layer Material for Solar Cell Application. *Sci. Rep.* **2020**, *10*, 1–11.
4. Gutiérrez, H.R.; Perea-López, N.; Elías, A.L.; Berkdemir, A.; Wang, B.; Lv, R.; López-Urías, F.; Crespi, V.H.; Terrones, H.; Terrones, M. Extraordinary room-temperature photoluminescence in triangular $WS_2$ monolayers. *Nano Lett.* **2013**, *13*, 3447–3454. [CrossRef] [PubMed]

5. Tanoh, A.O.A.; Alexander-Webber, J.; Xiao, J.; Delport, G.; Williams, C.A.; Bretscher, H.; Gauriot, N.; Allardice, J.; Pandya, R.; Fan, Y.; et al. Enhancing photoluminescence and mobilities in $WS_2$ monolayers with oleic acid ligands. *Nano Lett.* **2019**, *19*, 6299–6307. [CrossRef] [PubMed]
6. Yuan, L.; Huang, L. Exciton dynamics and annihilation in $WS_2$ 2D semiconductors. *Nanoscale* **2015**, *7*, 7402–7408. [CrossRef]
7. Zhu, B.; Chen, X.; Cui, X. Exciton binding energy of monolayer $WS_2$. *Sci. Rep.* **2015**, *5*, 9218. [CrossRef]
8. Ye, Z.; Cao, T.; O'brien, K.; Zhu, H.; Yin, X.; Wang, Y.; Louie, S.G.; Zhang, X. Probing excitonic dark states in single-layer tungsten disulphide. *Nature* **2014**, *513*, 214–218. [CrossRef]
9. Peimyoo, N.; Shang, J.; Cong, C.; Shen, X.; Wu, X.; Yeow, E.K.; Yu, T. Nonblinking, intense two-dimensional light emitter: Monolayer $WS_2$ triangles. *ACS Nano* **2013**, *7*, 10985–10994. [CrossRef]
10. Lan, F.; Yang, R.; Xu, Y.; Qian, S.; Zhang, S.; Cheng, H.; Zhang, Y. Synthesis of large-scale single-crystalline monolayer $WS_2$ using a semi-sealed Method. *Nanomaterials* **2018**, *8*, 100. [CrossRef]
11. Zhang, Q.; Lu, J.; Wang, Z.; Dai, Z.; Zhang, Y.; Huang, F.; Bao, Q.; Duan, W.; Fuhrer, M.S.; Zheng, C. Reliable synthesis of large-area monolayer $WS_2$ single crystals, films, and heterostructures with extraordinary photoluminescence induced by water intercalation. *Adv. Opt. Mater.* **2018**, *6*, 1701347. [CrossRef]
12. Liu, P.; Luo, T.; Xing, J.; Xu, H.; Hao, H.; Liu, H.; Dong, J. Large-area $WS_2$ film with big single domains grown by chemical vapor deposition. *Nanoscale Res. Lett.* **2017**, *12*, 558. [CrossRef] [PubMed]
13. Wang, Q.H.; Kalantar-Zadeh, K.; Kis, A.; Coleman, J.N.; Strano, M.S. Electronics and optoelectronics of two-dimensional transition metal dichalcogenides. *Nat. Nanotechnol.* **2012**, *7*, 699. [CrossRef] [PubMed]
14. Dong, R.; Kuljanishvili, I. Progress in fabrication of transition metal dichalcogenides heterostructure systems. *J. Vac. Sci. Technol. B* **2017**, *35*, 030803. [CrossRef] [PubMed]
15. Yuan, L.; Ge, J.; Peng, X.; Zhang, Q.; Wu, Z.; Jian, Y.; Xiong, X.; Yin, H.; Han, J. A reliable way of mechanical exfoliation of large scale two dimensional materials with high quality. *AIP Adv.* **2016**, *6*, 125201. [CrossRef]
16. Ghorai, A.; Midya, A.; Maiti, R.; Ray, S.K. Exfoliation of $WS_2$ in the semiconducting phase using a group of lithium halides: A new method of Li intercalation. *Dalton Trans.* **2016**, *45*, 14979–14987. [CrossRef]
17. Nicolosi, V.; Chhowalla, M.; Kanatzidis, M.G.; Strano, M.S.; Coleman, J.N. Liquid exfoliation of layered materials. *Science* **2013**, *340*, 1226419. [CrossRef]
18. Elías, A.L.; Perea-López, N.; Castro-Beltrán, A.; Berkdemir, A.; Lv, R.; Feng, S.; Long, A.D.; Hayashi, T.; Kim, Y.A.; Endo, M.; et al. Controlled synthesis and transfer of large-area $WS_2$ sheets: From single layer to few layers. *ACS Nano* **2013**, *7*, 5235–5242. [CrossRef]
19. Cao, S.; Liu, T.; Hussain, S.; Zeng, W.; Peng, X.; Pan, F. Hydrothermal synthesis of variety low dimensional $WS_2$ nanostructures. *Mater. Lett.* **2014**, *129*, 205–208. [CrossRef]
20. Alonso, G.; Petranovskii, V.; Del Valle, M.; Cruz-Reyes, J.; Licea-Claverie, A.; Fuentes, S. Preparation of WS2 catalysts by in situ decomposition of tetraalkylammonium thiotungstates. *Appl. Catal. A* **2000**, *197*, 87–97. [CrossRef]
21. Balasubramanyam, S.; Shirazi, M.; Bloodgood, M.A.; Wu, L.; Verheijen, M.A.; Vandalon, V.; Kessels, W.M.; Hofmann, J.P.; Bol, A.A. Edge-site nanoengineering of $WS_2$ by low-temperature plasma-enhanced atomic layer deposition for electrocatalytic hydrogen evolution. *Chem. Mater.* **2019**, *31*, 5104–5115. [CrossRef] [PubMed]
22. Loh, T.A.; Chua, D.H.; Wee, A.T. One-step synthesis of few-layer $WS_2$ by pulsed laser deposition. *Sci. Rep.* **2015**, *5*, 18116. [CrossRef] [PubMed]
23. Tian, K.; Baskaran, K.; Tiwari, A. Growth of two-dimensional $WS_2$ thin films by pulsed laser deposition technique. *Thin Solid Film.* **2018**, *668*, 69–73. [CrossRef]
24. Koçak, Y.; Akaltun, Y.; Gür, E. Magnetron sputtered $WS_2$; optical and structural analysis. *J. Phys. Conf. Ser.* **2016**, *707*, 012028. [CrossRef]
25. Gao, Y.; Liu, Z.; Sun, D.M.; Huang, L.; Ma, L.P.; Yin, L.C.; Ma, T.; Zhang, Z.; Ma, X.L.; Peng, L.M.; et al. Large-area synthesis of high-quality and uniform monolayer $WS_2$ on reusable Au foils. *Nat. Commun.* **2015**, *6*, 8569. [CrossRef] [PubMed]
26. Xu, Z.Q.; Zhang, Y.; Lin, S.; Zheng, C.; Zhong, Y.L.; Xia, X.; Li, Z.; Sophia, P.J.; Fuhrer, M.S.; Cheng, Y.B.; et al. Synthesis and transfer of large-area monolayer $WS_2$ crystals: Moving toward the recyclable use of sapphire substrates. *ACS Nano* **2015**, *9*, 6178–6187. [CrossRef]
27. Yu, J.; Li, J.; Zhang, W.; Chang, H. Synthesis of high quality two-dimensional materials via chemical vapor deposition. *Chem. Sci.* **2015**, *6*, 6705–6716. [CrossRef]
28. Rong, Y.; Fan, Y.; Koh, A.L.; Robertson, A.W.; He, K.; Wang, S.; Tan, H.; Sinclair, R.; Warner, J.H. Controlling sulphur precursor addition for large single crystal domains of $WS_2$. *Nanoscale* **2014**, *6*, 12096–12103. [CrossRef]
29. Okada, M.; Okada, N.; Chang, W.H.; Endo, T.; Ando, A.; Shimizu, T.; Kubo, T.; Miyata, Y.; Irisawa, T. Gas-source CVD growth of atomic layered $WS_2$ from $WF_6$ and $H_2S$ precursors with high grain size uniformity. *Sci. Rep.* **2019**, *9*, 1–10. [CrossRef]
30. Lu, Y.; Chen, T.; Ryu, G.H.; Huang, H.; Sheng, Y.; Chang, R.J.; Warner, J.H. Self-limiting growth of high-quality 2D monolayer $MoS_2$ by direct sulfurization using precursor-soluble substrates for advanced field-effect transistors and photodetectors. *ACS Appl. Nano Mater.* **2018**, *2*, 369–378. [CrossRef]
31. Kim, Y.; Song, J.G.; Park, Y.J.; Ryu, G.H.; Lee, S.J.; Kim, J.S.; Jeon, P.J.; Lee, C.W.; Woo, W.J.; Choi, T.; et al. Self-limiting layer synthesis of transition metal dichalcogenides. *Sci. Rep.* **2016**, *6*, 18754. [CrossRef] [PubMed]

32. Zhang, Y.; Zhang, Y.; Ji, Q.; Ju, J.; Yuan, H.; Shi, J.; Gao, T.; Ma, D.; Liu, M.; Chen, Y.; et al. Controlled growth of high-quality monolayer WS2 layers on sapphire and imaging its grain boundary. *ACS Nano* **2013**, *7*, 8963–8971. [CrossRef] [PubMed]
33. Cong, C.; Shang, J.; Wu, X.; Cao, B.; Peimyoo, N.; Qiu, C.; Sun, L.; Yu, T. Synthesis and optical properties of large-area single-crystalline 2D semiconductor WS$_2$ monolayer from chemical vapor deposition. *Adv. Opt. Mater.* **2014**, *2*, 131–136. [CrossRef]
34. Li, S.; Wang, S.; Tang, D.M.; Zhao, W.; Xu, H.; Chu, L.; Bando, Y.; Golberg, D.; Eda, G. Halide-assisted atmospheric pressure growth of large WSe$_2$ and WS$_2$ monolayer crystals. *Appl. Mater. Today* **2015**, *1*, 60–66. [CrossRef]
35. Kang, K.N.; Godin, K.; Yang, E.H. The growth scale and kinetics of WS$_2$ monolayers under varying H$_2$ concentration. *Sci. Rep.* **2015**, *5*, 1–9. [CrossRef] [PubMed]
36. Liu, Z.; Murphy, A.W.A.; Kuppe, C.; Hooper, D.C.; Valev, V.K.; Ilie, A. WS$_2$ Nanotubes, 2D nanomeshes, and 2D in-plane films through one single chemical vapor deposition route. *ACS Nano* **2019**, *13*, 3896–3909. [CrossRef] [PubMed]
37. Lee, Y.H.; Zhang, X.Q.; Zhang, W.; Chang, M.T.; Lin, C.T.; Chang, K.D.; Yu, Y.C.; Wang, J.T.W.; Chang, C.S.; Li, L.J.; et al. Synthesis of large-area MoS$_2$ atomic layers with chemical vapor deposition. *Adv. Mater.* **2012**, *24*, 2320–2325. [CrossRef]
38. Abid; Sehrawat, P.; Islam, S.S.; Mishra, P.; Ahmad, S. Reduced graphene oxide (rGO) based wideband optical sensor and the role of temperature, defect states and quantum efficiency. *Sci. Rep.* **2018**, *8*, 1–13. [CrossRef]
39. Sehrawat, P.; Islam, S.S.; Mishra, P. Reduced graphene oxide based temperature sensor: Extraordinary performance governed by lattice dynamics assisted carrier transport. *Sens. Actuators B* **2018**, *258*, 424–435. [CrossRef]
40. Sehrawat, P.; Islam, S.S. An ultrafast quantum thermometer from graphene quantum dots. *Nanoscale Adv.* **2019**, *1*, 1772–1783. [CrossRef]
41. Zhang, X.; Nan, H.; Xiao, S.; Wan, X.; Gu, X.; Du, A.; Ni, Z.; Ostrikov, K.K. Transition metal dichalcogenides bilayer single crystals by reverse-flow chemical vapor epitaxy. *Nat. Commun.* **2019**, *10*, 1–10. [CrossRef] [PubMed]
42. Yan, J.; Xia, J.; Wang, X.; Liu, L.; Kuo, J.L.; Tay, B.K.; Chen, S.; Zhou, W.; Liu, Z.; Shen, Z.X. Stacking-dependent interlayer coupling in trilayer MoS$_2$ with broken inversion symmetry. *Nano Lett.* **2015**, *15*, 8155–8161. [CrossRef] [PubMed]
43. Jeong, H.Y.; Jin, Y.; Yun, S.J.; Zhao, J.; Baik, J.; Keum, D.H.; Lee, H.S.; Lee, Y.H. Heterogeneous defect domains in single-crystalline hexagonal WS$_2$. *Adv. Mater.* **2017**, *29*, 1605043. [CrossRef] [PubMed]
44. Yue, Y.; Chen, J.; Zhang, Y.; Ding, S.; Zhao, F.; Wang, Y.; Zhang, D.; Li, R.; Dong, H.; Hu, W.; et al. Two-dimensional high-quality monolayered triangular WS$_2$ flakes for field-effect transistors. *ACS Appl. Mater. Interfaces* **2018**, *10*, 22435–22444. [CrossRef] [PubMed]
45. Chen, F.; Ding, S.; Su, W. A feasible approach to fabricate two-dimensional WS$_2$ flakes: From monolayer to multilayer. *Ceram. Int.* **2018**, *44*, 22108–22112. [CrossRef]
46. McCreary, K.M.; Hanbicki, A.T.; Jernigan, G.G.; Culbertson, J.C.; Jonker, B.T. Synthesis of large-area WS$_2$ monolayers with exceptional photoluminescence. *Sci. Rep.* **2016**, *6*, 19159. [CrossRef]
47. Boson, A.J. Chemical Vapor Deposition of Two-Dimensional Materials and Heterostructures. Ph.D. Thesis, University of Nebraska-Lincoln, Lincoln, NE, USA, 2017. Available online: https://digitalcommons.unl.edu/cgi/viewcontent.cgi?article=1083&context=chemistrydiss (accessed on 28 April 2017).
48. Xiao, J.; Zhao, M.; Wang, Y.; Zhang, X. Excitons in atomically thin 2D semiconductors and their applications. *Nanophotonics* **2017**, *6*, 1309–1328. [CrossRef]
49. Mitioglu, A.A.; Plochocka, P.; Jadczak, J.N.; Escoffier, W.; Rikken, G.L.J.A.; Kulyuk, L.; Maude, D.K. Optical manipulation of the exciton charge state in single-layer tungsten disulfide. *Phys. Rev. B* **2013**, *88*, 245403. [CrossRef]
50. Paur, M.; Molina-Mendoza, A.J.; Bratschitsch, R.; Watanabe, K.; Taniguchi, T.; Mueller, T. Electroluminescence from multi-particle exciton complexes in transition metal dichalcogenide semiconductors. *Nat. Commun.* **2019**, *10*, 1–7. [CrossRef]
51. Chernikov, A.; Berkelbach, T.C.; Hill, H.M.; Rigosi, A.; Li, Y.; Aslan, O.B.; Reichman, D.R.; Hybertsen, M.S.; Heinz, T.F. Exciton binding energy and nonhydrogenic Rydberg series in monolayer WS$_2$. *Phys. Rev. Lett.* **2014**, *113*, 076802. [CrossRef]
52. Shang, J.; Shen, X.; Cong, C.; Peimyoo, N.; Cao, B.; Eginligil, M.; Yu, T. Observation of excitonic fine structure in a 2D transition-metal dichalcogenide semiconductor. *ACS Nano* **2015**, *9*, 647–655. [CrossRef] [PubMed]
53. Ren, D.D.; Qin, J.K.; Li, Y.; Miao, P.; Sun, Z.Y.; Xu, P.; Zhen, L.; Xu, C.Y. Photoluminescence inhomogeneity and excitons in CVD-grown monolayer WS$_2$. *Opt. Mater.* **2018**, *80*, 203–208. [CrossRef]
54. Carozo, V.; Wang, Y.; Fujisawa, K.; Carvalho, B.R.; McCreary, A.; Feng, S.; Lin, Z.; Zhou, C.; Perea-López, N.; Elías, A.L.; et al. Optical identification of sulfur vacancies: Bound excitons at the edges of monolayer tungsten disulfide. *Sci. Adv.* **2017**, *3*, e1602813. [CrossRef] [PubMed]
55. Zhao, W.; Ghorannevis, Z.; Chu, L.; Toh, M.; Kloc, C.; Tan, P.H.; Eda, G. Evolution of electronic structure in atomically thin sheets of WS$_2$ and WSe$_2$. *ACS Nano* **2013**, *7*, 791–797. [CrossRef] [PubMed]
56. Mak, K.F.; He, K.; Lee, C.; Lee, G.H.; Hone, J.; Heinz, T.F.; Shan, J. Tightly bound trions in monolayer MoS$_2$. *Nat. Mater.* **2013**, *12*, 207–211. [CrossRef]
57. Ross, J.S.; Wu, S.; Yu, H.; Ghimire, N.J.; Jones, A.M.; Aivazian, G.; Yan, J.; Mandrus, D.G.; Xiao, D.; Yao, W.; et al. Electrical control of neutral and charged excitons in a monolayer semiconductor. *Nat. Commun.* **2013**, *4*, 1–6. [CrossRef]
58. Zeng, H.; Liu, G.B.; Dai, J.; Yan, Y.; Zhu, B.; He, R.; Xie, L.; Xu, S.; Chen, X.; Yao, W.; et al. Optical signature of symmetry variations and spin-valley coupling in atomically thin tungsten dichalcogenides. *Sci. Rep.* **2013**, *3*, 1608. [CrossRef]

59. McCreary, A.; Berkdemir, A.; Wang, J.; Nguyen, M.A.; Elías, A.L.; Perea-López, N.; Fujisawa, K.; Kabius, B.; Carozo, V.; Cullen, D.A.; et al. Distinct photoluminescence and Raman spectroscopy signatures for identifying highly crystalline WS$_2$ monolayers produced by different growth methods. *J. Mater. Res.* **2016**, *31*, 931–944. [CrossRef]
60. McCreary, K.M.; Hanbicki, A.T.; Singh, S.; Kawakami, R.K.; Jernigan, G.G.; Ishigami, M.; Ng, A.; Brintlinger, T.H.; Stroud, R.M.; Jonker, B.T. The effect of preparation conditions on Raman and photoluminescence of monolayer WS$_2$. *Sci. Rep.* **2016**, *6*, 35154. [CrossRef]
61. Liang, J.; Zhang, L.; Li, X.; Pan, B.; Luo, T.; Liu, D.; Zou, C.; Liu, N.; Hu, Y.; Yang, K.; et al. Carbon-nanoparticle-assisted growth of high quality bilayer WS$_2$ by atmospheric pressure chemical vapor deposition. *Nano Res.* **2019**, *12*, 2802–2807. [CrossRef]
62. Okada, M.; Sawazaki, T.; Watanabe, K.; Taniguch, T.; Hibino, H.; Shinohara, H.; Kitaura, R. Direct chemical vapor deposition growth of WS$_2$ atomic layers on hexagonal boron nitride. *ACS Nano* **2014**, *8*, 8273–8277. [CrossRef] [PubMed]
63. Molas, M.R.; Nogajewski, K.; Potemski, M.; Babiński, A. Raman scattering excitation spectroscopy of monolayer WS$_2$. *Sci. Rep.* **2017**, *7*, 1–8. [CrossRef] [PubMed]
64. Botello Méndez, A.R.; Perea López, N.; Elías Arriaga, A.L.; Crespi, V.; López Urías, F.; Terrones Maldonado, H.; Terrones Maldonado, M. Identification of individual and few layers of WS$_2$ using Raman spectroscopy. *Sci. Rep.* **2013**, *3*, 1755.
65. Gołasa, K.; Grzeszczyk, M.; Bożek, R.; Leszczyński, P.; Wysmołek, A.; Potemski, M.; Babiński, A. Resonant Raman scattering in MoS$_2$—From bulk to monolayer. *Solid State Commun.* **2014**, *197*, 53–56. [CrossRef]
66. Buscema, M.; Steele, G.A.; van der Zant, H.S.; Castellanos-Gomez, A. The effect of the substrate on the Raman and photoluminescence emission of single-layer MoS$_2$. *Nano Res.* **2014**, *7*, 561–571. [CrossRef]
67. Chien, C.T.; Li, S.S.; Lai, W.J.; Yeh, Y.C.; Chen, H.A.; Chen, I.S.; Chen, L.C.; Chen, K.H.; Nemoto, T.; Isoda, S.; et al. Tunable photoluminescence from graphene oxide. *Angew. Chem. Int. Ed.* **2012**, *51*, 6662–6666. [CrossRef]
68. Tripathi, N.; Mishra, P.; Joshi, B.; Islam, S.S. Catalyst free, excellent quality and narrow diameter of CNT growth on Al$_2$O$_3$ by a thermal CVD technique. *Phys. E* **2014**, *62*, 43–47. [CrossRef]
69. Chakraborty, B.; Matte, H.R.; Sood, A.K.; Rao, C.N.R. Layer-dependent resonant Raman scattering of a few layer MoS$_2$. *J. Raman Spectr.* **2013**, *44*, 92–96. [CrossRef]
70. Wang, Y.; Cong, C.; Qiu, C.; Yu, T. Raman spectroscopy study of lattice vibration and crystallographic orientation of monolayer MoS$_2$ under uniaxial strain. *Small* **2013**, *9*, 2857–2861. [CrossRef]
71. Talib, M.; Tabassum, R.; Islam, S.S.; Mishra, P. Improvements in the performance of a visible–NIR photodetector using horizontally aligned TiS$_3$ nanoribbons. *ACS Omega* **2019**, *4*, 6180–6191. [CrossRef]
72. Abid; Sehrawat, P.; Islam, S.S.; Gulati, P.; Talib, M.; Mishra, P.; Khanuja, M. Development of highly sensitive optical sensor from carbon nanotube-alumina nanocomposite free-standing films: CNTs loading dependence sensor performance analysis. *Sens. Actuators A* **2018**, *269*, 62–69. [CrossRef]

Article

# GFET Asymmetric Transfer Response Analysis through Access Region Resistances

Alejandro Toral-Lopez [1,*], Enrique G. Marin [1,2], Francisco Pasadas [3], Jose Maria Gonzalez-Medina [1], Francisco G. Ruiz [1,4], David Jiménez [3] and Andres Godoy [1,4,*]

1 Departamento de Electrónica, Facultad de Ciencias, Universidad de Granada, 18071 Granada, Spain
2 Dipartimento di Ingegneria dell'Informazione, Università di Pisa, 56122 Pisa, Italy
3 Departament d'Enginyeria Electrònica, Escola d'Enginyeria, Universitat Autònoma de Barcelona, 08193 Bellaterra, Spain
4 Pervasive Electronics Advanced Research Laboratory, CITIC, Universidad de Granada, 18017 Granada, Spain
\* Correspondence: atoral@ugr.es (A.T.-L.); agodoy@ugr.es (A.G.)

Received: 23 June 2019; Accepted:15 July 2019; Published: 18 July 2019

**Abstract:** Graphene-based devices are planned to augment the functionality of Si and III-V based technology in radio-frequency (RF) electronics. The expectations in designing graphene field-effect transistors (GFETs) with enhanced RF performance have attracted significant experimental efforts, mainly concentrated on achieving high mobility samples. However, little attention has been paid, so far, to the role of the access regions in these devices. Here, we analyse in detail, via numerical simulations, how the GFET transfer response is severely impacted by these regions, showing that they play a significant role in the asymmetric saturated behaviour commonly observed in GFETs. We also investigate how the modulation of the access region conductivity (i.e., by the influence of a back gate) and the presence of imperfections in the graphene layer (e.g., charge puddles) affects the transfer response. The analysis is extended to assess the application of GFETs for RF applications, by evaluating their cut-off frequency.

**Keywords:** GFET; RF; access region

## 1. Introduction

Two-dimensional materials (2DMs) have awakened the great interest of the nanotechnology community during the last decade [1]. Their striking physical properties, intrinsically different from their 3D counterparts, open a vast field of opportunities only partially exploited so far. Among these alternatives, 2DMs find a natural spot in electronics, where their monoatomic thickness makes them especially attractive to overcome the hurdles related to the transistor scaling-down [2].

Graphene is not only the pioneer, but also the most singular member of the 2DM family [3]. It is characterized by a gapless Dirac-cone bandstructure, where electrons and holes have symmetric dispersion relationships. The literature is abundant in Graphene Field-Effect Transistors (GFETs) [4–6], where this particular band structure is manifested in an ambipolar behaviour and a poor $I_{ON}/I_{OFF}$ ratio (direct consequence of the easiness to switch the carrier transport from electrons to holes and vice versa). This issue jeopardizes the use of GFETs in digital electronics, although a successful demonstration has been achieved in [7]. In radio-frequency (RF), however, graphene has revealed itself as an interesting candidate [8], and devices with cut-off frequencies of hundreds of GHz have already been demonstrated [9,10], even reaching wafer scale integration [11], or being applied for flexible electronics [12,13]. The main strategies to boost GFETs performance have consisted of the scaling-down of the gate oxide thickness [4,14], the encapsulation in hexagonal boron nitride [15] or the improvement in the quality of the graphene-insulator stack [7,16]. In particular, clean self-aligned fabrication, based in pre-deposited gold, has been proposed in [17]; while the self-aligned transfer of the gate stack (processed in a sacrificial substrate) has been detailed in [18].

The transfer characteristic of experimental GFETs is V-shaped, but very often shows an asymmetry with respect to the Dirac voltage [19], usually associated with different electron and hole mobilities. These mobility dissimilarities are the common path to handle the device response asymmetry, leaving out of the spot the relevance of the gate underlapped areas [15,20,21]. These access regions (intended to minimize the capacitance coupling between the gate and the source and drain) impact, however, strongly on the GFET electrical behaviour, as they constitute a noticeable resistance pathway for carrier transport. Partial attempts on the modelling of this issue have been discussed from an analytical resistance-based perspective in [20,22], but a comprehensive study of their impact in the GFET performance is still lacking [18]. In this work, we direct our attention to this asymmetric response of GFETs and, by means of detailed numerical simulations, we explain such effect studying the impact of the access regions in the transfer characteristic as well as in the RF performance of such devices.

The rest of the document is organized as follows. Section 2.1 presents the numerical model employed for this study. To check and validate it we compare, in Section 2.2, the simulated transfer response of two GFETs against the corresponding experimental measurements. Section 2.3 contains a thorough analysis of the access resistances and a discussion of its influence on the cut-off frequency, $f_T$. Finally, the main conclusions are drawn in Section 3.

## 2. Results

### 2.1. Device Simulation

A schematic depiction of the physical structure of the simulated GFET is shown in Figure 1. The graphene flake is sandwiched in between a top insulator layer, with thickness $t_{TOX}$ and dielectric permittivity $\varepsilon_{TOX}$, and an insulating substrate, with thickness $t_{BOX}$ and dielectric permittivity $\varepsilon_{BOX}$. Both oxides are assumed thick enough as to neglect any tunnelling current through them. A four-terminal device is considered, with a front gate extending over a length $L_{Chn}$ (the device channel length), giving rise to two under-lapped regions of length $L_{Acc}$ (the access region length) that connect it with the source and drain terminals. The back gate, when considered, extends all along the structure including the channel as well as the access regions. $V_{FG}$, $V_{BG}$, and $V_D$ stand for the front gate, back gate, and drain terminal biases respectively, while the source terminal, $V_S$, is assumed to be grounded. The total resistance of this structure, $R_T$, can be schematically split into the series combination of three resistances corresponding to the source access region ($R_{S,Acc}$), the channel region ($R_{Chn}$) and the drain access region ($R_{D,Acc}$).

To determine the $I - V$ response of GFET devices, we have self-consistently solved the coupled Poisson, Drift-Diffusion and continuity equations [23,24]. For the device modelling, we have considered a longitudinal $x - y$ section of the GFET, assuming invariance along the device width ($z$). The resulting 2D Poisson equation is given by:

$$\nabla \left( \varepsilon(x,y) \nabla V(x,y) \right) = -\rho(x,y) \tag{1}$$

where $V$ is the electrostatic potential; $\rho$ is the net charge density in the structure, that comprises the mobile (electrons and holes) and fixed (dopants) charges; and $\varepsilon$ is the dielectric permittivity.

The Drift-Diffusion transport equation is formulated in terms of the pseudo-Fermi level ($E_F$) as proposed in [25]:

$$J(x) = q \left[ \mu_n n_{1D}(x) + \mu_p p_{1D}(x) \right] \frac{dV_{E_F}}{dx} \tag{2}$$

where $V_{E_F}$ is the potential associated with this level and $n_{1D}$ ($p_{1D}$) is the graphene electron (hole) 1D density profile. Here, $\mu_n$ ($\mu_p$) stands for the electron (hole) mobility. Due to the extreme confinement, the carriers are supposed to move only along the transport direction ($x$). $J$ must comply with the continuity equation that, under steady-state conditions, is formulated as: $\nabla \cdot J = 0$. Ohmic contacts are assumed at the source and drain terminals, with the Fermi level at the source grounded, $E_{F,S} = 0$, and at the drain given by $E_{F,D} = -qV_{DS}$. The equation system is then iteratively solved for each set of terminal biases, until a convergence threshold is achieved for the potential and charge concentrations.

In addition to the mobile charge and dopants in the graphene layer, we account for the existence of puddles [26,27]. Their associated charge density, $N_p$, is assumed constant and added to both electron and hole charge densities [28]. In this way, puddles impact on the overall graphene layer conductivity while conserving a neutral net charge character.

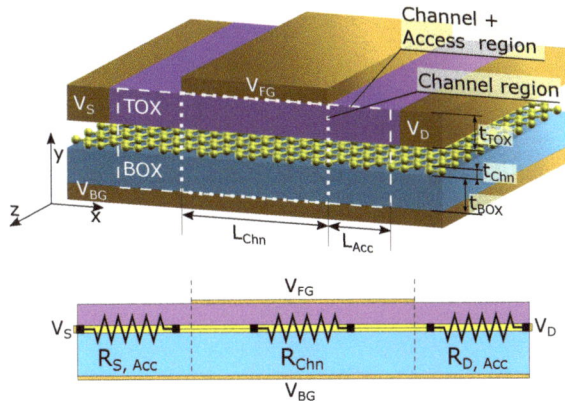

**Figure 1.** Schematic of the simulated GFET and the characteristic resistances of the device. The dashed and dotted rectangles indicate the regions used for the different simulations. While the dotted rectangle only encompasses the channel region, the dashed one includes the access regions.

## 2.2. Validation

To assess the capability of the numerical simulator to reproduce and explain the experimental results, we have first validated it against the devices fabricated in [29,30]. Both are GFETs based on monolayer graphene embedded between a $SiO_2$ layer, which acts as a substrate, and a $Y_2O_3$ layer, which acts as a front gate dielectric. In both cases, this $Y_2O_3$ layer is 5 nm thick while the substrate is 300 nm thick in [29], and 286 nm thick in [30]. For the device presented in [29], the distance between the source and drain contacts is 1.5 μm and the front gate length is 600 nm, while in [30] the device is 8.2 μm long and its front gate is 7 μm long. In other words, in both experimental devices the gate contact does not cover the whole region between source and drain contacts, thus creating two symmetrical under-lapped regions at both channel edges; namely, the device access regions. To reproduce the data reported in [29], the same mobility is assumed for both types of carriers, electrons and holes ($\mu = \mu_n = \mu_p$) with a value of 90 cm$^2$/Vs, and a puddle charge density of $7 \cdot 10^{11}$ cm$^{-2}$ is considered. N-type chemical doping of $10^{12}$ cm$^{-2}$ is defined for the graphene layer. To account for the graphene-metal contact resistances, which are in series with the total resistance of the structure, $R_T$, we include two additional 100 nm long N-type doped regions ($5 \cdot 10^{10}$ cm$^{-2}$) in both source and drain ends [31]. The back gate is grounded and $V_{DS}$ is set to 0.1 V. To fit the data presented in [30], the values used are $\mu = 1091$ cm$^2$/Vs, $N_p = 8 \cdot 10^{11}$ cm$^{-2}$ and the graphene layer chemical doping is set to $10^{11}$ cm$^{-2}$. The back gate is also grounded and $V_{DS}$ is set to 0.05 V. The experimental and simulated transfer characteristics are shown in Figure 2a [29] and Figure 2b [30]. The simulated I-V characteristics match very accurately with the experimental results in the whole range of biases and are able to catch the transfer response of the electron and hole branches, especially in Figure 2b.

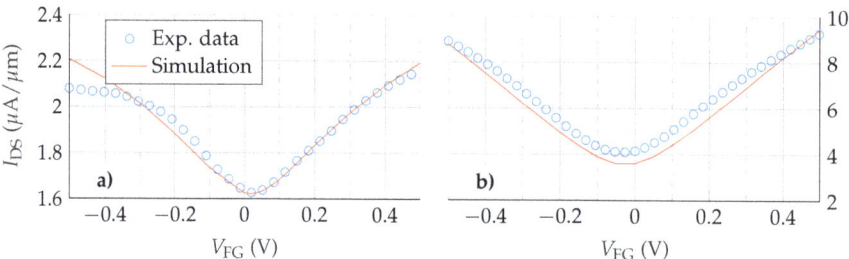

**Figure 2.** Comparison between the simulation results and the experimental data extracted from [29] (**a**) and [30] (**b**).

## 2.3. Access Region Analysis

As mentioned in Section 1, the existence of access regions and puddles is a very common scenario in the experimental realization of GFETs due to the difficulties to precisely control the fabrication process in this early stage of the technology. They modify the behaviour of the transistors, in many cases determining their performance, and therefore deserving a particular attention that is usually obliterated. Hence, once the numerical simulator has been validated, we now proceed to analyse the effect of the access regions.

### 2.3.1. Including the Access Regions

To begin with, we have considered a test structure where the front gate covers the whole device length (i.e., suppressing the access regions) and compared the results with those obtained later when access regions are included. These scenarios are illustrated in Figure 1 by the dotted and dashed frames respectively. The material stack comprises a monolayer graphene sandwiched between a 3 nm thick $HfO_2$ layer (front gate insulator) and a 27 nm thick $SiO_2$ layer (back gate insulator). The front gate, which determines the channel length ($L_{Chn}$), is 100 nm long and both access regions are 35 nm long ($L_{Acc}$). Electron and hole mobilities are equal ($\mu = 1500$ cm$^2$/Vs) and no chemical doping or puddle charge density is considered in the graphene layer.

The transfer characteristic of the device without access regions is depicted in Figure 3a for different values of $V_{DS}$. As can be observed, the device exhibits the ambipolar V-shaped $I - V$ response of an ideal GFET. The minimum of the $I - V$ curve defines the Dirac voltage ($V_{Dirac}$) that is shifted to larger $V_{FG}$ when $V_{DS}$ increases. The behaviour is perfectly symmetric with respect to $V_{Dirac}$, reflecting the symmetry between electron and hole properties.

Next, the GFET including the access regions is investigated. The resulting transfer characteristic is shown in Figure 3b. Comparing Figure 3b and Figure 3a, a marked variation of the GFET response is observed. First, there is a notable decrease in the values of $I_{DS}$, around a factor ×100. Second, the transfer characteristic shows a saturation trend for high $|V_{FG}|$ which resembles much better the experimental response. Third, and more important, the $I - V$ characteristic is no longer symmetric with respect to $V_{Dirac}$, though the mobility is identical for both kinds of carriers.

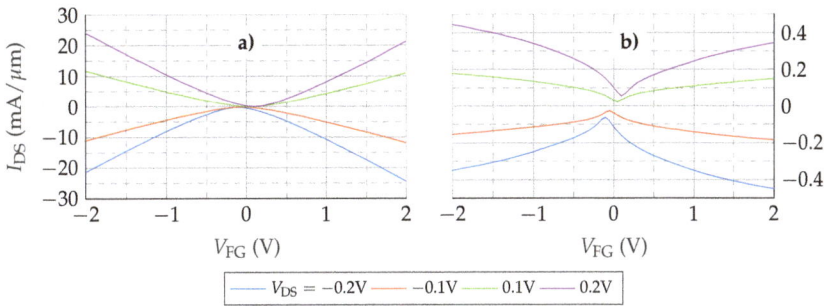

**Figure 3.** $I_{DS} - V_{FG}$ curves of the device without (**a**) and with (**b**) access regions.

To provide insights into these changes, the resistance of the different regions of the device are calculated. Figure 4 shows their values for $V_{DS} = -0.1$ V and $V_{DS} = -0.2$ V. Mirror symmetric behaviour is observed for positive $V_{DS}$. The access region resistances, $R_{S,Acc}$ and $R_{D,Acc}$, show values comparable with the channel resistance, $R_{Chn}$. At the Dirac voltage, where the channel resistivity is the highest, $R_{Chn}$ commands the series association, but still the access regions have a noticeable contribution. For $|V_{FG} - V_{Dirac}| > 0.1$ V the total resistance is mainly determined by $R_{S,Acc}$ and $R_{D,Acc}$. Consequently, the total resistance ($R_T$) is not controlled just by the channel conductivity and, therefore, by the gate terminal. The weak dependence of $R_{S,Acc}$ and $R_{D,Acc}$ on $V_{FG}$ is reflected in the $I_{DS}$ trend to saturation. As the values of $R_{S,Acc}$ and $R_{D,Acc}$ are higher than the channel resistance, a larger fraction of $V_{DS}$ drops in the access regions. This fact reduces the potential at the channel edges with respect to the no-access-regions scenario, reducing the output current. In addition, the $R_{Acc} - V_{FG}$ dependence is not symmetric, so neither are the access region potential drops, resulting into a non-symmetric reduction of the output current, that is, an asymmetric $I_{DS} - V_{FG}$ curve shown in Figure 3b. This lack of equivalence between the source and drain access regions is explored in detail in the following section.

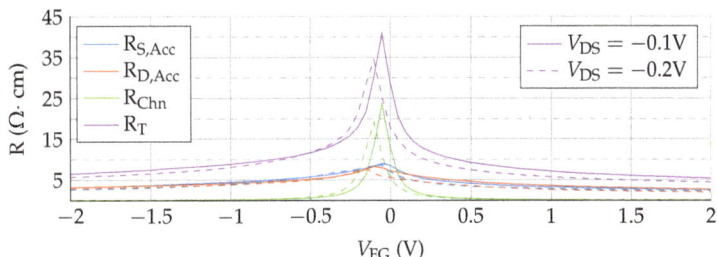

**Figure 4.** Resistance of the three device regions (channel, source and drain access regions) compared with the total resistance as a function of the gate potential, for two $V_{DS}$ values: $-0.1$ V (solid) and $-0.2$ V (dashed).

### 2.3.2. Gate Misalignment

In the previous section, we assumed that the gate is perfectly aligned in the middle of the channel leading to identical source and drain access regions ($L_S = L_D = L_{Acc}$) at both ends. A more realistic scenario should consider the impact of having non-equal $L_S$ and $L_D$, enabling us to test the non-equivalent role of $R_{S,Acc}$ and $R_{D,Acc}$ on the GFET response. For this purpose, we have analysed GFETs where the top gate contact is not placed in the centre of the structure, resulting in access regions of different length. In particular, we have kept $L_S$ (or $L_D$) equal to 35 nm while $L_D$ (or $L_S$) is modified. Specifically, we considered four scenarios: (i) short source, (ii) short drain, (iii) long source and (iv) long drain. The length of the short and long regions is set to 17.5 nm and 70 nm, respectively. The $I_{DS}-V_{FG}$ curves, along with the resistances $R_{S,Acc}$, $R_{D,Acc}$ and $R_{Chn}$ obtained in each case, are depicted in Figure 5.

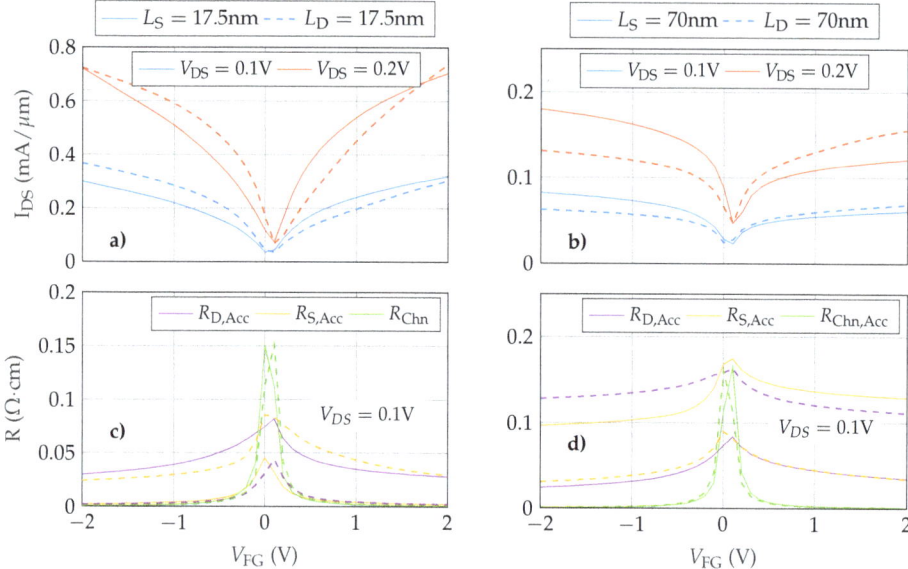

**Figure 5.** Transfer response (**a,b**) and structure resistances (**c,d**) as a function of the gate bias. These results are obtained reducing the length of either the source (**a,c**, solid lines) or drain access region (**b,d**, dashed lines) down to 17.5 nm, and increasing the length of either the source (**a,c**, solid lines) or the drain access region (**b,d**, dashed lines) up to 70 nm.

As expected, there are significant differences between devices. Shortening either the source or the drain access regions results in a higher output current (Figure 5a) and reduces both its saturation and its asymmetry with respect to the elongated scenario (Figure 5b). When comparing the shorter regions (Figure 5a) it is clearly observable that the $L_S = 17.5$ nm device (solid lines) has a more symmetric response than the $L_D = 17.5$ nm (dashed lines). This is more evident for $V_{DS} = 0.1$ V and emphasizes the role of the source access region with respect to the drain access region. An equivalent conclusion can be achieved from the elongated devices (Figure 5b). The longer $L_S$ results in an increased asymmetry between both branches. These results can be explained by analysing the resistances of the structure. Figure 5c,d show $R_{S,Acc}$, $R_{D,Acc}$ and $R_{Chn}$ as a function of $V_{FG}$ for $V_{DS} = 0.1$ V. When any access region is shortened (Figure 5c), its resistance is similar or lower than the channel resistance regardless $V_{FG}$. The longer region resistance controls the total current (except for $V_{FG}$ close to zero). When one of the regions is enlarged this effect is emphasized. The transfer responses in Figure 5b are clearly saturated due to the dominant role in the total conductivity of the longer access region.

### 2.3.3. Impact of Electrostatic Doping and Puddles

To reduce the impact of the access regions in the overall device performance, it is possible to increase their conductivity by means of an electrostatic doping using the back-gate terminal. In the following we analyse how the back gate influences the GFET behaviour. Figure 6 shows the transfer characteristic for three different values of $V_{BG}$: $-1$ V, 0 V and 1 V (solid lines). For $V_{BG} = 0$ V the results are quite similar to the scenario without back gate. In the other two cases, depending on the polarity of $V_{BG}$, electrons or holes are accumulated in the graphene layer. As a result, the P-type (N-type) branch is enhanced for $V_{BG} = -1$ V ($V_{BG} = 1$ V), regardless the value of $V_{DS}$. As in the previous scenario, the origin of this behaviour can be traced back to the resistance associated with the access regions.

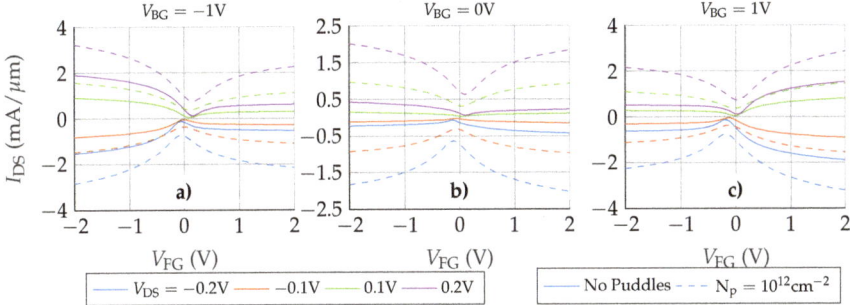

**Figure 6.** $I_{DS} - V_{FG}$ characteristics of the complete structure when three different back gate potentials are used ($-1$ V (**a**), 0 V (**b**) and 1 V (**c**)). Solid lines correspond to the device without puddles and dashed lines to the device with $N_p = 10^{12}$ cm$^{-2}$.

Figure 7 depicts the device resistances for different $V_{BG}$ and $V_{DS} = -0.1$ V (without puddles, solid lines). For $|V_{BG}| = 1$ V the total resistance near the Dirac voltage is dominated by $R_{Chn}$. When $V_{FG}$ is increased above $V_{Dirac}$, the symmetry of $R_{Chn}$ is kept since it is mostly controlled by the front gate, while the asymmetry of $R_{S,Acc}$ and $R_{D,Acc}$ is exacerbated due to the electrostatic doping, giving rise to the large asymmetry observed in the transfer response, in Figure 6. In particular, the asymmetric step-like dependence of the access resistances on $V_{FG}$ (for $V_{BG} \neq 0$ V) is the result of the electrostatic competition between the front and back gates to control the access regions closer to the channel. When $V_{FG}$ and $V_{BG}$ have the same polarity, they add their electric forces to increase the carrier density in the aforementioned zones, increasing the conductivity and therefore lowering the whole access resistance. However, if $V_{FG}$ is opposite to $V_{BG}$, both gates compete to accumulate different types of charges, resulting in a depleted region close to the channel edges that decreases the conductivity and increases the overall access region resistances. An equivalent conclusion was achieved in [26] where a strong modulation of the total resistance by two additional gates is observed, as in Figure 7.

An additional aspect that cannot be overlooked is the effect of the presence of puddles in the graphene layer [27,32]. To shed light on this issue Figure 6 includes the $I_{DS} - V_{FG}$ response when a puddle charge density of $N_p = 10^{12}$ cm$^{-2}$ is considered (dashed lines). Two major changes are observed after including the puddles: (i) the total current is increased, and (ii) the asymmetry is clearly reduced. These changes derive from the equal contribution of puddles to the conductivity of both electrons and holes, and explain why the $I - V$ curves of some experimental devices are reasonably symmetric close to the Dirac voltage, where the conductivity of puddles is dominant. In this situation, the conductivity of the whole graphene layer is increased for electrons and holes, in contrast with the electrostatic doping generated by the back gate. This non-selective improvement of the conductivity is translated into the resistances of the device: Figure 7 includes the $R - V_{FG}$ relation for $N_p = 10^{12}$ cm$^{-2}$ (dashed lines). The step-like behaviour of $R_{S,Acc}$ and $R_{D,Acc}$ is softened when the puddles are included, resembling the $V_{BG} = 0$ V case.

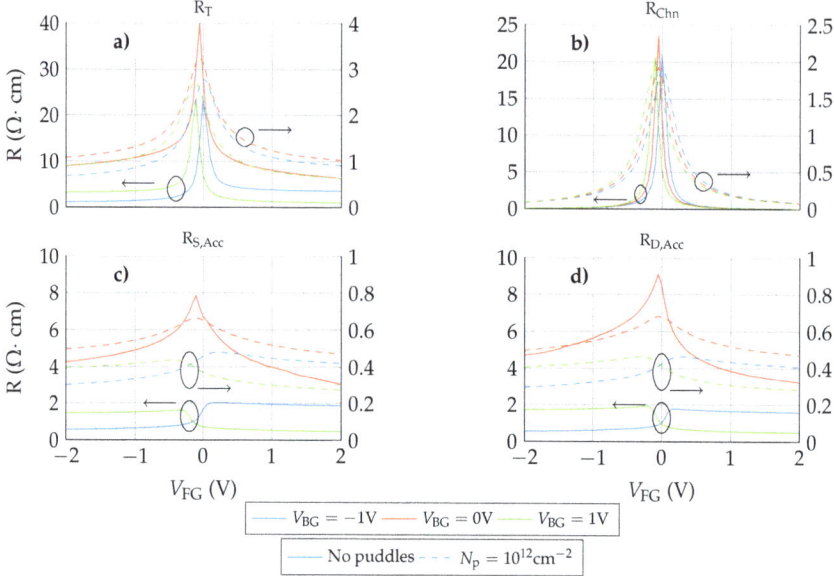

**Figure 7.** Total (**a**), channel (**b**), source (**c**) and drain (**d**) resistances for different back gate biases and $V_{DS} = -0.1$ V. Solid lines (referred to the left axis) correspond to the no puddles scenario while dashed lines (referred to the right axis) depict the values obtained when a puddle concentration of $N_P = 10^{12}$ cm$^{-2}$ is considered.

### 2.3.4. RF Performance

Finally, to determine the impact of the access regions in the RF performance, we evaluate the cut-off frequency, $f_T$, as a RF figure of merit (FoM). The value of $f_T$ is calculated as in [33,34]:

$$f_T = \frac{1}{2\pi} \frac{g_m}{C_{fg}} \qquad (3)$$

where $g_m$ is the transconductance and $C_{fg}$ the front gate capacitance.

Figure 8 shows $f_T$ as a function of $V_{FG}$ under two scenarios: no puddles (solid lines) and $N_P = 10^{12}$cm$^{-2}$ (dash-dotted lines). To assess the impact of the access regions, the performance of the intrinsic device (structure indicated by the dotted rectangle in Figure 1) is depicted too (dashed lines). In addition, to evaluate the magnitude of the calculated values, the experimental measurements of $f_T$ reported in [35] and [36] are indicated by the arrows on the right side axis of Figure 8. Despite the device structure and the bias conditions are different, the channel lengths of these experimental devices are similar to the ones simulated here (144 nm [35] and 140 nm [36]), and therefore constitute a good reference. Importantly, a de-embedding procedure was carried out for the RF measurements of these experimental devices by using specific "short" and "open" structures with identical layouts in order to remove the effects of the parasitics associated with the pads and connections, but not the contact and access region resistances.

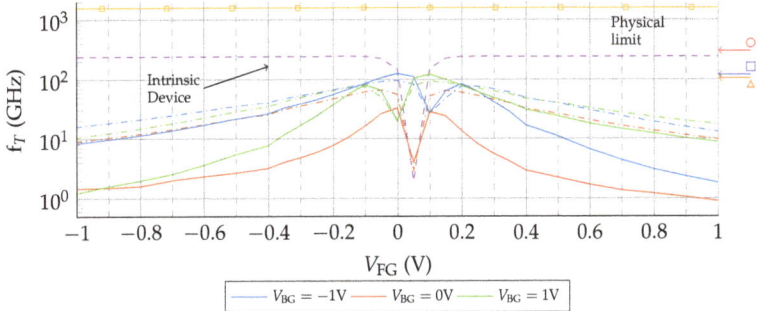

**Figure 8.** $f_T$ of the back-gated device with access regions under two scenarios: no puddles (solid lines) and $N_p = 10^{12}$ cm$^{-2}$ (dash-dotted lines). The values obtained for the intrinsic device are depicted by the purple dashed line. The arrows labelled by marks on the right side axis indicate the values of $f_T$ extracted from [35] (circle) and [36] (square and triangle). The yellow line indicates the physical limit for graphene $v_F/2\pi L$, determined by the transit time $L/v_F$, with the Fermi velocity $v_F \approx 10^8$ cm/s and $L = 100$ nm (squares).

Including the access regions results in a quite different response compared with the intrinsic device, as the associated parasitic resistances provoke a bias dependent decay of $f_T$. Considering the scenario without puddles, when the back gate is properly biased, $f_T$ is considerably improved. If we analyse Figure 8 in combination with Figure 7, those combinations of $V_{FG}$, $V_{BG}$ for which the $R_S - V_{FG}$ ($R_D - V_{FG}$) curve shows its minimum values, are those for which $f_T$ shows a greater improvement. When $R_S$ ($R_D$) is higher, $f_T$ is spoiled with respect to the $V_{BG} = 0$ V case. This relation between the access region conductivity and the improvement of the RF performance was experimentally observed in [21] where a higher $f_T$ was demonstrated when a GFET with two additional electrodes was properly biased to control such conductivity. When puddles are included, the channel conductivity increases, what reduces the control of the back-gate bias, and simultaneously results in a more symmetric $f_T - V_{FG}$ dependence.

## 3. Conclusions

GFETs have been thoroughly studied in order to assess the impact of the access regions in the device performance. The validation of our approach against two experimental devices spotlights the importance of these regions as well as the presence of puddles to reproduce the state-of-the-art technology. When the access regions are considered, the transfer response reveals a lower, saturated and asymmetric $I_{DS} - V_{FG}$ characteristic that is not observed in their absence. To explore the impact of a variable conductivity of these regions we have included a back gate in the structure able to introduce an electrostatic doping. The back gate increases the output current as well as the asymmetry of the transfer characteristic. The latter effect is explained in terms of the competition of the back and front gates that results in a depletion of the amount of carriers close to the channel edges when both biases have an opposite polarity. The influence of puddles is also theoretically investigated, observing that they reduce the asymmetry of $I_{DS} - V_{FG}$.

The analysis of the impact of the access regions and puddles have been extended to the prediction of the cut-off frequency to assess the properties of GFETs for potential RF applications. Our results reveal an important degradation of the $f_T - V_{FG}$ relation due to access regions. The application of an appropriate back gate bias can tune the access region conductivity generating a remarkable improvement in the RF performance. The presence of puddles also mitigates this degradation, but neglects the possibility of tuning the access regions conductivity.

**Author Contributions:** A.T.-L., E.G.M., F.G.R. and A.G. conceived the work. A.T.-L., F.P., and J.M.G.-M. performed the numerical simulations under the supervision of E.G.M., F.G.R., D.J. and A.G. All authors analysed the results, contributed to the discussion and wrote the manuscript.

**Funding:** This research was founded by Spanish government grant numbers TEC2017-89955-P (MINECO/AEI/FEDER, UE), TEC2015-67462-C2-1-R (MINECO), IJCI-2017-32297 (MINECO/AEI), FPU16/04043 and FPU14/02579, and the European Union's Horizon 2020 Research and Innovation Program under Grant GrapheneCore2 785219.

**Conflicts of Interest:** The authors declare no conflict of interest.

## Abbreviations

The following abbreviations are used in this manuscript:

| | |
|---|---|
| 2DM | Two-dimensional material |
| MOSFET | Metal-Oxide-Semiconductor Field-Effect Transistor |
| GFET | Graphene Field-Effect Transistors |
| RF | Radio-Frequency |

## References

1. Fiori, G.; Bonaccorso, F.; Iannaccone, G.; Palacios, T.; Neumaier, D.; Seabaugh, A.; Banerjee, S.K.; Colombo, L. Electronics based on two-dimensional materials. *Nat. Nanotechnol.* **2014**, *9*, 768–779. [CrossRef] [PubMed]
2. Lee, S.; Zhong, Z. Nanoelectronic circuits based on two-dimensional atomic layer crystals. *Nanoscale* **2014**, *6*, 13283–13300. [CrossRef] [PubMed]
3. Neto, A.H.C.; Guinea, F.; Peres, N.M.R.; Novoselov, K.S.; Geim, A.K. The electronic properties of graphene. *Rev. Mod. Phys.* **2009**, *81*, 109–162. [CrossRef]
4. Guerriero, E.; Pedrinazzi, P.; Mansouri, A.; Habibpour, O.; Winters, M.; Rorsman, N.; Behnam, A.; Carrion, E.A.; Pesquera, A.; Centeno, A.; et al. High-Gain Graphene Transistors with a Thin AlOx Top-Gate Oxide. *Sci. Rep.* **2017**, *7*, 2419. [CrossRef] [PubMed]
5. Lin, Y.M.; Jenkins, K.A.; Valdes-Garcia, A.; Small, J.P.; Farmer, D.B.; Avouris, P. Operation of Graphene Transistors at Gigahertz Frequencies. *Nano Lett.* **2009**, *9*, 422–426. [CrossRef]
6. Meric, I.; Han, M.Y.; Young, A.F.; Ozyilmaz, B.; Kim, P.; Shepard, K.L. Current saturation in zero-bandgap, top-gated graphene field-effect transistors. *Nat. Nanotechnol.* **2008**, *3*, 654–659. [CrossRef] [PubMed]
7. Rizzi, L.G.; Bianchi, M.; Behnam, A.; Carrion, E.; Guerriero, E.; Polloni, L.; Pop, E.; Sordan, R. Cascading Wafer-Scale Integrated Graphene Complementary Inverters under Ambient Conditions. *Nano Lett.* **2012**, *12*, 3948–3953. [CrossRef] [PubMed]
8. Pandey, H.; Shaygan, M.; Sawallich, S.; Kataria, S.; Wang, Z.; Noculak, A.; Otto, M.; Nagel, M.; Negra, R.; Neumaier, D.; et al. All CVD Boron Nitride Encapsulated Graphene FETs With CMOS Compatible Metal Edge Contacts. *IEEE Trans. Electron Devices* **2018**, *65*, 4129–4134. [CrossRef]
9. Wu, Y.; Zou, X.; Sun, M.; Cao, Z.; Wang, X.; Huo, S.; Zhou, J.; Yang, Y.; Yu, X.; Kong, Y.; et al. 200 GHz Maximum Oscillation Frequency in CVD Graphene Radio Frequency Transistors. *ACS Appl. Mater. Interfaces* **2016**, *8*, 25645–25649. [CrossRef]
10. Cheng, R.; Bai, J.; Liao, L.; Zhou, H.; Chen, Y.; Liu, L.; Lin, Y.C.; Jiang, S.; Huang, Y.; Duan, X. High-frequency self-aligned graphene transistors with transferred gate stacks. *Proc. Natl. Acad. Sci. USA* **2012**, *109*, 11588–11592. [CrossRef]
11. Lin, Y.M.; Dimitrakopoulos, C.; Jenkins, K.A.; Farmer, D.B.; Chiu, H.Y.; Grill, A.; Avouris, P. 100-GHz Transistors from Wafer-Scale Epitaxial Graphene. *Science* **2010**, *327*, 662. [CrossRef] [PubMed]
12. Georgiou, T.; Jalil, R.; Belle, B.D.; Britnell, L.; Gorbachev, R.V.; Morozov, S.V.; Kim, Y.J.; Gholinia, A.; Haigh, S.J.; Makarovsky, O.; et al. Vertical field-effect transistor based on graphene–WS2 heterostructures for flexible and transparent electronics. *Nat. Nanotechnol.* **2013**, *8*, 100–103. [CrossRef] [PubMed]
13. Wang, Z.; Uzlu, B.; Shaygan, M.; Otto, M.; Ribeiro, M.; Marín, E.G.; Iannaccone, G.; Fiori, G.; Elsayed, M.S.; Negra, R.; et al. Flexible One-Dimensional Metal–Insulator–Graphene Diode. *ACS Appl. Electron. Mater.* **2019**, *1*, 945–950. [CrossRef]
14. Liao, L.; Bai, J.; Cheng, R.; Lin, Y.C.; Jiang, S.; Huang, Y.; Duan, X. Top-Gated Graphene Nanoribbon Transistors with Ultrathin High-kDielectrics. *Nano Lett.* **2010**, *10*, 1917–1921. [CrossRef] [PubMed]

15. Mayorov, A.S.; Gorbachev, R.V.; Morozov, S.V.; Britnell, L.; Jalil, R.; Ponomarenko, L.A.; Blake, P.; Novoselov, K.S.; Watanabe, K.; Taniguchi, T.; et al. Micrometer-Scale Ballistic Transport in Encapsulated Graphene at Room Temperature. *Nano Lett.* **2011**, *11*, 2396–2399. [CrossRef] [PubMed]
16. Farmer, D.B.; Lin, Y.M.; Avouris, P. Graphene field-effect transistors with self-aligned gates. *Appl. Phys. Lett.* **2010**, *97*, 013103. [CrossRef]
17. Feng, Z.; Yu, C.; Li, J.; Liu, Q.; He, Z.; Song, X.; Wang, J.; Cai, S. An ultra clean self-aligned process for high maximum oscillation frequency graphene transistors. *Carbon* **2014**, *75*, 249–254. [CrossRef]
18. Fiori, G.; Iannaccone, G. Multiscale Modeling for Graphene-Based Nanoscale Transistors. *Proc. IEEE* **2013**, *101*, 1653–1669. [CrossRef]
19. Di Bartolomeo, A.; Giubileo, F.; Romeo, F.; Sabatino, P.; Carapella, G.; Iemmo, L.; Schroeder, T.; Lupina, G. Graphene field effect transistors with niobium contacts and asymmetric transfer characteristics. *Nanotechnology* **2015**, *26*, 475202. [CrossRef]
20. Jain, S.; Dutta, A.K. Resistance-Based Approach for Drain Current Modeling in Graphene FETs. *IEEE Trans. Electron Devices* **2015**, *62*, 4313–4321. [CrossRef]
21. Al-Amin, C.; Karabiyik, M.; Pala, N. Fabrication of Graphene Field-effect Transistor with Field Controlling Electrodes to improve $f_T$. *Microelectron. Eng.* **2016**, *164*, 71–74. [CrossRef]
22. Wang, H.; Hsu, A.; Kong, J.; Antoniadis, D.A.; Palacios, T. Compact Virtual-Source Current–Voltage Model for Top- and Back-Gated Graphene Field-Effect Transistors. *IEEE Trans. Electron Devices* **2011**, *58*, 1523–1533. [CrossRef]
23. Ancona, M.G. Electron Transport in Graphene From a Diffusion-Drift Perspective. *IEEE Trans. Electron Devices* **2010**, *57*, 681–689. [CrossRef]
24. Curatola, G.; Doornbos, G.; Loo, J.; Ponomarev, Y.; Iannaccone, G. Detailed Modeling of Sub-100-nm MOSFETs Based on Schrödinger DD Per Subband and Experiments and Evaluation of the Performance Gap to Ballistic Transport. *IEEE Trans. Electron Devices* **2005**, *52*, 1851–1858. [CrossRef]
25. Feijoo, P.C.; Jiménez, D.; Cartoixà, X. Short channel effects in graphene-based field effect transistors targeting radio-frequency applications. *2D Mater.* **2016**, *3*, 025036. [CrossRef]
26. Wilmart, Q.; Inhofer, A.; Boukhicha, M.; Yang, W.; Rosticher, M.; Morfin, P.; Garroum, N.; Fève, G.; Berroir, J.M.; Plaçais, B. Contact gating at GHz frequency in graphene. *Sci. Rep.* **2016**, *6*, 21085. [CrossRef]
27. Martin, J.; Akerman, N.; Ulbricht, G.; Lohmann, T.; Smet, J.H.; von Klitzing, K.; Yacoby, A. Observation of electron–hole puddles in graphene using a scanning single-electron transistor. *Nat. Phys.* **2007**, *4*, 144–148. [CrossRef]
28. Fregonese, S.; Magallo, M.; Maneux, C.; Happy, H.; Zimmer, T. Scalable Electrical Compact Modeling for Graphene FET Transistors. *IEEE Trans. Nanotechnol.* **2013**, *12*, 539–546. [CrossRef]
29. Wang, Z.; Xu, H.; Zhang, Z.; Wang, S.; Ding, L.; Zeng, Q.; Yang, L.; Pei, T.; Liang, X.; Gao, M.; et al. Growth and Performance of Yttrium Oxide as an Ideal *High-k* Gate Dielectric for Carbon-Based Electronics. *Nano Lett.* **2010**, *10*, 2024–2030. [CrossRef]
30. Zhang, Z.; Xu, H.; Zhong, H.; Peng, L.M. Direct extraction of carrier mobility in graphene field-effect transistor using current-voltage and capacitance-voltage measurements. *Appl. Phys. Lett.* **2012**, *101*, 213103. [CrossRef]
31. Venica, S.; Zanato, M.; Driussi, F.; Palestri, P.; Selmi, L. Modeling electrostatic doping and series resistance in graphene-FETs. In Proceedings of the 2016 International Conference on Simulation of Semiconductor Processes and Devices (SISPAD), Nuremberg, Germany, 6–8 September 2016.
32. Zhang, Y.; Brar, V.W.; Girit, C.; Zettl, A.; Crommie, M.F. Origin of spatial charge inhomogeneity in graphene. *Nat. Phys.* **2009**, *5*, 722–726. [CrossRef]
33. Marian, D.; Dib, E.; Cusati, T.; Marin, E.G.; Fortunelli, A.; Iannaccone, G.; Fiori, G. Transistor Concepts Based on Lateral Heterostructures of Metallic and Semiconducting Phases of $MoS_2$. *Phys. Rev. Appl.* **2017**, *8*, 054047. [CrossRef]
34. Schwierz, F. Graphene Transistors: Status, Prospects, and Problems. *Proc. IEEE* **2013**, *101*, 1567–1584. [CrossRef]

35. Liao, L.; Lin, Y.C.; Bao, M.; Cheng, R.; Bai, J.; Liu, Y.; Qu, Y.; Wang, K.L.; Huang, Y.; Duan, X. High-speed graphene transistors with a self-aligned nanowire gate. *Nature* **2010**, *467*, 305–308. [CrossRef]
36. Wu, Y.; Jenkins, K.A.; Valdes-Garcia, A.; Farmer, D.B.; Zhu, Y.; Bol, A.A.; Dimitrakopoulos, C.; Zhu, W.; Xia, F.; Avouris, P.; et al. State-of-the-Art Graphene High-Frequency Electronics. *Nano Lett.* **2012**, *12*, 3062–3067. [CrossRef]

© 2019 by the authors. Licensee MDPI, Basel, Switzerland. This article is an open access article distributed under the terms and conditions of the Creative Commons Attribution (CC BY) license (http://creativecommons.org/licenses/by/4.0/).

Article

# Calculations of Some Doping Nanostructurations and Patterns Improving the Functionality of High-Temperature Superconductors for Bolometer Device Applications

Jose C. Verde [1], Alberto S. Viz [1,2], Martín M. Botana [1,2], Carlos Montero-Orille [2,3] and Manuel V. Ramallo [1,2,*]

1. Quantum Materials and Photonics Research Group, Department of Particle Physics, University of Santiago de Compostela, ES-15782 Santiago de Compostela, Spain; josecasver@hotmail.com (J.C.V.); aseviz@mundo-r.com (A.S.V.); martin14441@gmail.com (M.M.B.)
2. Strategic Grouping in Materials AeMAT, University of Santiago de Compostela, ES-15782 Santiago de Compostela, Spain; carlos.montero@usc.es
3. Quantum Materials and Photonics Research Group, Department of Applied Physics, University of Santiago de Compostela, ES-15782 Santiago de Compostela, Spain
* Correspondence: ramallo@cond-mat.eu or mv.ramallo@usc.es; Tel.: +34-881813965

Received: 26 November 2019; Accepted: 30 December 2019; Published: 3 January 2020

**Abstract:** We calculate the effects of doping nanostructuration and the patterning of thin films of high-temperature superconductors (HTS) with the aim of optimizing their functionality as sensing materials for resistive transition-edge bolometer devices (TES). We focus, in particular, on spatial variations of the carrier doping into the $CuO_2$ layers due to oxygen off-stoichiometry, (that induce, in turn, critical temperature variations) and explore following two major cases of such structurations: First, the random nanoscale disorder intrinsically associated to doping levels that do not maximize the superconducting critical temperature; our studies suggest that this first simple structuration already improves some of the bolometric operational parameters with respect to the conventional, nonstructured HTS materials used until now. Secondly, we consider the imposition of regular arrangements of zones with different nominal doping levels (patterning); we find that such regular patterns may improve the bolometer performance even further. We find one design that improves, with respect to nonstructured HTS materials, both the saturation power and the operating temperature width by more than one order of magnitude. It also almost doubles the response of the sensor to radiation.

**Keywords:** superconducting devices; photodetectors; nanostructured materials, nanostructured and microstructured superconductors; high temperature superconductors; bolometers

---

## 1. Introduction

Bolometers are radiation sensors that detect incident energy via the increase of the temperature $T$ caused by the absorption of incoming photons [1–16]. Bolometers are often used, e.g., for thermal infrared cameras (see, e.g., [1–10]), mm-wave sensing [1–6,8–13], space-based [12,13], laboratory far-infrared spectroscopy [13], etc. [1–16]. Superconductors are among the best candidate materials for bolometers, due to their extreme sensitivity to $T$ near the superconducting transition, measurable for instance through the sharp variations of the electrical resistance $R$ (resistive transition-edge bolometer—TES). For resistive TES bolometers, a key figure for performance is the so-called "temperature coefficient of resistance" (TCR), given by [1–19]:

$$\text{TCR} = \left| \frac{1}{R} \frac{dR}{dT} \right|. \tag{1}$$

High bolometric sensitivity requires a large value of TCR. For instance, structures of vanadium oxides $V_xO_y$, commonly used in semiconductor-based bolometers, present TCR $\sim 0.025\,\text{K}^{-1}$ [20]. Much larger TCR may be achieved with superconductor materials kept at base temperatures coincident with their normal–superconducting transition, $T_c$. This is the case mainly when using conventional low-temperature superconductors with $T_c \leq 1\,\text{K}$ (the so-called low-$T_c$ TES bolometers), that achieve TCR $\sim 1000\,\text{K}^{-1}$ or even more [17–19], making them a technology of choice for detecting the most faint radiations, as the cosmic infrared background or in quantum entanglement and cryptography applications [17–19]. Note that for these measurements the very low temperature required to operate the low-$T_c$ TES is often not seen as a major problem, because cryogenizing the sensor below a few Kelvin is required anyway in order to minimize the thermal noise coming from the bolometer itself. However, the requirement of a highly-stabilized liquid-helium-based cryogenics is a serious difficulty for adoption of low-$T_c$ TES in other applications.

After the discovery of high-$T_c$ cuprate superconductors (HTS), various authors have explored their use for resistive bolometers with simpler liquid-nitrogen-based cryogenics (the so-called resistive HTS TES bolometers [1–16]). The compound $YBa_2Cu_3O_\delta$ (YBCO) is the HTS material usually considered for this application, usually with maximum-$T_c$ doping, i.e., stoichiometry $\delta \simeq 6.93$. Such YBCO thin films provide TCR $\sim 1.5\,\text{K}^{-1}$, low noise at an operational temperature $T_c \sim 90\,\text{K}$, and also favorable values for the rest of parameters contributing to good bolometric performance (thermal conductivity, infrared absorbance, response time, etc.) [1–16].

Besides the cryogenics, the other difference with respect to low-$T_c$ TES is that in actual implementations [1–16] the resistive HTS TES operate under current bias and usually in the ohmic regime (instead of non-ohmic resistance and the voltage bias employed in low-$T_c$ TES to avoid thermal runaways [17–19]).

However, the HTS TES until now proposed still share some of the significant shortcomings of low-$T_c$ TES: First, thermal stability of the cryogenic bath is still challenging (liquid-nitrogen systems are simpler but tend to thermally oscillate more than those based on liquid helium). Secondly, both types of TES have useful TCR only at the superconducting transition, corresponding to operational temperature intervals $\Delta T$ of just $\sim 0.1\,\text{K}$ or less for low-$T_c$ TES, and $\sim 1\,\text{K}$ for the resistive HTS TES proposed until now [1–19].

The HTS TES systems proposed until today are homogeneous in nominal composition and critical temperature [1–16]. However, in the recent years different novel techniques have been developed to impose regular patterns on HTS thin films, creating custom designs, down to the micro- and the nano-scales [21–30]. This allows custom-engineering regular variations of the critical temperature over the film surface. Realization of these regular and controlled patterning has been experimentally achieved using, e.g., local ferroelectric field-effect [21], nanodeposition [22], focused ion beam [23], etc. In fact, the nanostructuring of HTS has become the specific subject of recent conferences [24–27] and networks [28,29] funded by the European Union.

However, the use of nanostructured films for optimizing HTS TES has been considered only very marginally up to now, the only precedent to our knowledge being Reference [6] by Oktem et al., who considered films with random distributions of nonsuperconducting incrustations producing limited increases of $\Delta T$ up to only $\sim 2\,\text{K}$ (and also small, and not always favorable, TCR variations).

Our aim in the present work is to propose that certain custom nanostructurating and patterning of HTS materials may improve their functionality for resistive HTS TES sensors. In particular, we calculate the case of nanostructuring and patterning of the local carrier doping level $p$ (the number of carriers per $CuO_2$ unit cell) in the prototypical HTS compound YBCO via local variations of oxygen stoichiometry (as realizable, e.g., via local desoxigenation, ion bombardment with different masks, etc.). Our main objective will be to obtain an increase of the operational temperature interval, $\Delta T$, in which (i) the TCR is large and (ii) $R$ is linear with $T$ (i.e., $dR/dT$ constant with $T$, that is another desirable feature that simplifies both the electronic control of the bolometer and the required stability of the cryogenic setup).

Accompanying this $\Delta T$ increase we will also obtain improvements of other bolometric characteristics, such as the saturation power and in some cases the TCR itself.

We organize our studies of the structured HTS materials in two parts: First we study the simplest case of carrier doping nanostructuring, namely the random nanoscale structuration that appears by just using oxygen stoichiometries that do not maximize $T_c$. We present our methods for those randomly structured HTS in Section 2; these consists of finite-element computations (and also, to confirm their validity, analytical estimates using effective-medium approximations [31]) that we apply to calculate the performance of the material in various example bolometer device implementations. The results following these methods in random nanoscale structurations are presented in Section 4. These results indicate that this first simple structuration may already improve some of the bolometric parameters with respect to conventional, nonstructured HTS materials

The rest of the paper considers structurations that include not only the unavoidable random disorder but also the additional imposition of custom regular arrangements of zones with different nominal doping levels (patterning), studying different examples aimed to progressively improve the bolometric performance. The additional methods needed to calculate this added patterning are presented in Section 3, and the results are discussed in Sections 5 to 7 for various custom pattern designs, each of them improving the previous one. The most optimized pattern design (Section 7) is a four-step discretized exponential-like dependence of nominal doping with the longitudinal position. This arrangement should be also the easier one to fabricate. With respect to conventional nonstructured HTS TES materials, it improves by more than one order of magnitude the $\Delta T$ and the saturation power, and it also doubles the TCR sensitivity.

## 2. Methods for Structured Nonpatterned Resistive HTS TES

Our methodology consists of computing the electrical resistance $R$ versus temperature $T$ of each of the structured HTS materials considered by us, and then using such $R(T)$ to calculate the corresponding performance for bolometric operation.

For completeness we will, in fact, consider various example bolometer-device designs, including simple square-shaped sensors such as those in [7,16] (that may be a micrometric size as appropriate for building megapixel cameras; we shall also consider two different substrates for completeness) and also larger sensors for millimeter-wavelength sensing using a meander geometry (as those built, always with nonstructured HTS, in [1–4,6,8–10,12,13]). While naturally we could not calculate in this work the whole range of possible device designs for a bolometer, our results in these example implementations show that our proposed nano optimizations of the materials should lead to improvements in at least some popular types of resistive HTS TES device designs.

Also, for our $R(T)$ calculations we shall use two alternative calculations, so as to be confident about the validity of the results: Finite-element computations first, and then effective-medium formulae (both paths have been successful in other studies of structured HTS [30–35], and we shall also include some confirming example comparisons with real data). Let us provide the details of all such procedures in the following sections.

### 2.1. Main Operational Parameters for Resistive HTS TES Devices

We consider in this work, a HTS TES of resistive type, i.e., the temperature increase is sensed through the measurement of the electrical resistance, as in [1–16]. Contrarily to the most common case of low-$T_c$ TES, the measurement is in current-bias ($I$-bias) configuration in all experimentally implemented resistive HTS TES published to our knowledge (the experimental difficulties for voltage-bias ($V$-bias) sensing in HTS TES were explained, e.g., by Khrebtov et al. [15]). Also the $I$ value usually employed [1,7,9,10] is sufficiently small as to correspond to the ohmic regime ($R = V/I$ constant with $I$) in all the operational $T$-range (see also below; this is also in contrast to low-$T_c$ TES).

As already mentioned in the Introduction, for ohmic resistive TES a main parameter of merit is the TCR, that may be also expressed as

$$\text{TCR} = \frac{R(T^+) - R(T^-)}{\Delta T \, R(T^-)}, \qquad (2)$$

where $T^-$ is the base operation temperature (the one in absence of radiation), $T^+$ is the maximum temperature up to which the ohmic $R(T)$ maintains the strong and constant slope with temperature, and

$$\Delta T = T^+ - T^- \qquad (3)$$

will be henceforth called the operational temperature interval.

The other important parameter is $P^{\max}$, the maximum power measurable without saturation. In a $I$-bias resistive TES, it is possible to obtain $P^{\max}$ at good aproximation [18,19] by just applying the heat flow equilibrium condition at saturation:

$$P^{\max} + I^2 R(T^+) = G\Delta T, \qquad (4)$$

where $I^2 R(T^+)$ is the heat rate due to the Joule effect, $G\Delta T$ is the power dissipated towards the cryobath, and $G$ is the thermal conductance between the film and the bath.

We shall consider in this work three example resistive HTS TES device designs, to probe the effects of our proposed material optimizations in them. In particular, we consider two cases of microsensor bolometers, plus one case adapted to millimeter-wavelength sensing that we specify in the following section.

2.1.1. Microsensor Device Design

The first resistive HTS TES device design consists of depositing a thin layer of YBCO HTS material over a substrate, the area of the HTS and the substrate being micrometric. In particular, we consider the convenient area $(6 \, \mu m)^2$, that makes possible building a 1 megapixel array of sensors in $\sim 1 \, cm^2$. Each substrate is in direct contact with a cryogenic liquid-nitrogen bath and we shall consider two possible substrate compositions: $SrTiO_3$ (STO, most appropriate to grow HTS films) and a CMOS-type substrate of interest for technological integration (note that HTS TES over CMOS substrates, in particular silicon/Yttria-stabilized zirconia (YSZ)/zirconia, have been already fabricated [10], using nonstructured YBCO). The experimental value of $G$ for both types of substrate can be obtained from [10,36]. We consider YBCO thickness 100 nm and substrate thickness 1 mm. Also, we consider a bias current of $I = 6 \, \mu A$, that corresponds to a current density $j = 10^3 \, A/cm^2$, a value used in [13,15] and that corresponds to the ohmic range in all the $T$-range of operation [13,15,37].

2.1.2. Millimeter-Wave Sensor Device Design

The second device design we shall consider corresponds to the one most employed by experimentalists having produced resistive HTS TES [1–6,8–10,12,13]. It corresponds to a larger design using, as substrate, a suspended membrane of millimetric surface and CMOS-type composition; on top of such thin (micrometric thickness) membrane substrate a single meander of YBCO material is deposited. The larger area precludes building small megapixel sensors, but this is not important, e.g., for sensing millimeter wavelengths (that could not be constrained in smaller pixel sizes anyway, and that are among the main applications of bolometers). The meander geometry allows instead the ability to optimize the so-called "static voltage responsivity", $S_V$, an important parameter defined by:

$$S_V = \frac{\varepsilon L_0}{I(1 - L_0)}, \qquad (5)$$

where $\varepsilon$ is the absorbance of the sample, $I$ is the bias current, and

$$L_0 = \frac{\text{TCR } I^2 R}{G} \tag{6}$$

is the so-called loop gain coefficient, which is a relative measure of the positive electrothermal feedback of the device [15] and $G$ is again the thermal conductance towards the bath (whose experimental value may be found, e.g., in [13]); we consider (3 mm)$^2$ membranes for that evaluation. For a stable operation, the loop gain coefficient $L_0$ should be smaller than 1, the value $L_0 = 0.3$ being usually taken as optimal. Therefore, the maximum static responsivity is obtained by tuning the geometry of the meander so to tune the $I^2R$ contribution to $L_0$ in Equation (6) (Let us also note here that for $I$-bias the $L_0$ may remain constant, and $L_0 = 0.3$, only if $R$ is linear with $T$, so that maximizing $\Delta T$ is also interesting in this respect).

In our calculations, we will use for the meander section the same size 6 μm × 100 nm as previously for μm-sensors. We then choose the meander length for each sensing material so that always $L_0 \sim 0.3$. We also consider the same bias current and current density, I = 6 μm and $j = 10^3$ A/cm$^2$, than for μm-sensors (again corresponding to the ohmic range [13,15,37] and comparable to values used in experimental meander resistive HTS TES [13,15]). These choices not only are realistic but also they will allow us to use the same computer calculations of $R(T)$ for both μm- and mm-device designs (as only a geometric correction prefactor is needed to change $R$ from one design to the other) and the same pair of bias current and current density, $I = 6$ μA and $j = 10^3$ A/cm$^2$.

## 2.2. R(T) in the Normal State of Nonstructured HTS

In HTS materials, the ohmic resistance versus temperature, $R(T)$, markedly varies with the doping level $p$ (number of carriers per CuO$_2$ unit cell that for instance in YBCO may be changed through the oxygen content). This is true both for the value of the critical temperature $T_c(p)$ below which, the superconductivity transition occurs, and for the $R(T)$ magnitude and $T$-dependence in the normal state $T > T_c(p)$. The $R(T)$-versus-$p$ phase diagram has been extensively studied in many works such as the review [38] (see also, e.g., [39,40]). Here, let us recall that the superconducting critical temperature is maximum at $p \sim 0.155$ (separating the so-called underdoped $p < 0.155$ and overdoped $p > 0.155$ compositions). Above $T_c(p)$, the material presents a normal-state background electrical resistivity, $\rho_b(T, p)$, that is linear on $T$ above a certain so-called pseudogap temperature $T^*$, and is pseudoparabolic semiconducting-like [38] for $T_c < T < T^*$. In YBCO, it is $T^*(K) \approx 270 - 3000(p - 0.1)$ [38], so that for $p \gtrsim 0.16$, it is $T^* < T_c$ and the semiconducting-like region disappears. Instead of these rapid crude approximations, we will use in our analysis, all through the present work, the detailed quantitative results for $T_c(p)$, $T^*(p)$, and $\rho_b(T, p)$ given in reference [38] for YBCO.

Near $T_c(p)$, obviously $R(T)$ undergoes the superconducting transition towards $R(T) = 0$. This transition is not fully sharp, instead, a sizable rounding of $R(T)$ occurs in the vicinity of $T_c(p)$. This rounding is known to have two contributions: critical fluctuations and doping inhomogeneities, that we describe in the following subsections.

## 2.3. Rounding of R(T) Near the Superconducting Transition Due to Critical Phenomena

The critical fluctuations around the transition play an important role in HTS and have been studied in detail, e.g., in [32,41–48]. The effects of critical fluctuations in the resistance curves are commonly summarized via the so-called paraconductivity, $\Delta\sigma$, defined as the additional contribution to the electrical conductivity due to fluctuations: In particular, the total conductivity $\sigma(T)$ near the transition becomes

$$\sigma = \Delta\sigma + 1/\rho_b, \tag{7}$$

where $\rho_b$ is the normal-state background resistivity (see previous subsection). Because $\Delta\sigma$ follows critical-divergence laws near the transition, its effect far from $T_c$ (for $T \gtrsim 1.7T_c$) is totally negligible.

Closer to $T_c$, however, $\Delta\sigma$ becomes progressively important and two $T$ ranges may be distinguished. For $1.01T_c \lesssim T \lesssim 1.7T_c$, i.e., the so-called Gaussian fluctuations region, $\Delta\sigma$ is well described by the Lawrence–Doniach paraconductivity equation for layered superconductors: [41–45,49]

$$\Delta\sigma = \frac{e^2}{16\hbar d}\left\{\frac{1}{t}\left(1+\frac{B_{LD}}{t}\right)^{-1/2} - \frac{2}{c} + \frac{t+B_{LD}/2}{c^2}\right\}, \qquad (8)$$

where $e$ is the electron charge, $\hbar$ is the reduced Planck constant, $t = \ln(T/T_c)$ is the reduced temperature, $B_{LD} = (2\xi_c(0)/d)^2$ is the Lawrence–Doniach [49] layering parameter, $\xi_c(0)$ is the Ginzburg–Landau coherence length amplitude in the out-of-plane direction ($\simeq 1.1$ Å in YBCO [44,45]), $d$ is the superconducting layer periodicity length ($\simeq 5.85$ Å in YBCO [44,45]) and $c$ is a high-temperature cutoff constant $\simeq 0.7$ [43,44,50,51].

Closer to $T_c$, for $T_{BKT} \lesssim T \lesssim 1.01T_c$ we find the strong phase fluctuation regime, dominated by the Berezinskii–Kosterlitz–Thouless (BKT) transition temperature $T_{BKT}$ ($\sim T_c - 2K$ in YBCO) [42,52]. In this regime, the paraconductivity can be obtained using the equation: [33–35,47,53]

$$\Delta\sigma = A_{BKT}\exp\left[4\sqrt{\frac{T_c - T_{BKT}}{T - T_{BKT}}}\right], \qquad (9)$$

where $A_{BKT}$ is a constant, obtainable by requiring continuity of Equations (8) and (9) at the intersection of the Gaussian and BKT regimes, i.e., at $T = 1.01T_c$.

## 2.4. R(T) Transition Rounding Due to Intrinsic Structuration of the Carrier Doping Level; Nominal vs. Local Doping

As it has been explicitly demonstrated in various relatively recent experimental and theoretical works [32,46,47,54,55], an additional (and crucial for some doping levels) ingredient to understand the phenomenology of the resistive transition in HTS is to take into account the random $T_c$-inhomogeneities associated with the intrinsic disorder of the doping level. This intrinsic structuration is due to the fact that HTS compounds are non-stoichiometric, and therefore each dopant ion has at its disposal various lattice positions to occupy. For concreteness, we focus our present article in the case of the $YBa_2Cu_3O_\delta$ superconductor with oxygen as a dopant ion. Experimental measurement indicates that a typical size of each local inhomogeneity is about $(30\text{ nm})^2$ for HTS [32,54,55]. This produces, therefore, a certain randomness in the doping at the local scale, unavoidably present in even the more carefully grown HTS samples. A relatively easy geometrical calculation [32,54,55] reveals that this intrinsic structuration shall produce a Gaussian distribution of local dopant levels, as

$$\omega(p,\bar{p}) = \frac{2\sqrt{\ln 2}}{\sqrt{\pi}\Delta p}\exp\left[-\left(\frac{p-\bar{p}}{\Delta p/(2\sqrt{\ln 2})}\right)^2\right], \qquad (10)$$

where $\omega(p,\bar{p})$ is the fraction distribution of local doping levels, $p$, for a film with average doping level $\bar{p}$ (henceforth called nominal doping), and $\Delta p$ is the FWHM of the Gaussian distribution. This $\Delta p$ may be obtained, in turn, on the grounds of coarse-graining averages (see, e.g., Equation (6) of References [32,54]) and for YBCO it is $\Delta p \sim 0.006$ (with a small dependence on $\bar{p}$ that may be considered in excellent approximation linear $\Delta p = 0.0032 + 0.0189\bar{p}$) [32,54].

Due to the $T_c(p)$ dependence in HTS, the above distribution of local $p$ values leads, in turn, to a corresponding distribution of local critical temperatures around the nominal value $\bar{T}_c = T_c(\bar{p})$. The corresponding full width at half maximum (FWHM) for such intrinsic $T_c$ structuration has been also considered, e.g., in [32,54]. Not surprisingly, it becomes quite negligible ($\sim 1$ K in YBCO) for the nominal dopings $\bar{p} \simeq 0.155$ that maximize $T_c$ (and that has been used up to now for HTS TES; $\bar{p} \simeq 0.155$ corresponds to $YBa_2Cu_3O_{6.93}$ stoichiometry at which $T_c(p)$ is maximum and $dT_c/dp \sim 0$). However, for other dopings the situation may become very different and the $T_c$ distribution can reach FWHM values as large as, e.g., ~5 K for $\bar{p} = 0.13$, significantly influencing the $R(T)$ roundings [32,54,55].

## 2.5. Obtainment of the $R(T)$ Curve of Nonpatterned HTS TES Using Finite-Element Computations

To calculate the resistance transition curves, $R(T)$, of the $T_c$-structured HTS material, we have used software (TOSERIS, available by request to authors) that numerically solves the electrical mesh-current matrix equations of a film modeled as a $200 \times 200$ square lattice of monodomains, where each domain $i$ may have its own doping $p_i$, and thus its own $T_{ci}$ and resistivity curve. We have used Equations (7)–(9) for the $\rho_i(T,p)$ functionality of each monodomain $i$. The model also includes an I-bias power source and a voltmeter connected with zero-resistance contacts to opposite edges of the sample (see, e.g., scheme in Figure 1) and the $R(T)$ of the film will be obtained as the external $V/I$. Calculating the circuit requires to numerically invert, for each temperature, the sparse matrix with dimensions $40,001 \times 40,001$ that defines the mesh-current equations. This is a parallelizable computation for which we employed a 31 Tflops supercomputer (LBTS-$\varepsilon$psilon, that comprises about 12,000 floating-point units and is described in [56]). It was 100% allocated to run our software during several weeks.

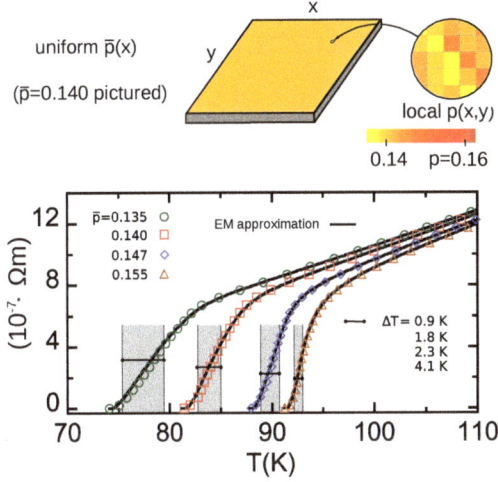

**Figure 1.** Electrical resistivity $\rho$ versus temperature $T$ obtained for YBa$_2$Cu$_3$O$_\delta$ (YBCO) films with a single, uniform value for the nominal doping level $\bar{p}$, including the case with negligible $T_c$ nanostructuration (or maximum-$T_c$ doping, $\bar{p} = 0.155$, in which $T_c$ saturates near its maximum value and the $T_c$ disorder is negligible) and various cases in which the $\bar{p}$ value corresponds to significant $T_c$ nanostructuration (see Section 4 for details). The data points correspond to the finite-element computations, and the continuous lines to the analytical effective-medium (EM) equations. The shaded gray region signals the operational temperature range $\Delta T$ (in which $\rho$ is strongly dependent and linear in $T$). In the upper drawing we illustrate the simulated sample and setup, also including a zoom at smaller length scales, imaging the spatial variation of the local doping level $p(x,y)$ (each $p(x,y)$ monodomain has typical size $(30 \text{ nm})^2$ and the distribution is Gaussian around the average $\bar{p}(x)$, see main text for details).

We have performed our calculations with numerical values representative of the HTS compound YBCO and therefore for the area of a finite-element monodomain $i$ we used $(30 \text{ nm})^2$, that is expected to correspond to the size of a doping $T_c$ inhomogeneity in YBCO. [32,54,55] Therefore, the surface of the simulated HTS film is going to be $(6 \text{ μm})^2$, in agreement with the microsensor HTS TES device implementation of Section 2.1.1.

In the case of the nonpatterned HTS considered in this section, the only spatial variation of doping and $T_c$ is the unavoidable intrinsic dopant ion structuration and, thus, we assign the local $p_i$ and $T_{ci}$ value to each of our $200 \times 200$ monodomains $i$ as follows: We first build a set of 40,000 values of dopings following the Gaussian distribution given by Equation (10). We then assign each of those $p$-values to each node $i$ randomly. Finally, those $p_i$ are transformed to $T_{ci}$ values (and corresponding $\rho_i(T)$ functions) following the quantitative results of [38]. A scheme of an example of the resulting spatial distribution is provided in Figure 1 (note the random nanostructuration in the zoomed area).

## 2.6. Analytical Estimates Using an Effective-Medium Approximation

To additionally probe the consistency of our computations, we will use, as a useful test, semi-analytical results that we calculate using the so-called effective-medium equations (EM approximation). The EM approximation was first introduced by Bruggeman [57] for general random inhomogeneous materials, and then adapted, e.g., by Maza and coworkers [31] for HTS with Gaussian random $T_c$ distributions. As shown in those early works, the EM approximation is a coarse-averaging model that may be considered accurate for temperatures not too close to the $R \to 0$ point (at which percolation effects may be expected to invalidate the approximation). In the case of our 2D media, the EM equations may be summarized as the following implicit condition for the conductivity $\sigma$ of each region with random doping inhomogeneities [31,33–35]:

$$\int_0^\infty \frac{\sigma_p - \sigma}{\sigma_p + \sigma} w(p, \bar{p}) dp = 0. \tag{11}$$

Here, $p$, $\bar{p}$ and $w(p, \bar{p})$ retain the same meaning as in Equation (10), and $\sigma_p$ is the electrical conductivity corresponding to doping level $p$. The above equation has to be numerically solved to obtain $\sigma$; however, the computational weight is much lower than the finite-element computation method (seconds versus hours or even days in our parallel computer [56]).

## 3. Additional Methods for Structured and Patterned Resistive HTS TES

We now describe the additional methods needed to obtain the $R(T)$ curve of HTS films in which, additional to the random nanostructuration considered in previous section, also a regular pattern of nominal doping levels is imposed, with the aim to obtain designs that optimize the bolometric functionality. In these films, a regular spatial variation of the nominal doping level $\bar{p}$ is created by the samples' grower by using any of the different methods for micro- and nanostructuration developed in the recent years by experimentalists in HTS films (see, e.g., [21–30]; for instance, for YBCO, this is possible by local deoxygenation using cover masks, ion bombardment, etc.). In particular, all the specific example patterns considered in this work will be expressible as functions $\bar{p}(x)$, where $x$ is the coordinate in the direction parallel to the external bias current (see scheme in Figure 1) and thus it will be useful to introduce the corresponding function $\lambda(\bar{p})$, or relative length weight of each nominal $\bar{p}$ value in the film, defined as

$$\lambda(\bar{p}) = \frac{1}{L} \frac{dx}{d\bar{p}}, \tag{12}$$

where $L$ is the total length of the film in the $x$-direction. Crucial for our studies, one has still to add to these nominal $\bar{p}(x)$ variations the unavoidable nanometric-scale randomness of the doping level (considered in the previous sections), i.e.,

$$p(x,y) = \bar{p}(x) + p_{\text{random}}(x,y), \tag{13}$$

with $p_{\text{random}}(x,y)$ consistent with Equation (10) evaluated using the local $\bar{p}(x)$.

## 3.1. Obtainment of the R(T) Curve of Patterned HTS Using Finite-Element Computations

To obtain the $R(T)$ curves of patterned resistive HTS TES, we use the finite-element software TOSERIS already described in Section 2.5. We again use a 200 × 200 simulation mesh and now we assign to each of those finite elements a local doping as follows: First, we associate to each element $i$ a nominal doping $\bar{p}_i$ corresponding to the pattern to be simulated. Then we randomly calculate the local doping $p_i$ following the Gaussian distribution given by Equation (10), evaluated with the nominal doping $\bar{p}_i$ of each node. Finally, to each node we assign the $T_{ci}$ and $\rho_i(T)$ corresponding to their local $p_i$ as per the quantitative results of [38] for the HTS material YBCO (see Sections 2.2 and 2.3).

We also tested that the sets of nodes sharing the same $\bar{p}_i$ value follow the Gaussian distribution, and each $R(T)$ simulation was repeated for several so-generated samples to verify their reproducibility. These checks indicate that our choice of a 200 × 200 node mesh provides enough statistical size. If we attribute to each node the size $(30\text{ nm})^2$ corresponding to each $T_c$-monodomain in YBCO (see Section 2.4 and [32,54]), the whole 200 × 200 sample corresponds to $(6\text{ μm})^2$, that is realistic for a microbolometric pixel.

Unless stated otherwise, we will again use in our calculations the numerical values in Sections 2.2 to 2.5 for the common material characteristics, such as, e.g., a film thickness of 100 nm or values for the critical-fluctuation parameters as per Section 2.3.

## 3.2. Analytical Estimates Using an Extended-EM Approximation

Besides performing finite-element computations, we will test our results against estimates based on the EM approach. For that purpose, we must suitably extend this approximation to account for the 1D gradient of nominal dopings corresponding to each example pattern to be considered in this work. For that, we consider the film as an association in a series of domains, each one with its own resistance and nominal doping $\bar{p}$, so that:

$$R(T) = \int_{x=0}^{x=L} \frac{d\bar{p}}{\sigma(\bar{p}(x),T)S}, \tag{14}$$

where $L$ is again the total length of the superconductor, $S$ is its transversal surface, and $\sigma(\bar{p}(x),T)$ is the ohmic conductivity obtained using the monodomain-EM approach, i.e., using Equation (11) for each doping $\bar{p}(x)$. Equation (14) can be also written as the following integration over nominal doping, with the help of the $\lambda(\bar{p})$ function defined in Equation (12):

$$R(T) = L \int_{\bar{p}_0}^{\bar{p}_L} \lambda(\bar{p}) \frac{dx}{\sigma(\bar{p}(x),T)S}, \tag{15}$$

For a discrete distribution (stepwise function $\bar{p}(x)$), the above equation becomes instead a summation:

$$R(T) = \sum_{i=1}^{N} \frac{L_i}{\sigma(\bar{p}_i,T)S}, \tag{16}$$

where $N$ is the number of discrete domains, each with its own nominal doping $\bar{p}_i$ and length $L_i$.

Note that Equations (14) to (16) do not explicitly take into account the transverse currents when associating the different domains $\bar{p}_i$ and $L_i$. Non-longitudinal transport inside each domain is built-in by using the EM approach for each $\sigma(\bar{p}_i,T)$. However, this approximation may be expected to fail when it has to describe percolations (because both the sum in a series of domains and the EM approximation do not take them into account). Therefore it could be expected to overestimate the value of $R(T)$ in the very close proximity to the fully superconducting $R(T) \to 0^+$ state.

## 4. Results for Structured Nonpatterned HTS Materials

In the reminder of this article, we describe the results of applying our methods to different structured HTS materials. We consider first the case of nonpatterned HTS materials, i.e., those with a uniform nominal doping $\bar{p}$. As already mentioned, the doping level $\bar{p} \simeq 0.155$ (corresponding to the stoichiometry YBa$_2$Cu$_3$O$_{6.93}$) is the one that has been used up to now to experimentally produce HTS TES, and, due to the saturation of $T_c$ near such doping level, it corresponds to a HTS film without a $T_c$-nanostructure. However, the cases with uniform $\bar{p} < 0.155$ correspond to films with random $T_c$-nanostructuration.

## 4.1. Results for the $R(T)$ Profile and Operational Parameters for Resistive TES Case

In Figure 1 we show the $R(T)$ resulting from our finite-element computations for the case of YBCO films with nominal dopings $\bar{p} = 0.135, 0.140, 0.147$ and $0.155$, represented as circles, squares, diamonds, and triangles, respectively. As previously mentioned, to these nominal dopings, a random intrinsic structuration has to be added (following a Gaussian distribution as per Equation (10)) in order to obtain the local $p(x,y)$ values; this is illustrated by the zoom in the pictured drawn in Figure 1.

As it is clearly shown in that figure, the reduction of $\bar{p}$ induces not only a shift of the transitions towards somewhat lower temperatures (as expected from the $T_c$-vs-$\bar{p}$ phase diagram of HTS), but also a widening of the $T$-width of the transition region. The gray areas in Figure 1 are the $T$-range, $\Delta T$, in which the $R(T)$ transition occurs and $R$-vs-$T$ is linear, i.e., the operational interval $\Delta T$ of Equation (3). This $\Delta T$ increases as $\bar{p}$ decreases, as may be noticed both in Figure 1 and also in Table 1. In this table we summarize the bolometric operational parameters obtained by using such $R(T)$ results and the methods in Section 2 for three example resistive HTS TES devices designs (described in Sections 2.1.1 and 2.1.2).

It is clear that the improvement that the $T_c$-nanostructure may provide for such bolometric characteristics: Notably, the increase of $\Delta T$ (about five times higher for the more nanostructured case than in the nonstructured one) is translated in an enhancement of $P^{max}$ of the bolometer device. This means the ability to receive a higher amount of radiation without saturating the sensing material. Note that a larger $\Delta T$ also implies a less demanding cryogenic setup in terms of required stability.

Therefore, our studies suggest that this first simple $T_c$ nanostructuration already improves some of the bolometric operational parameters with respect to the conventional, nonstructured HTS materials proposed until now.

**Table 1.** Summary of the main operation parameters for resistive high-$T_c$ cuprate superconductors (HTS) transition-edge bolometer devices (TES) devices using, as sensing materials, YBCO superconductors with the various doping nanostructurations and patterns explored in this work. These include the usual nonstructured YBCO ($\bar{p} = 0.155$) and the novel options considered by us: structured nonpatterned YBCO ($\bar{p} \leq 0.155$, Section 4) and structured patterned YBCO (Sections 5 to 7). The $\Delta T$ and TCR follow from the $\rho(T)$ curves presented in Figures 1 and 3–5. The $P^{max}$ values were calculated for the three example device implementations described in Sections 2.1.1 and 2.1.2 (microbolometers with direct cooling and SrTiO$_3$(STO) or silicon/Yttria-stabilized zirconia (YSZ)/Zirconia (CMOS)-type substrates, plus millimeter-wave sensors using a meander geometry).

| Sensing Material | $\Delta T$ (K) | TCR (K$^{-1}$) | $P^{max}$ ($\mu$W) μm-sensor over STO | $P^{max}$ ($\mu$W) μm-sensor over CMOS | $P^{max}$ ($\mu$W) mm-sensor over CMOS |
|---|---|---|---|---|---|
| nonstructured YBCO: $\bar{p} = 0.155$ | 0.9 | 3.05 | 0.5 | 0.037 | 13 |
| structured nonpatterned YBCO: | | | | | |
| $\bar{p} = 0.147$ | 1.8 | 2.67 | 1.1 | 0.080 | 31 |
| $\bar{p} = 0.140$ | 2.3 | 2.15 | 1.3 | 0.095 | 38 |
| $\bar{p} = 0.135$ | 4.1 | 2.16 | 2.3 | 0.17 | 72 |
| structured patterned YBCO: | | | | | |
| linear $\bar{p}(x)$ | 1.4 | 0.25 | 0.8 | 0.062 | 4.2 |
| exponential-like $\bar{p}(x)$ | 8.3 | 0.18 | 4.9 | 0.35 | 120 |
| 4-step exponential-like $\bar{p}(x)$ | 12.7 | 5.13 | 7.2 | 0.55 | 230 |

## 4.2. Verification Using the Analytical EM Approximation and Against Existing Measurements

Figure 1 also shows (as continuous lines) the results obtained by applying the EM approach, i.e., Equation (11), to the same parameter values and doping levels as used in the previous subsection. It can be seen in that figure that the coincidence between the finite-element computation and the EM approximation is excellent, even in the $R \to 0^+$ tails (a log–log zoom of such tails evidences moderate deviations in relative values, negligible in the absolute scale of Figure 1, as coherent with the expectation that the EM approximation is less accurate when percolative current paths appear [31,57]; see also Figure 2 for better evidence of these $R \sim 0^+$ deviations. This comparison gives, then, a first argument supporting the validity, at least concerning the main features, of our calculation methods for the doping structuring effects.

A second argument supporting such validity is the comparison with actual measurements for $R(T)$. In the case of structured nonpatterned HTS films considered in this section, measurements valid for such a comparison do exist. In particular, we have plotted in Figure 2 the data measured in reference [48] in high-quality YBCO (YBa$_2$Cu$_3$O$_\delta$) films comprised by a single zone of nominal oxygen stoichiometries $O_{6.78}$ and $O_{6.85}$ (i.e., $\bar{p} \simeq 0.140$ and $\bar{p} \simeq 0.156$ respectively; to get the relations between oxygen ratio and doping we have interpolated the experimental data described in reference [58]). We can see in that figure the good accuracy of the theoretical (EM approach) and computational (finite-element) methods used in this article to reproduce the experimental resistance curves of nonpatterned YBCO films in the studied doping range.

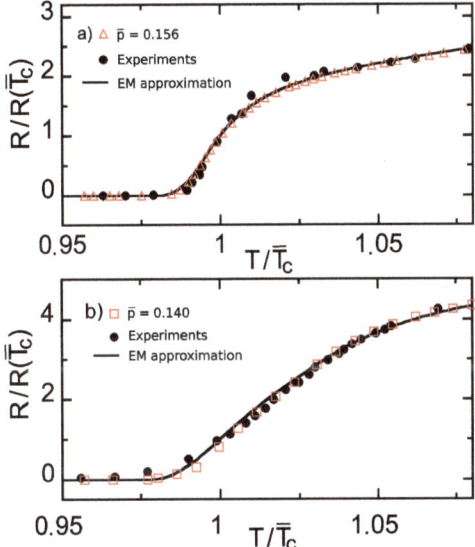

**Figure 2.** Comparison between The electrical resistance vs. temperature curves resulting from our methodology (open symbols for the finite-element computations and solid line for the EM analytical approximation) and the measurements of reference [48] (solid symbols), for YBCO films with uniform nominal oxygen stoichiometry corresponding to: in panel a) to $\bar{p} = 0.156$, i.e., very near the maximum-$T_c$ doping level; in panel b) to $\bar{p} = 0.140$, i.e., a $T_c$-nanostructured nonpatterned HTS. Note that the normalization of the axes significantly zooms the transition region with respect to Figure 1.

## 5. Results for Structured HTS Materials Patterned with a Linear $\bar{p}(x)$ Variation

Let us now study different instances of doping-patterned HTS, seeking to progressively identify pattern designs optimizing the performance as bolometric sensor materials. We start by considering in this section, a simple linear variation of $\bar{p}$ along the longitudinal direction (the direction of the overall externally-applied electrical current, see the scheme in Figure 3):

$$\bar{p}(x) = \bar{p}_0 + \left(\frac{\bar{p}_L - \bar{p}_0}{L}\right) x, \qquad (17)$$

where $\bar{p}_0$ and $\bar{p}_L$ are the $\bar{p}$-values at the opposite ends of the film $x = 0$ and $x = L$. In terms of the $\lambda(\bar{p})$ function of Equation (12), this linear-in-$x$ $\bar{p}$-pattern simply becomes the constant value

$$\lambda(\bar{p}) = \frac{1}{\bar{p}_L - \bar{p}_0}. \qquad (18)$$

For our computations we chose the rather typical values $\bar{p}_0 = 0.135$ and $\bar{p}_L = 0.161$.

### 5.1. Results for the R(T) Profile and Operational Parameters for Resistive TES Use

The results of our numerical finite-element evaluation for this $\bar{p}$-pattern are displayed in Figure 3 (see also Table 1 for a comparative summary). As evidenced in the Figure 3, this type of structuring of the HTS film significantly broadens the $R(T)$ transition (compare, e.g., with Figure 1 that represents, in the same $T$-scale, the results for HTS with comparable, but uniform, $\bar{p}$-values). However, this structuring does not lead to a linear dependence of $R$ vs. $T$ in that transition region. This may pose a difficulty in resistive TES applications, that ideally require a $R(T)$ variation both large (i.e., large TCR) and linear (i.e., constant $dR/dT$). The range $\Delta T$ in which both conditions are met is merely about 1.4 K for this type of $\bar{p}$-pattern, already suggesting that further structuring optimizations would be desirable (see next section). In Table 1, we summarize the operational parameters obtained for the linear $\bar{p}(x)$ resistive bolometer. We can conclude that they are of the same order or worse than the parameters obtained for the typical already existing resistive HTS TES (the case $\bar{p} \simeq 0.155$). This even includes the TCR, that is lower due to the increase of the operational temperature $T^-$ and then of $R(T^-)$. The maximum energy and power may be somewhat higher due to the small increase of the width of the linear regime.

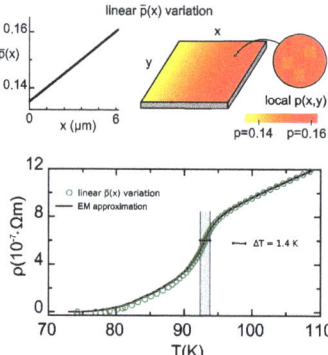

**Figure 3.** In the upper row, we illustrate a YBCO film patterned following the linear variation of the nominal doping $\bar{p}(x)$ studied by us in Section 5 (see Equations (17) and (18)). We also illustrate doping across the film as a 2D color map, taking into account that the local doping level $p(x, y)$ (zoom in the picture) results from accumulating the lineal $\bar{p}(x)$ and the random Gaussian disorder at smaller length scales of about $(30 \text{ nm})^2$ (see main text for details). In the lower row, we plot the resistivity vs. temperature $\rho(T)$ that we obtain for such film (data points for finite-element computations, continuous line for the analytical EM approximation, see Equation (19)). Note that the transition widens considerably with respect to Figure 1, but the operational $\Delta T$ range (shaded gray region) is small due to the nonlinearity of $\rho$ with $T$ in most of the transition.

We can conclude that this first patterning does not effectively optimize the operational parameters of the resistive HTS TES, mainly because it broadens the $R(T)$ transition but does not achieve $R(T)$ linearity in it.

### 5.2. Verification Using the Extended-EM Analytical Approximation

To check the validity of our results for the linear $\bar{p}(x)$ variation, we also have used the formulae described in Section 3.2. For that, our first step has been to combine Equation (15) with the $\lambda(\bar{p})$ formula for this type of pattern (Equation (18)). This leads us to the new equation:

$$R(T) = \frac{L}{S(\bar{p}_L - \bar{p}_0)} \int_{\bar{p}_0}^{\bar{p}_L} \frac{d\bar{p}}{\sigma(\bar{p}, T)} \quad \text{(linear } \bar{p}(x) \text{ pattern)}, \tag{19}$$

where $\sigma(\bar{p}, T)$ results from Equation (11). The result of this analytical estimate is displayed in Figure 3 as a continuous line. As in the case described for constant nominal doping, this estimate achieves good agreement with the finite-element computation, confirming the basic accuracy of our results.

## 6. Results for Structured HTS Materials Patterned with a Continuous Exponential-Like Doping Variation

Seeking to find a $\bar{p}(x)$ profile producing a $R(T)$ transition that improves the bolometric operational characteristics, we have explored numerous $\bar{p}(x)$ options beyond the simple linear function discussed above. In the present section we present the results that we obtained with the continuous $\bar{p}(x)$ functionality that led us to better bolometric performance (and a step-like, noncontinuous variation will be later discussed, in Section 7). This continuous $\bar{p}(x)$ profile is more intuitively described by means of the length weight function $\lambda(\bar{p})$. In particular, we consider $\bar{p}$-profiles leading to the following exponential $\lambda(\bar{p})$ function:

$$\lambda(\bar{p}) = A \exp\left(\frac{\bar{p}_0 - \bar{p}}{\delta \bar{p}}\right), \tag{20}$$

where $\delta \bar{p}$ and $A$ are constants, the latter being easy to obtain by normalization considerations as

$$A = \frac{1}{\delta \bar{p}} \frac{1}{1 - \exp\left(\frac{\bar{p}_0 - \bar{p}_L}{\delta \bar{p}}\right)}. \tag{21}$$

In these equations, $\bar{p}_0$ and $\bar{p}_L$ are, as in the previous sections, the nominal doping at $x = 0$ and $x = L$ respectively, being $L$ the size of the film. Note that, by applying Equation (12), this corresponds to:

$$p(x) = \bar{p}_0 - \delta \bar{p} \ln\left\{1 - \frac{x}{L}\left[1 - \exp\left(\frac{\bar{p}_0 - \bar{p}_L}{\delta \bar{p}}\right)\right]\right\}. \tag{22}$$

For the case of YBCO films considered in this article, and for $\bar{p}_0 = 0.135$ and $\bar{p}_L = 0.161$ as in the previous section, we found that the $\delta \bar{p}$ value that best optimizes the bolometric characteristics (most notably $\Delta T$) is $\delta \bar{p} = 0.007$. We also employed in our evaluations the same common parameter values as described in Sections 2.3 to 2.5.

In the upper row of Figure 4, the corresponding doping profile is pictured, both as a $\bar{p}(x)$ representation and as a 2D color density plot. It may be noticed that at the qualitative level the $\bar{p}(x)$ function itself is not too dissimilar to an exponential (however a purely exponential dependence of $\bar{p}$ with $x$ would produce less optimized bolometric performance).

### 6.1. Results for the R(T) Profile and Operational Parameters for Resistive TES Use

The results of our numerical finite-element evaluation for this $\bar{p}$-pattern are displayed in the second raw of Figure 4 (see also Table 1). As evidenced in that Figure 4, not only the transition is significantly broadened with respect to nonpatterned HTS but also (unlike what happened in the case of a linear $\bar{p}(x)$ variation) $\Delta T$ is highly increased. In particular, the $\Delta T$ region is increased up to 8.3 K, almost 10 times more than for nonstructured HTS.

As may be seen in Table 1, the improvements also occur in the $P^{\text{max}}$ parameter, that increase about one order of magnitude with respect to nonstructured HTS. However, note that the TCR value is one order of magnitude worse than in the case of such conventional, nonstructured HTS. This shortcoming and other improvements will be addressed in Section 7 with an evolved $\bar{p}$-pattern design.

### 6.2. Verification Using the Extended-EM Analytical Approximation

We have checked our results also using an analytical estimate, by adapting to this pattern the effective-medium approach described in Section 3.2. For that, we have combined Equation (15) with the Equation (22) defining this $\bar{p}$-pattern, to obtain the new formula:

$$R(T) = \frac{AL}{S} \int_{\bar{p}_0}^{\bar{p}_L} \exp\left(\frac{\bar{p}_0 - \bar{p}}{\delta \bar{p}}\right) \frac{d\bar{p}}{\sigma(\bar{p}, T)} \quad \text{(exp-like pattern),} \quad (23)$$

where $\sigma(\bar{p}, T)$ results from the Equation (11). The result of this analytical estimate is displayed in Figure 4 as a continuous line. Again it slightly overestimates $R(T)$ in the tail of the transition, but basically confirms the finite-element results. As already mentioned, the overestimation is expected to be linked to precursor percolation effects.

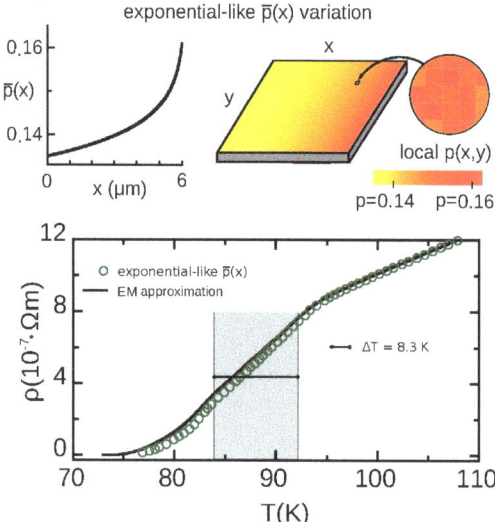

**Figure 4.** In the upper row, we illustrate a YBCO film patterned following the exponential-like variation of nominal doping $\bar{p}(x)$ studied by us in Section 6 (see Equations (20) to (22)). We also illustrate doping across the film as a 2D color map, taking into account that the local doping level $p(x, y)$ (zoom in the picture) results from accumulating the exponential-like $\bar{p}(x)$ and the random Gaussian disorder at smaller length scales of about $(30\text{ nm})^2$ (see main text for details). In the lower row, we plot the resistivity vs. temperature $\rho(T)$ that we obtain for such film (data points for finite-element computations, continuous line for the analytical EM approximation, adapted in this work to this $\bar{p}(x)$ case, see Equation (23)).

## 7. Results for Structured HTS Materials Patterned with a Four-Step Exponential-Like Doping Variation

While the $\bar{p}(x)$-pattern design considered in the previous section produced notable improvements of the bolometric features, at least two concerns may be expressed about it: First, any current structuration experimental technique [21–30] may have difficulties producing such a smooth and exponential-like variation of $\bar{p}$ with $x$ (Equations (20) to (22)). Instead, it would be preferable a simpler and, mainly, *discrete*-pattern, i.e., one comprised of a few zones, each with a single $\bar{p}$. This would ease fabrication, e.g., by means of several stages of deoxygenation of YBCO films using different cover masks in each stage. Secondly, the continuous-pattern of the previous section presents somewhat worsened TCR value with respect to some of the nonpatterned resistive HTS.

To address both issues, we consider now the discrete $\bar{p}(x)$ pattern described in the upper row of Figure 5. This pattern defines four zones, each with a single uniform $\bar{p}$ chosen to optimize the linear region of the transition. These values of $\bar{p}$ follow a discretized version of the exponential pattern:

$$L_i = B \exp\left(\frac{\overline{p}_0 - \overline{p}_i}{\delta \overline{p}}\right), \tag{24}$$

where $L_i$ is the length of the zone of nominal doping $\bar{p}_i$, and $B$ is a constant so that $\sum_i L_i = L$.

We tested the bolometric performance for various doping levels $\bar{p}_i$ of the four zones. We obtained the best results with the set $\bar{p}_i = \{0.136, 0.141, 0.145, 0.160\}$, that we describe next.

### 7.1. Results for the R(T) Profile and Operational Parameters for Resistive TES Use

The results for our numerical finite-element evaluation for this $\bar{p}$-pattern are displayed in Figure 5 (see also Table 1). As evidenced there, the $R(T)$ transition becomes significantly broad and linear, with such linear region conveniently starting at $T^- = 76.6$ K (so that the HTS TES could be operated with the simplest liquid-nitrogen bath, at 77 K). The corresponding $\Delta T$ is now almost 13 K, the largest obtained in this paper. Also the TCR value $> 5$ K$^{-1}$ is the largest obtained in this work, being almost double than for conventional nonstructured (i.e., maximum $T_c$) YBCO. The $P^{max}$ values (see Table 1) also reflect these improvements, being again the best among the HTS options considered in this work and more than one order of magnitude larger than for the nonstructured HTS.

To sum up, these finite-element computations reveal that this relatively simple-to-fabricate $\bar{p}$-pattern produces order-of-magnitude improvements over nonstructured HTS materials in $\Delta T$ and $P^{max}$, and also a 66% improvement in TCR.

### 7.2. Verification Using the Extended-EM Analytical Approximation

We have checked our results for this four-step $\bar{p}(x)$ pattern also using an analytical estimate, by adapting to this pattern the approach described in Section 3.2. In this case we used their discretized version, given by Equations (16). By combining it with the $\bar{p}(x)$-pattern given by Equation (24) we now obtain:

$$R = \frac{B}{S} \sum_{i=1}^{N} \frac{1}{\sigma(\overline{p}_i, T)} \exp\left(\frac{\overline{p}_0 - \overline{p}_i}{\delta \overline{p}}\right), \tag{25}$$

where the $\bar{p}_i$ are the nominal dopings of each of the $i$ zones, and $\sigma(\bar{p}_i, T)$ results from Equation (11). This analytical estimate is displayed in Figure 5 as a continuous line. It fully confirms the main features obtained by the finite-element computations. Similarly to the case of the other $\bar{p}$-patterns considered in our work, the estimate is expected to be less reliable in the lower part of the transition.

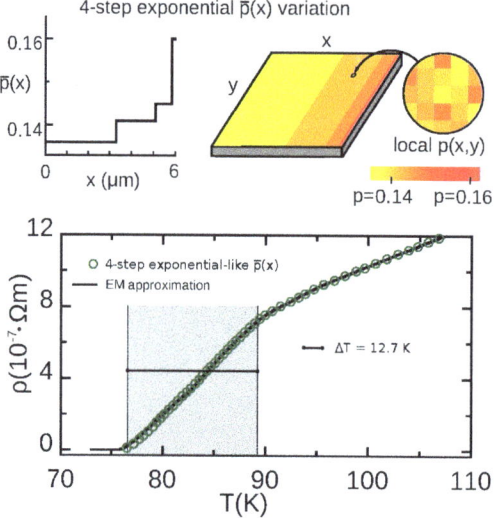

**Figure 5.** In the upper row, we illustrate a YBCO film patterned following the discretized four-step exponential-like variation of the nominal doping $\bar{p}(x)$ studied by us in Section 7. We also illustrate doping across the film as a 2D color map, taking into account that the local doping level $p(x,y)$ (zoom in the picture) results from accumulating the four-step exponential $\bar{p}(x)$ and the random Gaussian disorder at smaller length scales of about (30 nm)$^2$ (see main text for details). In the lower row, we plot the resistivity vs. temperature $\rho(T)$ that we obtain for such film (data points for finite-element computations, continuous line for analytical EM approximation, see Equation (25)). This is the most optimized design found in this work for the use in resistive HTS TES devices (see also Table 1).

## 8. Conclusions

To sum up, we considered the advantages of structuring and patterning of the doping level (and hence of the critical temperature) in high-temperature superconductors with respect to their operational characteristics as resistive bolometric sensors (resistive HTS TES) of electromagnetic radiation. In particular we studied some chosen examples of spatial variations of the carrier doping into the CuO$_2$ superconducting layers due to oxygen off-stoichiometry. Our main results are (see also Table 1 for a quantitative account):

(i) Non-patterned structured HTS materials (i.e., those with a nominal doping level uniform in space but that does not maximize the critical temperature, thus having random $T_c$-nanostructuring) may already provide some benefit for bolometric use with respect to the nonstructured HTS materials used up to now for those devices. In particular, they present a widened transition leading to a larger operational temperature interval $\Delta T$ and also larger $P^{max}$ (corresponding to the larger maximum detectable radiation power before sensor saturation). However, these improvements come at the expense of a certain reduction of the sensibility of the sensor as measured by the TCR value.

(ii) The bolometric performance may be significantly more optimized with the use of HTS materials including an additional regular dependence on the position of the nominal doping level, $\bar{p}(x)$ (doping-level patterning). In that case, ad-hoc pattern designs may be found by progressively seeking widened and linear $R(T)$ transitions. Our more optimized design is shown in Figure 5 and consists of just four zones of different sizes and doping levels (related by the exponential-like Equation (24)) evaluated at $\bar{p}_i = 0.136, 0.141, 0.145$, and $0.160$). With this design the operational temperature is conveniently located at $T^- = 76.6$ K, the operational temperature interval $\Delta T$ is almost 13 K (more than one order of magnitude larger than for the conventional nonstructured YBa$_2$Cu$_3$O$_{6.93}$), the TCR value is $> 5$ K$^{-1}$ (almost double than for the nonstructured case), and the $P^{max}$ values are also optimized about one order of magnitude.

**Author Contributions:** J.C.V. and M.V.R. derived the EM equations. J.C.V., A.S.V., M.M.B., and M.V.R. wrote the manuscript. J.C.V., A.S.V., C.M.-O., and M.V.R. contributed to the design of the studied patterns. All authors contributed to the computations and analyses of the results.

**Acknowledgments:** This work was supported by projects FIS2016-79109-P (AEI/FEDER, UE) and AYA2016-78773-C2-2-P(AEI/FEDER,UE), by the Xunta de Galicia under grants ED431D 2017/06 and ED431C 2018/11, the Consellería de Educación Program for Development of a Strategic Grouping in Materials AeMAT under Grant No. ED431 2018/08, Xunta de Galicia, and by the CA16218 nanocohybri COST Action. JCV thanks the Spanish Ministry of Education for grant FPU14/00838.

**Conflicts of Interest:** "The authors declare no conflict of interest."

## Abbreviations

The following abbreviations are used in this manuscript:

| | |
|---|---|
| TCR | Temperature coefficient resistance |
| YBCO | $YBa_2Cu_3O_\delta$ |
| STO | $SrTiO_3$ |
| CMOS | silicon/YSZ/Zirconia |
| YSZ | Yttria-stabilized zirconia |
| TES | Transition-edge sensor |
| HTS | High-temperature superconductor |
| FWHM | Full width at half maximum |
| EM | Effective medium |
| BKT | Berezinskii–Kosterlitz–Thouless |

## References

1. Mohajeri, R.; Opata, Y.A.; Wulff, A.C.; Grivel, J.C.; Fardmanesh, M. All Metal Organic Deposited High-Tc Superconducting Transition Edge Bolometer on Yttria-Stabilized Zirconia Substrate. *J. Supercond. Nov. Magn.* **2017**, *30*, 1981–1986. [CrossRef]
2. Moftakharzadeh, A.; Kokabi, A.; Banzet, M.; Schubert, J.; Fardmanesh, M. Detectivity Analysis and Optimization of Large-Area Freestanding-Type HTS Bolometers. *IEEE Tran. Appl. Supercond.* **2012**, *22*, 2100107. [CrossRef]
3. Hosseini, M.; Moftakharzadeh, A.; Kokabi, A.; Vesaghi, M.A.; Kinder, H.; Fardmanesh, M. Characterization of a Transition-Edge Bolometer Made of YBCO Thin Films Prepared by nonfluorine Metal-Organic Deposition. *IEEE Tran. Appl. Supercond.* **2011**, *21*, 3587–3591. [CrossRef]
4. Moftakharzadeh, A.; Kokabi, A.; Ghodselahi, T.; Vesaghi, A.; Khorasani, S.; Banzet, M.; Schubert, J.; Fardmanesh, M. Investigation of Bias Current and Modulation Frequency Dependences of Detectivity of YBCO TES and the Effects of Coating of Cu-C Composite Absorver Layer. *IEEE Tran. Appl. Supercond.* **2009**, *19*, 3688–3693. [CrossRef]
5. Hosseini, M.; Moftakharzadeh, A.; Kokabi, A.; Vesaghi, M.A.; Kinder, M.; Fardmanesh, M. 2D Analysis of the Effects of Geometry on the Response of High-$T_c$ Superconductive Bolometric Detectors. *IEEE Tran. Appl. Supercond.* **2009**, *19*, 484–488.
6. Oktem, B.; Bozbey, A.; Avci, I.; Tepe, M.; Abukay, D.; Fardmanesh, M. The superconducting transition width and illumination wavelength dependence of the response of MgO substrate YBCO transition edge bolometers. *Phys. C* **2007**, *458*, 6–11. [CrossRef]
7. Lakew, B.; Brasunas, J.C.; Aslam, S.; Pugel, D.E. High-Tc transition edge superconducting (TES) bolometer on a monolithic saphire membrane– construction and performance. *Sensors Actuators A.* **2004**, *114*, 36–40. [CrossRef]
8. Delerue, J.; Gaugue, A.; Testé, P.; Caristan, E.; Klisnick, G.; Redon, M.; Kreisler, A. YBCO Mid-Infrared Bolometer Arrays. *IEEE Tran. Appl. Supercond.* **2003**, *13*, 176–179. [CrossRef]
9. Khrebtov, I.A.; Tkachenko, A.D. High-Temperature superconductor bolometers for the IR region. *J. Opt. Technol.* **1999**, *66*, 735–741. [CrossRef]
10. Kaiser, G.; Thurk, M.; Seidel, P. Signal-to-noise ratio improvement of HTSC bolometers for cryocooler operation using a thermal compensation principle. *Cryogenics* **1995**, *35*, 463–465. [CrossRef]

11. Zakar, E.; Wikner, D.; Dubey, M.; Amirtharaj, P. Thin Film YBCO Pixels for MMW Detector. *Adv. Sci. Technol. Res. J.* **2008**, *54*, 434–438.
12. Mohajeri, R.; Nazifi, R.; Wulff, A.C.; Vesaghi, M.A.; Grivel, J.C.; Fardmanesh, M. Investigation of $CeO_2$ Buffer Layer Effects on the Voltage Response of YBCO Transition Edge Bolometers. *IEEE Tran. Appl. Supercond.* **2016**, *26*, 1–4. [CrossRef]
13. de Nivelle, M.J.M.E.; Bruijn, M.P.; de Vries, R.; Wijnbergen, J.J.; de Korte, P.A.J.; Sánchez, S.; Elwenspoek, M.; Heidenblut, T.; Schwierzi, B.; Michalke, W.; et al. Low noise high-$T_c$ superconducting bolometers on silicon nitride membranes for far-infrared detection. *J. Appl. Phys.* **1997**, *82*, 4719–4726. [CrossRef]
14. Zhang, Z.M.; Frenkel, A. Thermal and Nonequilibrium Responses of Superconductors for Radiation Detectors. *J. Supercond.* **1994**, *7*, 871–884. [CrossRef]
15. Khrebtov, I.A. Noise Properties of High Temperature Superconducting Bolometers. *Fluct. Noise Lett.* **2002**, *2*, 51–69. [CrossRef]
16. Ivanov, K.V.; Khokhlov, D.A.; Khrebtov, I.A.; Kulikov, Y.V.; Malyarov, V.G.; Nikolenko, A.D.; Pindyurin, V.F.; Zerov, V.Y. Characterization of the composite bolometer with a high-Tc superconductor thermometer for an absolute radiometer of synchrotron radiation. *Nucl. Instrum. Methods Phys. Res. A.* **2007**, *575*, 272–275. [CrossRef]
17. Eaton, H.A.C. Observing Photons in Space, chapter 29. In *Infrared Imaging Bolometers*; Huber, M.C.E., Pauluhn, A., Culhane, J.L., Timothy, J.G., Wilhelm, K., Zehnder, A., Eds.; AG of the Series ISSI Scientific Report Series; Springer: Basel, Switzerland, 2013; Volume 9, pp. 515–524.
18. Irwin, K.D. An application of electrothermal feedback for high resolution cryogenic particle detection. *Appl. Phys. Lett.* **1995**, *66*, 1998–2000. [CrossRef]
19. Irwin, K.D.; Hilton, G.C. Transition-Edge Sensors in Cryogenic Particle Detection, edited by C. Enss, Springer-Verlag, Berlin Heidelberg. *Top. Appl. Phys.* **2005**, *99*, 63–149.
20. Abdel-Rahman, M.; Ilahi, S.; Zia, M.F.; Alduraibi, M.; Debbar, N.; Yacoubi, N.; Ilahi, B. Temperature coefficient of resistance and thermal conductivity of Vanadium oxide 'Big Mac' sandwich structure. *Infrared Phys. Technol.* **2015**, *71*, 127–130. [CrossRef]
21. Crassous, A.; Bernard, R.; Fusil, S.; Bouzehouane, K.; Bourdais, D.L.; Enouz-Vedrenne, S.; Briatico, J.; Bibes, M.; Barthélémy, A.; Villegas, J.E. Nanoscale electrostatic manipulation of magnetic flux quanta in ferroelectric/superconductor $BiFeO_3/YBa_2Cu_3O_{7-\delta}$ heterostructures. *Phys. Rev. Lett.* **2011**, *107*, 247002. [CrossRef]
22. Katzer, C.; Stahl, C.; Michalowski, P.; Treiber, S.; Schmidl, F.; Seidel, P.; Albrecht, J.; Schütz, G. Gold nanocrystals in high-temperature superconducting films: Creation of pinning patterns of choice. *New J. Phys.* **2013**, *15*, 113029. [CrossRef]
23. Vestgården, J.I.; Yurchenko, V.V.; Wördenweber, R.; Johansen, T.H. Mechanism for flux guidance by micrometric antidot arrays in superconducting films. *Phys. Rev. B* **2012**, *85*, 014516. [CrossRef]
24. Moschalkov, V.V. Nanostructured superconductors: quantum matter at low temperatures. In Proceedings of the Workshop on vortex behavior in unconventional superconductors, Braga, Portugal, 7–12 October 2018.
25. Feuiller-Palma, C. High-Tc superconducting devices. In Proceedings of the Coherent Superconducting Hybrids and Related Materials, Les Arcs, France, 26–29 March 2018.
26. García-Serrano, I.; Córdoba, R.; Sesé, J.; Ibarra, M.R.; Guillamón, I.; Suderow, H.; Vieira, S.; De Teresa, J.M. Superconducting nanostructures grown by focused ion beam induced deposition. In Proceedings of the International conference on nano confined superconductors and their application, Garmish, Germany, 3–7 September 2016.
27. Ramallo, M.V.; Carballeira, C.; Cotón, N.; Mosqueira, J.; Ramos-Álvarez, A.; Vidal, F. Influence of disorder and reduced dimensionality on the critical phenomena around the superconducting transition in cuprates. In Proceedings of the International workshop on advances in nanostructured superconductors: materials, properties and theory, Madrid, Spain, 4–7 May 2014.
28. European network NanoSC. Available online: http://www.cost.eu/actions/MP1201 (accessed on 1 January 2020).
29. European network NanoCoHybri. Available online: http://www.cost.eu/actions/CA16218 (accessed on 1 January 2020).

30. Verde, J.C.; Doval, J.M.; Ramos-Álvarez, A.; Sóñora, D.; Ramallo, M.V. Resistive Transition of High-$T_c$ Superconducting Films With Regular Arrays of $T_c$-Domains Induced by Micro- or Nanofunctionalization. *IEEE Tran. Appl. Supercond.* **2016**, *26*, 8800204. [CrossRef]
31. Maza, J.; Vidal, F. Critical-temperature inhomogeneities and resistivity rounding in copper oxide superconductors. *Phys. Rev. B* **1991**, *43*, 10560. [CrossRef] [PubMed]
32. Cotón, N; Mercey, B.; Mosqueira, J.; Ramallo, M.V.; Vidal, F. Synthesis from separate oxide targets of high quality $La_{2-x}Sr_xCuO_4$ thin films and dependence with doping of their superconducting transition width. *Supercond. Sci. Technol.* **2013**, *26*, 075011.
33. Cotón, N.; Ramallo, M.V.; Vidal, F. Critical temperatures for superconducting phase-coherence and condensation in $La_{2-x}Sr_xCuO_4$. *arXiv* **2013**, arXiv:1309.5910v3.
34. Benfatto, L.; Castellani, C.; Giamarchi, T. Doping dependence of the vortex-core energy in bilayer films of cuprates. *Phys. Rev. B* **2008**, *77*, 100506. [CrossRef]
35. Caprara, S.; Grilli, M.; Benfatto, L.; Castellani, C. Effective medium theory for superconducting layers: A systematic analysis including space correlation effects. *Phys. Rev. B* **2011**, *84*, 014514. [CrossRef]
36. Yu, C.; Scullin, M.L.; Ramamoorthy, M.H.; Majumdar, A. Thermal conductivity reduction in oxygen-deficient strontium titanates. *Appl. Phys. Lett.* **2008**, *92*, 191911 [CrossRef]
37. Lang, W.; Puica, I.; Zechner, G.; Kitzler, T.; Bodea, M.A.; Siraj, K.; Pedaring, J.D. All Non-ohmic electrical transport properties above the critical temperature in optimally and underdoped superconducting $YBa_2Cu_3O_{6+x}$. *J. Supercond. Nov. Magn.* **2012**, *25*, 1361–1364. [CrossRef]
38. Barišić, M.; Chan, M.K.; Li, Y.; Yu, G.; Zhao, X.; Dressel, M.; Smontara, A.; Greven, M. Universal sheet resistance and revised phase diagram of the cuprate high-temperature superconductors. *Proc. Natl. Acad. Sci. USA* **2013**, *110*, 12235–12240. [CrossRef] [PubMed]
39. Barišić, N.; Badoux, S.; Chan, M.K.; Dorow, C.; Tabis, W.; Vignolle, B.; Yu, G.; Béard, J.; Zhao, X.; Proust, C.; et al. Universal quantum oscillations in the underdoped cuprate superconductors. *Nat. Phys.* **2013**, *9*, 761–764. [CrossRef]
40. Tafti, F.F.; Laliberté, F.; Dion, M.; Gaudet, J.; Fournier, P.; Taifeller, L. Nernst effect in the electron-doped cuprate superconductor $Pr_{2-x}Ce_xCuO_4$: Superconducting fluctuations, upper critical field $H_{c2}$, and the origin of the $T_c$ dome. *Phys. Rev. B* **2014**, *90*, 024519. [CrossRef]
41. Pomar, A.; Ramallo, M.V.; Maza, J.; Vidal F. Measurements of the fluctuation-induced magnetoconductivity in the a-direction of an untwinned $Y_1Ba_2Cu_3O_{7-\delta}$ single-crystal in the weak magnetic field limit. *Phys. C* **1994**, *225*, 287–293. [CrossRef]
42. Ramallo, M.V.; Vidal, F. On the width of the full-critical region for thermal fluctuations around the superconducting transition in layered superconductors. *Europhys. Lett.* **1997**, *39*, 177–182. [CrossRef]
43. Viña, J.; Campá, J.A.; Carballeira, C.; Currás, S.R.; Maignan, A.; Ramallo, M.V.; Rasines, I.; Veira, J.A.; Wagner, P.; Vidal, F. Universal behavior of the in-plane paraconductivity of cuprate superconductors in the short-wavelength fluctuation regime. *Phys. Rev. B* **2002**, *65*, 212509-1–212509-4. [CrossRef]
44. Carballeira, C.; Currás, S.R.; Viña, J.; Veira, J.A.; Ramallo, M.V.; Vidal, F. Paraconductivity at high reduced temperatures in $YBa_2Cu_3O_{7-\delta}$ superconductors. *Phys. Rev. B* **2001**, *63*, 144515. [CrossRef]
45. Ramallo, M.V.; Pomar, A.; Vidal, F. In-plane paraconductivity and fluctuation-induced magnetoconductivity in biperiodic layered superconductors: Application to $YBa_2Cu_3O_{7-\delta}$. *Phys. Rev. B.* **1996**, *54*, 4341–4356. [CrossRef]
46. Mosqueira, J.; Recolevschi, A.; Torrón, C.; Ramallo, M.V.; Vidal, F. Crossing point of the magnetization versus temperature curves and the Meissner fraction in granular $La_{1.9}Sr_{0.1}CuO_4$ superconductors: Random orientation and inhomogeneity effects. *Phys. Rev. B* **1999**, *59*, 4394–4403. [CrossRef]
47. Cotón, N.; Ramallo, M.V.; Vidal, F. Effects of critical temperature inhomogeneities on the voltage-current characteristics of a planar superconductor near the Berezinskii-Kosterlitz-Thouless transition. *Supercond. Sci. Technol.* **2011**, *24*, 085013. [CrossRef]
48. Solov'ev, A.L.; Dmitriev, V.M. Fluctuation conductivity and pseudogap in YBCO high-temperature superconductors (Review). *J. Low Temp. Phys.* **2009**, *35*, 169–197. [CrossRef]
49. Lawrence, W.E.; Doniach, S. Theory of layer structure superconductors. In *Proceedings of the Twelfth International Conference on Low-Temperature Physics*, Kyoto, Japan, 4–10 September 1970; Kanda, E., Ed.; Keigatu: Tokyo, Japan, 1971; p. 361.

50. Carballeira, C.; Mosqueira, J.; Ramallo, M.V.; Veira, J.A.; Vidal, F. Fluctuation-induced diamagnetism in bulk isotropic superconductors at high reduced temperatures. *J. Phys. Condens. Matter* **2001**, *13*, 9271–9279. [CrossRef]
51. Mosqueira, J.; Ramallo, M.V.; Currás, S.R.; Torrón, C.; Vidal, F. Fluctuation-induced diamagnetism above the superconducting transition in $MgB_2$. *Phys. Rev. B* **2002**, *65*, 174522-1–174522-7. [CrossRef]
52. Ying, Q.Y.; Kwook, H.S. Kosterlitz-Thouless transition and conductivity fluctuations in Y-Ba-Cu-O thin films. *Phys. Rev. B* **1990**, *42*, 2242–2247. [CrossRef] [PubMed]
53. Halperin, B.I.; Nelson, D.R. Resistive Transition in Superconducting Films. *J. Low Temp. Phys.* **1979**, *36*, 599–616. [CrossRef]
54. Mosqueira, J.; Cabo, L.; Vidal, F. Structural and $T_c$ inhomogeneities inherent to doping in $La_{2-x}Sr_xCuO_4$ superconductors and their effects on the precursor diamagnetism. *Phys. Rev. B* **2009**, *80*, 214527. [CrossRef]
55. Mihailovic, D.; Optical experimental evidence for a universal length scale for the dynamic charge inhomogeneityy of cuprate superconductors. *Phys. Rev. Lett.* **2005**, *94*, 201001. [CrossRef]
56. Verde, J.C.; Ramallo, M.V. Herramientas Computacionales en el laboratorio LBTS. In *Películas Micro- y Nanoestructuradas de Superconductores de alta Temperatura: Computación de su Transición Resistiva*; GIDFI: Santiago de Compostela, Spain, 2016; pp. 39–47, ISBN 978-1-68073-062-3.
57. Garland, J.C.; Tanner, B.D. (Eds.) *Electrical Transport and Optical Properties of Inhomogeneous Media*; AIP: New York, NY, USA, 1978; p. 2.
58. Tallon, J.L.; Bernhard, C.; Shaked, H. Generic superconducting phase behavior in high-$T_c$ cuprates: $T_c$ variation with hole concentration in $YBaCu_3O_{7-\delta}$. *Phys. Rev. B* **1995**, *51*, 12911–12914. [CrossRef]

© 2020 by the authors. Licensee MDPI, Basel, Switzerland. This article is an open access article distributed under the terms and conditions of the Creative Commons Attribution (CC BY) license (http://creativecommons.org/licenses/by/4.0/).

Article

# Transport and Point Contact Measurements on $Pr_{1-x}Ce_xPt_4Ge_{12}$ Superconducting Polycrystals

Paola Romano [1,2], Francesco Avitabile [1], Angela Nigro [3,4], Gaia Grimaldi [2], Antonio Leo [3,4], Lei Shu [5,6], Jian Zhang [5], Antonio Di Bartolomeo [2,3] and Filippo Giubileo [2,*]

[1] Science and Technology Department, Via De Sanctis, University of Sannio, I-82100 Benevento, Italy; promano@unisannio.it (P.R.); favitabile@unisa.it (F.A.)
[2] CNR-SPIN Salerno, via Giovanni Paolo II n. 132, 84084 Fisciano, Italy; gaia.grimaldi@spin.cnr.it (G.G.); adibartolomeo@unisa.it (A.D.B.)
[3] Physics Department "E. R. Caianiello", University of Salerno, via Giovanni Paolo II n. 132, 84084 Fisciano, Italy; nigro@sa.infn.it (A.N.); antonio.leo@fisica.unisa.it (A.L.)
[4] NANO_MATES Research Center, Università degli Studi di Salerno, I-84084 Fisciano (SA), Italy
[5] State Key Laboratory of Surface Physics, Department of Physics, Fudan University, Shanghai 200433, China; leishu@fudan.edu.cn (L.S.); 14110190050@fudan.edu.cn (J.Z.)
[6] Shanghai Research Center for Quantum Sciences, Shanghai 201315, China
* Correspondence: filippo.giubileo@spin.cnr.it

Received: 30 July 2020; Accepted: 7 September 2020; Published: 10 September 2020

**Abstract:** We performed a detailed investigation of the superconducting properties of polycrystalline $Pr_{1-x}Ce_xPt_4Ge_{12}$ pellets. We report the effect of Ce substitution, for x = 0.07, on magnetic field phase diagram H-T. We demonstrate that the upper critical field is well described by the Ginzburg–Landau model and that the irreversibility field line has a scaling behaviour similar to cuprates. We also show that for magnetic fields lower than 0.4 T, the activation energy follows a power law of the type $H^{-1/2}$, suggesting a collective pinning regime with a quasi-2D character for the Ce-doped compound with x = 0.07. Furthermore, by means of a point contact Andreev reflection spectroscopy setup, we formed metal/superconductor nano-junctions as small as tens of nanometers on the $PrPt_4Ge_{12}$ parent compound (x = 0). Experimental results showed a wide variety of conductance features appearing in the dI/dV vs. V spectra, all explained in terms of a modified Blonder–Tinkham–Klapwijk model considering a superconducting order parameter with nodal directions as well as sign change in the momentum space for the sample with x = 0. The numerical simulations of the conductance spectra also demonstrate that s-wave pairing and anisotropic s-waves are unsuitable for reproducing experimental data obtained at low temperature on the un-doped compound. Interestingly, we show that the polycrystalline nature of the superconducting $PrPt_4Ge_{12}$ sample can favour the formation of an inter-grain Josephson junction in series with the point contact junction in this kind of experiments.

**Keywords:** superconductivity; transport properties; energy gap; superconducting order parameter; proximity effect; nano-junction; Andreev reflection

## 1. Introduction

Filled skutterudite materials have attracted a great deal of attention for a large number of properties such as metal–insulator transitions, spin fluctuations, and heavy fermion behaviour [1–4]. Several compounds in the family of filled skutterudites also show the phenomenon of superconductivity [5–8]. They have the chemical formula $MT_4X_{12}$, where M is an electropositive metal (Sr, Ba, La, Pr, Th), T is a transition metal (Fe, Os, or Ru), and X usually represents a pnictogen (Sb, As, or P). The first Pr-based superconductor to be discovered was the heavy-fermion $PrOs_4Sb_{12}$, with a critical temperature $T_c$ = 1.85 K, showing intriguing properties such as a giant electronic specific heat coefficient [1]. Moreover, experiments of thermal transport [9] on single crystals evidenced the possible existence of a superconducting phase at high magnetic fields in which the energy gap has at least four point nodes, and a second phase at low magnetic fields in which the energy gap is characterized by only two point nodes. Recently, a new Pt-based family of skutterudite, with chemical formula $MPt_4Ge_{12}$, was synthetized, showing superconducting properties at relatively high temperatures. In particular, the compound with praseodymium (Pr) as metal shows a transition temperature $T_c$ = 7.9K, while for the compound with Lanthanum (M = La), $T_c$ = 8.3 K has been reported [10], as confirmed by electrical resistivity, magnetic susceptibility and specific heat measurements. Nuclear magnetic resonance experiments have given indications for conventional superconductivity in $LaPt_4Ge_{12}$ [11].

Lower superconducting critical temperature was previously reported for other $MPt_4Ge_{12}$ compounds such as $SrPt_4Ge_{12}$ ($T_c$ = 5.10 K) and $BaPt_4Ge_{12}$ ($T_c$ = 5.35 K) [12]. The higher critical temperatures for Pr and La compounds with respect to Sr and Ba compounds have been explained as the existence of a larger density of states at the Fermi level, as resulting from $^{73}Ge$ nuclear quadrupole resonance experiments at zero field [13]. It has also been suggested that $PrPt_4Ge_{12}$ and $LaPt_4Ge_{12}$ can be characterized by two superconducting gaps. Indeed, according to heat capacity measurements as a function of temperature and magnetic field, the superconducting state cannot be explained by considering a single isotropic or anisotropic energy gap [14]. The presence of two distinct linear regions in the magnetic field dependence of the Sommerfeld coefficient of electronic heat capacity was interpreted as a possible indication for two-gap superconductivity in these compounds. The critical current density and pinning force of superconducting $PrPt_4Ge_{12}$ was measured in magnetization experiments [15], revealing that dependence of both quantities with respect magnetic field can be explained using a double exponential model already developed to explain the properties of the two-band superconductor $MgB_2$ [16–19].

µSR experiments on $PrPt_4Ge_{12}$ showed a time-reversal symmetry breaking below $T_c$ [20–23], in contrast to the results on $LaPt_4Ge_{12}$, for which the time-reversal symmetry breaking is absent and a conventional superconductivity with a fully gapped density of states is supposed [21]. The superconducting order parameter of $LaPt_4Ge_{12}$ has also been studied using specific heat and thermal conductivity measurements [24], showing that the sharp transition in the specific heat and its zero-field temperature dependence are well described in a conventional BCS (Bardeen–Cooper–Schrieffer) scenario characterized by a single energy gap and s-wave symmetry [25]. On the other hand, de Haas–van Alphen measurements have been reported with state-of-the-art band-structure calculations showing that $LaPt_4Ge_{12}$ and $PrPt_4Ge_{12}$ have almost identical electronic structures, Fermi surfaces and effective masses [26]. So far, few investigations have been reported that probe the superconducting energy gap in the $PrPt_4Ge_{12}$ compound, with results supporting both nodal and nodeless energy gaps. Recently, electrical resistivity, magnetic susceptibility, specific heat, and thermoelectric power experiments were performed on $Pr_{(1-x)}Ce_xPt_4Ge_{12}$ to investigate the influence of the magnetic state of the Ce ions on the superconducting properties of the compound [27]. Interestingly, the results indicate a crossover from a nodal to a nodeless superconducting energy gap and that $PrPt_4Ge_{12}$ could be a two-band superconductor in which the electron scattering due to Ce substitution can suppress the superconductivity within one of the bands.

In this paper, we perform a detailed study of the superconducting transport properties of the $Pr_{1-x}Ce_xPt_4Ge_{12}$ compound for x = 0.07. We measured the resistive transitions for the sample with x = 0.07 in external applied magnetic fields. We deduced the H-T phase diagram of the Ce-doped sample $Pr_{0.93}Ce_{0.07}Pt_4Ge_{12}$, that is the upper critical field $H_{c2}$, as well as the irreversibility line. We also analysed the resistive transition data in the framework of the thermally assisted motion of vortices. We also performed direct measurements of the superconducting energy gap in the parent compound $PrPt_4Ge_{12}$ (x = 0) by means of point contact spectroscopy experiments, which made it possible to realize metal/superconductor nano-junctions with dimensions of few nanometres. We measured the conductance spectra of the point contact junction at low temperature (4.2 K) and we demonstrated that the conductance feature can be reproduced in a theoretical model that takes into account the symmetry of the superconducting order parameter with nodal directions and change of sign in the momentum space. We also estimated the superconducting energy gap for the sample PrPt$_4$Ge$_{12}$ in the range 0.55–0.95 meV.

## 2. Materials and Methods

Polycrystalline Pr$_{1-x}$Ce$_x$Pt$_4$Ge$_{12}$ pellets (with x = 0, 0.07, 0.1) were synthesized in argon atmosphere by arc melting, using Pr ingots, Ce rods, Pt sponge, and Ge pieces as preparation materials, weighed in stochiometric ratios. Arc melting and turning over were repeated five times to obtain high chemical homogeneity. The samples were then annealed in a sealed quartz tube in 200 Torr argon atmosphere at 800 °C for 14 days. X-Ray diffractometry (reported elsewhere [27]) confirmed the sample quality evidencing the expected cubic skutterudite crystal structure.

Measurements of sample resistance as a function of the temperature, $R(T)$, were carried out by standard four-probe offset-compensated technique inside a Cryogenic Ltd. cryogen-free magnet system, equipped with a variable temperature insert (vertically inserted inside a superconducting solenoid for fields up to 9T) in which the temperature can vary in the range 1.6 K–325 K. A Keithley 2430 DC current source was employed to bias the sample, while measuring the voltage by means of a Keithley 2182 nanovoltmeter.

Point Contact Spectroscopy experiments were performed by means of a home-built mechanical inset equipped with a screw-driven chariot to move a metallic tip towards the surface of the superconducting sample, in order to form a metal/superconductor nanometric constriction, the so-called point contact junction. The junction is then cooled down by immersing the inset in a liquid helium cryostat to perform current-voltage (I–V) measurements at low temperature by standard four-probe technique. Differential conductance (dI/dV vs. V) spectra are then obtained performing numerical derivative of the I–V curves.

## 3. Results and Discussion

### 3.1. Transport Properties

The dynamic behaviour of Abrikosov vortices in type II superconductors determines the transport properties of superconducting samples. In particular, vortices are set in motion when the Lorentz force, due to the bias current, exceeds the strength of vortex pinning forces, causing a nonzero Ohmic resistance. The presence of pinning, caused by any spatial inhomogeneity of the material like impurities, point defects, grain boundaries, etc., allows superconducting material to sustain current without flux motion and dissipation, giving rise to a nonzero critical current density. Different phases can be recognized in the magnetic field phase diagram H-T depending on the relative strengths of the pinning potential, the Lorentz driving energy, and the elastic energy of the vortex lattice, thermal energy and dimensionality. The interplay between these interactions results in several phase separation lines in the H-T phase diagram [28].

In the following, we characterize the H-T phase diagram of the sample Pr$_{0.93}$Ce$_{0.07}$Pt$_4$Ge$_{12}$, the upper critical field H$_{c2}$, and the irreversibility line, above which the critical current density becomes zero. Then, the resistive transitions in external applied magnetic fields are analysed in the framework of the thermally assisted motion of vortices.

#### 3.1.1. Magnetic Field Temperature Phase Diagram

In Figure 1a we report the resistance vs. temperature curves, $R(T)$, for Pr$_{1-x}$Ce$_x$Pt$_4$Ge$_{12}$ samples having x = 0, 0.07 and 0.10. The data were normalized to the normal state resistance, $R_N$, evaluated just before the onset of the superconducting transition. We measured $R_N$ = 4.3 mΩ for the undoped sample, $R_N$ = 34 mΩ for sample with x = 0.07 and $R_N$ = 63 mΩ for sample with x = 0.10. The superconducting critical temperature $T_c$ was estimated at 50% of the onset transition resistance, obtaining $T_c$ = 7.9 K for the undoped sample, $T_c$ = 4.7 K for samples with x = 0.07, and $T_c$ = 3.6 K for samples with x = 0.1.

The evolution of the critical temperature $T_c$ as a function of the Ce doping $x$ is summarized in Figure 1b. The effect on $T_c$ of the partial substitution of Pr by Nd has been also reported in samples with Nd content $x_{Nd}$ up to 0.1 [29]. The critical temperature is weakly dependent by Nd content, being reduced by only 10% at $x_{Nd} = 0.1$. On the other hand, the effect of the Ce substitution is much more important; the $T_c$ is reduced by 59% at $x = 0.07$ and by 45% at $x = 0.1$. The effect of externally applied magnetic field up to 1 T on the R(T) curve for sample with $x = 0.07$ is shown in Figure 1c.

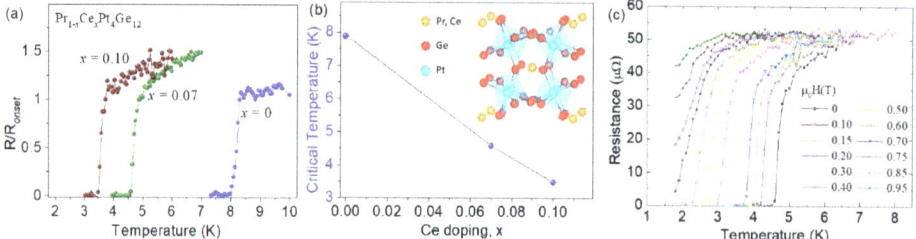

**Figure 1.** (**a**) The resistance as a function of the temperature normalized to the normal state resistance value for the three different Ce doping. (**b**) Evaluated critical temperature values as a function of the doping. The inset shows a schematic diagram of the $Pr_{1-x}Ce_xPt_4Ge_{12}$ crystal structure, showing the Pr,Ce atoms residing in icosahedral cages formed by tilted $PtGe_6$ octahedral. (**c**) Magnetic field dependence of the resistance versus temperature curve measured for the sample with $x = 0.07$ doping.

In Figure 2a, the resulting magnetic field–temperature (*H-T*) phase diagram is shown, together with the upper critical field line $H_{c2}(T)$, which separates the normal and the superconducting state, and the irreversibility line $H_{irr}(T)$. In the *H-T* phase diagram, the $H_{irr}(T)$ line separates the Abrikosov vortex pinned regime and the vortex liquid regime, which is at a given temperature; the critical current density goes to zero at the irreversibility field. To evaluate the upper critical field, $\mu_0 H_{c2}$, we employed to the 90% of normal state resistance $R_N$ criterion, while the irreversibility line, $\mu_0 H_{irr}$, was obtained using the 10% of $R_N$ criterion. To analyse the temperature dependence of the upper critical field, the $\mu_0 H_{c2}(T)$ data extracted by the *H-T* phase diagram are shown in Figure 2b.

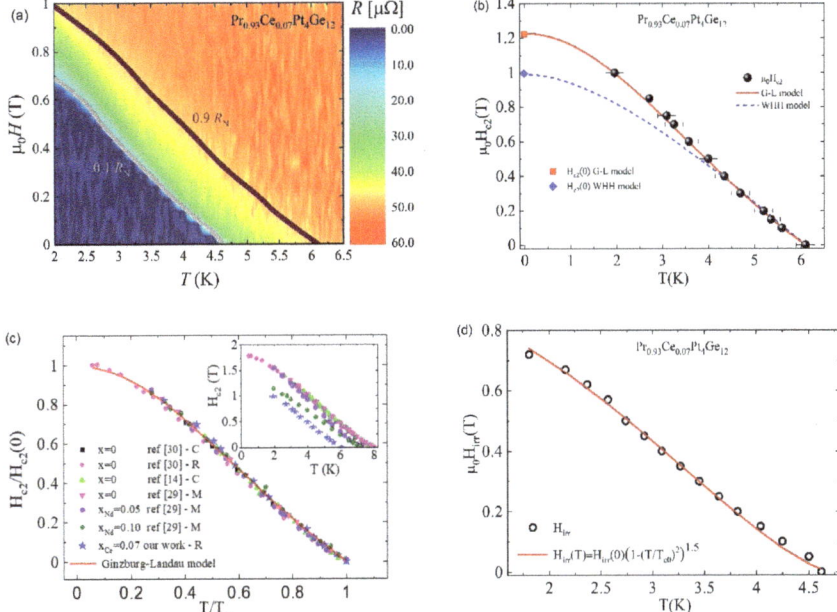

**Figure 2.** (a). The H-T phase diagram as obtained by R(T) measurements at different applied magnetic fields for the sample with the doping x = 0.07. The irreversibility line (0.1 $R_N$ curve) and the upper critical field behaviour (0.9 $R_N$ curve) are indicated. (b) The upper critical field $H_{c2}(T)$ data are shown as black spheres. The red solid line is a fit of the data by the Ginzburg–Landau Equation (Equation (1) in the text). The blue dashed line is obtained by the single band WHH model (Equation (2) in the text). (c) Scaling plots of the normalized upper critical field $H_{c2}(T)/H_{c2}(0)$ plotted as function of the reduced temperature $T/T_c$ for the parent compound $PrPt_4Ge_{12}$ [14,29,30], Nd-doped samples $Pr_{1-x}Nd_xPt_4Ge_{12}$ [29] and for our $Pr_{1-x}Ce_xPt_4Ge_{12}$ sample with x = 0.07. $H_{c2}(T)$ curves are obtained by resistivity, R, specific heat, C, and magnetization measurements, M. The inset shows the $H_{c2}$ data as a function of the temperature for the same samples in the main panel. (d) The irreversibility field $H_{irr}(T)$ data are shown as open circles. The red solid line is a fit of the data by Equation (5) in the test.

The red solid line in Figure 2b represents the best fit of the data by the Ginzburg–Landau (G-L) formula:

$$H_{c2}(T) = H_{c2}(0)\frac{(1-t^2)}{(1+t^2)} \quad (1)$$

where $H_{c2}(0)$ is the upper critical field at zero temperature and $t = T/T_C$ is the reduced temperature. The data are very well described by the G-L Equation with $\mu_0 H_{c2}(0) = 1.23$ T, as already reported for $(Pr,La)Pt_4Ge_{12}$ and $Pr_{1-x}Nd_xPt_4Ge_{12}$ compounds [14,24,29,31-34]. For comparison, in Figure 2b, we also show the temperature dependence of the upper critical field derived within the Werthamer–Helfand–Hohenberg (WHH) model (blue dashed line), which includes orbital and Zeeman pair breaking [35,36]. In particular, for a single band superconductor in a dirty limit, the model yields:

$$H_{c2} = \frac{2\Phi_0 k_B T_c}{hD_0} ht \quad (2)$$

where $\Phi_0$ is the magnetic flux quantum, $k_B$ the Boltzmann constant, $T_c$ the critical temperature in zero applied magnetic field, $h$ is the reduced Planck constant, $D_0 = h/2m_e$ with $m_e$ the electron mass, and h is a parameter that runs from 0 to ∞ as T varies from $T_c$ to 0, while the reduced temperature $t = T/T_c$ is given by:

$$\ln(t) = \Psi\left(\frac{1}{2}\right) - \text{Re}\Psi\left(\frac{1}{2} + h(i+d)\right) \quad (3)$$

where $\Psi$ is the digamma function, $d = D/D_0$, and $D$ the diffusivity of the band related to the slope of the $\mu_0 H_{c2}(T)$ experimental data near $T_c$, given by $D = 4k_B/\pi e\mu_0|dH_{c2}(T)/dT|$. For our sample, $\mu_0 dH_{c2}(T)/dT = -0.23$ TK$^{-1}$. Within this model, the zero-temperature upper critical field $H_{c2}(0)$ can be obtained by the well-known WHH formula:

$$H_{c2}(0) = 0.693 \times T_c \left|\frac{dH_{c2}(T)}{dT}\right| \quad (4)$$

We note that the WHH model underestimates the $H_{c2}$ field at low temperatures, with the WHH formula giving $\mu_0 H_{c2}(0) = 0.99$ T, corresponding to the value experimentally measured at T = 2.1 K ($\mu_0 H_{c2} = 1$ T).

The Ce substitution for Pr in PrPt$_4$Ge$_{12}$ does not seem to modify the behaviour of the temperature dependence of the upper critical field, showing a characteristic positive curvature near $T_c$, as for the parent compounds (Pr,La)Pt$_4$Ge$_{12}$ and the doped Pr$_{1-x}$Nd$_x$Pt$_4$Ge$_{12}$ material. To analyse the effects on the upper critical field $H_{c2}(T)$ curve of the partial substitution of Pr in PrPtGe in Figure 2c, we compare our findings for the sample with Ce doping x = 0.07 with the results reported in the literature for the un-doped parent compound PrPt$_4$Ge$_{12}$ [14,29,30] and for Nd-doped samples Pr$_{1-x}$Nd$_x$Pt$_4$Ge$_{12}$ [29]. A scaling behaviour described by the G-L formula, Equation (1), is obtained when the normalized upper critical field $H_{c2}(T)/H_{c2}(0)$ is plotted as a function of the reduced temperature t = T/Tc. We also point out that the figure includes $H_{c2}(T)$ curves obtained by resistivity, specific heat, and magnetization measurements. Furthermore, the scaling behaviour is the same for the two different doping, Ce and Nd, despite the different strength of critical temperature lowering induced by the two type of doping.

Different mechanisms have been proposed to explain this behaviour, such as strong coupling effects, multi-band electronic structure, and disorder [37,38].

Moreover, the coherence length at zero temperature was evaluated by $\mu_0 H_{c2}(0) = \Phi_0/4\pi\xi(0)^2$, with $\Phi_0$ being the magnetic flux quantum. A value of $\xi(0) \approx 12$ nm was obtained, which is close to the value reported for the un-doped compound, $\xi_{x=0}(0) \approx 14$ nm [39].

In Figure 2d, the temperature dependence of the irreversibility field is shown. The scaling relation,

$$H_{irr}(T) = H_{irr}(0)\left[1 - \left(\frac{T}{T_{C0}}\right)^2\right]^n \quad (5)$$

was adapted to the experimental data with $n = 1.5$ (red solid line in Figure 2c) and $\mu_0 H_{irr}(0) = 0.94T$. $T_{C0}$ is the zero field transition temperature, and the exponent $n$ is determined by the flux pinning mechanism [40]. At temperatures close to $T_{C0}$, the scaling Equation was reduced to $H_{irr} \sim (1 - T/T_{C0})^{1.5}$ as observed by Yeshumn et al. for single crystals of YBa$_2$Cu$_3$O$_7$ high-temperature superconductor and interpreted within the thermally activated flux-creep theory [41]. The exponent $n = 1.5$ is also consistent with the values found for the iron-based 122 and 1111-families and the TlSr$_2$Ca$_2$Cu$_3$O$_y$ compound [42–44].

In the field range between $H_{irr}(T)$ and $H_{c2}(T)$, the thermal fluctuations become important, and the superconducting state loses its zero-resistance behaviour. In type II superconductors, high-field and -current applications are limited by the irreversibility line $H_{irr}(T)$; for example, values of $H_{irr}$ at low temperatures from 50% to ~80% of the $H_{c2}$ have been observed in MgB$_2$ and up to 85% in (Y$_{0.77}$Gd$_{0.23}$)Ba$_2$Cu$_3$O$_y$ films [45,46]. In our sample, the irreversibility field was 70% of the upper critical field at low temperatures, and dropped to less than 20% of $H_{c2}$ close to the critical temperature $T_{C0}$.

### 3.1.2. Temperature Dependence of the Vortex Activation Energy

To further analyse the pinning properties of $Pr_{1-x}Ce_xPt_4Ge_{12}$, we analysed the field dependence of the pinning activation energy $U$. This physical parameter was evaluated by a linear fit of the transition region in the $R(T)$ curves represented in an Arrhenius plot, which are shown in Figure 3a. Indeed, the Arrhenius plots show that the resistivity is thermally activated over about two orders of magnitude at low fields; in this regime, the resistance's dependence on temperature and field can be written in the form: $R(T,H) = R_0 e^{-U(T,H)/k_B T}$ [47].

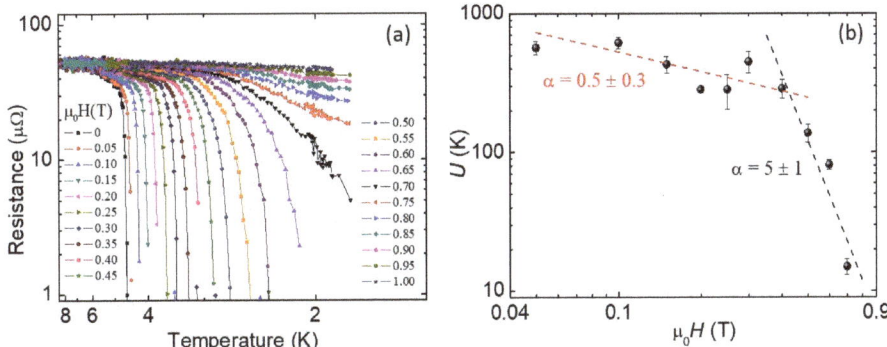

**Figure 3.** (a) The Arrhenius plot of the R(T) curves for the sample with the doping x = 0.07. (b) The pinning activation energy as a function of the applied magnetic field for the same sample. The dotted lines are obtained by a linear fit on the data in the log–log plot.

In Figure 3b, the resulting $U(H)$ curve is shown. In particular, small activation energies, up to 600 K, are reported, close to the values $\sim 10^3$ K observed in Bi2212 superconductor [48]. According to the literature [34,36], the dependence of the pinning activation energy on the applied magnetic field follows a power law of the type $H^{-\alpha}$, with the exponent $\alpha$, which assumes different values depending on the vortex pinning regime. In our case it is evident a crossover between two power law behaviours with different exponents. This crossover is at about 0.4 T, and the exponents are $\alpha \approx 0.5$ for $\mu_0 H < 0.4$ T and $\alpha \approx 5$ for $\mu_0 H > 0.4$ T. Both values can be associated with a collective pinning regime, with an exponent value between 0.5 and 1, which is usually found in cuprate superconductors and could be related to the quasi-2D character of these materials [41,49,50]. The existence of a crossover suggests the presence of two different pinning centres with different dimensions within a collective pinning regime, as was observed, for example, in undoped and Nd-doped $PrPt_4Ge_{12}$ samples [29], as well as $YBa_2Cu_3O_7$ compounds [50] and in $Nd_{2-x}Ce_xCuO_{4-\delta}$ thin films [51].

### 3.2. Point Contact Spectroscopy

Point contact Andreev Reflection spectroscopy (PCAR) is a very powerful technique, widely applied to investigate the fundamental properties of superconductors, such as the superconducting energy gap amplitude, the density of states (DOS) at the Fermi level, and the symmetry of the superconducting order parameter (OP) [52]. PCAR experiments have been reported to study conventional BCS superconductors [53], high Tc cuprates (both hole doped and electron doped) [54–59], multiband superconductors [60–64], ruthenocuprates [65], iron-pnicniteds [66], heavy fermion superconductors [67], non-centrosymmetric superconductors [68], and topological superconductors [69]. This technique has also been successfully applied for precise measurements of the thickness and of the polarization in thin ferromagnetic/superconductor multilayers [70–75]. The PCAR technique consists of realizing a nano-contact between a tip-shaped normal-metal (N) electrode and a superconductor (S), thus forming a N/S nano-junction. By tuning the transparency of the N/S interface (i.e., by changing the tip pressure on the sample surface) one can realize different tunnelling regimes, going from the Andreev reflection [76,77] regime (in the case of a low potential barrier at the interface, corresponding to high interface transparency) to quasiparticle tunnelling regime for low interface transparency (high potential barrier). In a typical PCAR experiment, an intermediate regime can be achieved, with both Andreev reflection processes and quasiparticle tunnelling contributing to current transport through the N/S interface. If an electron travels from the normal side of the junction, with an energy lower than the superconducting energy gap, towards the N/S interface, it can enter into the superconducting side only as a Cooper pair, i.e., forming a pair with another electron, while originating a reflected hole in N with the opposite momentum. Consequently, a single Andreev reflection event causes a charge transfer to the S side of 2e, with e the electron charge. From a theoretical point of view, the transport through a point contact junction between a normal metal and a conventional BCS superconductor (with isotropic s-wave symmetry of the superconducting OP) was described in the BTK theory [78], in which the interface barrier is modelled by a dimensionless parameter Z. The case Z = 0 corresponds to an N/S junction, with a completely transparent barrier, in which the Andreev process is the dominant mechanism responsible for the transport current. On the other hand, Z > 1 represents a junction with a low transparent barrier, corresponding to a dominant tunnelling current flowing through the junction.

The BTK theory was subsequently extended to the case of superconductors with amplitude variation of the OP in the k-space (as for an anisotropic s-wave) and to the case of unconventional superconductors, in which the sign of the OP may also change (as for d-wave symmetry) [79]. It has been demonstrated that if an incident quasiparticle at the N/S interface experiences a different sign of the OP, Andreev bound states are formed at the Fermi energy [80]. From an experimental point of view, the formation of Andreev bound states are seen in the differential conductance spectra as a peak at zero bias [81–85]. In the case of d-wave symmetry, conductance depends on both the incident angle $\varphi$ of the quasiparticle at the N/S interface and on the orientation angle $\alpha$ between the a-axis of the superconducting order parameter and the crystallographic axis. The conductance expression can be reduced to the model for anisotropic s-wave by simply assuming costant phase and assuming that only the OP amplitude changes in the k-space. We mention here that the BTK model and its extended version applied here do not consider the possible effects due to the case of energy-dependent DOS (the effects being mostly expected on the thermoelectric effects in NS junctions [86].

PCAR Experiment

The PCAR experiment was performed on the $Pr_{1-x}Ce_xPt_4Ge_{12}$ sample having x = 0 ($T_c$ = 7.9 K). We used a gold tip as a normal metal electrode, which was gently pushed onto the sample surface to realize the N/S nanoconstriction. The setup was then immersed in a helium liquid bath for low-temperature (T = 4.2 K) characterization. We measured the current–voltage characteristics I–V using a standard four-probe configuration, using a dc current supply to bias the junction and measuring the voltage by a nano-voltmeter. The conductance curves, dI/dV–V, were obtained by numerical derivation of the I–V curves. The PCAR setup also makes it possible to vary the tip pressure on the sample, obtaining a tuning of the barrier transparency and, consequently, different junction resistances. In our experiment, we obtained junction resistances $R_N$ in the range 0.1 Ω–50 Ω. We noticed here that we did not have a direct control of the geometrical dimensions of the N/S junction formed in the PCAR experiment. However, we estimated the junction size through the Sharvin formula $R_N = 4\rho\ell/(3\pi d^2)$, in which the normal resistance of the junction is related to the resistivity $\rho$ = 3.5 µΩcm [87] and the mean free path $\ell$ = 103 nm [87] in the superconducting material, as well as to contact dimension d.

In Figure 4, we report normalized dI/dV–V curves, measured at low temperature (T = 4.2 K) for different nano-junctions, realized by varying the tip pressure and/or position on the sample surface. The conductance curves in Figure 4a,b are characterized by a zero-bias conductance peak (ZBCP) and have normal resistance $R_N$ of 20 Ω and 0.2 Ω, respectively. Based on the Sharvin formula, we found the junction size to be d = 7 nm and d = 65 nm, respectively. In both cases, this confirms that the point contact is in the ballistic regime [52], in which the size of the junction is smaller than the mean free path in the superconductor (d << $\ell$). This corresponds to the physical conditions for which an electron can accelerate freely through the point contact, with no heat generated in the contact region, allowing energy-resolved spectroscopy.

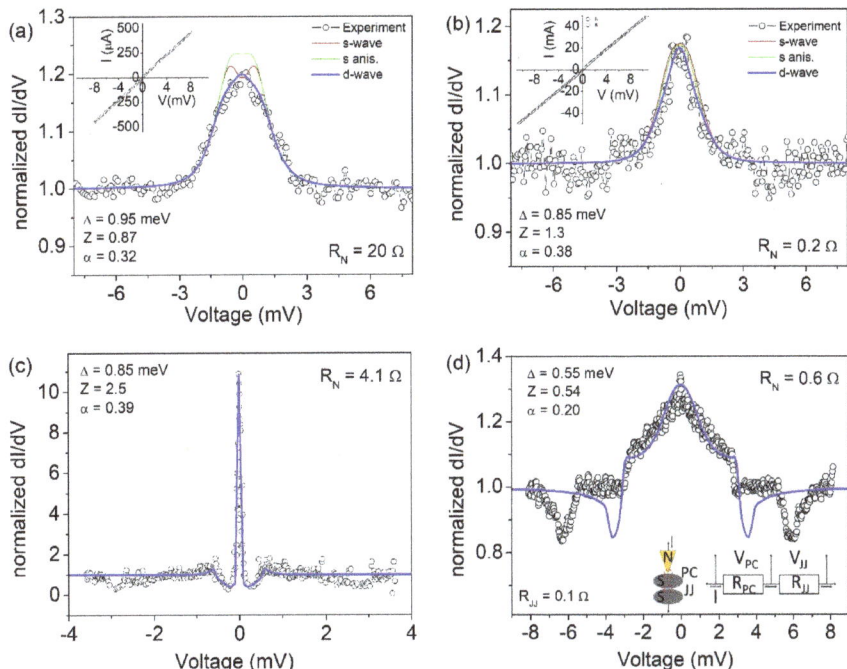

**Figure 4.** Normalized conductance spectra, dI/dV–V, measured at low temperature (T = 4.2 K) in different sample locations on the $Pr_{1-x}Ce_xPt_4Ge_{12}$ (with x = 0) sample. Experimental data (empty symbols) in (**a,b**) are compared to numerically calculated curves for the three different symmetries. The I–V curve is shown in the inset. Experimental data (empty symbols) in (**c,d**) are compared to numerically calculated curves for d-wave symmetry only. Inset in (**d**) represent the schematic of model in which an inter-grain Josephson junction is formed in series with the point contact junction.

The ZBCPs reported in Figure 4a,b have similar height (~1.2) and energy width (~ ±3 meV), while presenting a quite different shape. Experimental data are compared to theoretical fittings obtained for the three mentioned symmetries of the OP. We notice that s-symmetries are not able to completely reproduce the observed features. This discrepancy is more evident in Figure 4a, where the blue solid line represents the simulation obtained assuming a d-wave symmetry, with $\Delta$ = 0.95 meV, Z = 0.87 and $\alpha$ = 0.32 as fitting parameters. The Z value gives an indication of an intermediate regime, in which both Andreev reflection and quasiparticle tunnelling contribute to the conduction mechanism. The $\alpha$ value is an indication that the current direction is in between the nodal direction ($\alpha = \pi/4$) and $\alpha = 0$ (corresponding to maximum energy gap amplitude). In Figure 4b, very similar fitting curves are obtained for the different symmetries, although in this case, too, the d-wave symmetry seems to better reproduce the experimental behaviour, with fitting parameters $\Delta$ = 0.85 meV, Z = 1.3 and $\alpha$ = 0.38.

On the other side, the spectra reported in Figure 4c,d appear very different. Indeed, in Figure 5c the ZBCP is very narrow and its amplitude is above 10, a value that cannot be obtained in s- or s-anisotropic fitting models, the maximum height being limited to 2. Moreover, at the side of the ZBCP, conductance minima are present, at voltages below ±1 mV. Such a feature is usually expected only when the superconducting OP is characterized by a sign change, as in the d-wave symmetry. Accordingly, we succeeded to simulate the experimental data by using the extended BTK model for a d-wave superconductor, assuming $\Delta$ = 0.85 meV, Z = 2.5 and $\alpha$ = 0.39. It was not possible to obtain similar features by applying the s-wave or s-anisotropic symmetry of the OP. We notice here that all experimental data have been simulated without introducing the so-called Γ-Dynes smearing factor [88] typically used to take into account possible pair-breaking effects of various origins (impurities, inelastic scattering, magnetic field, etc.).

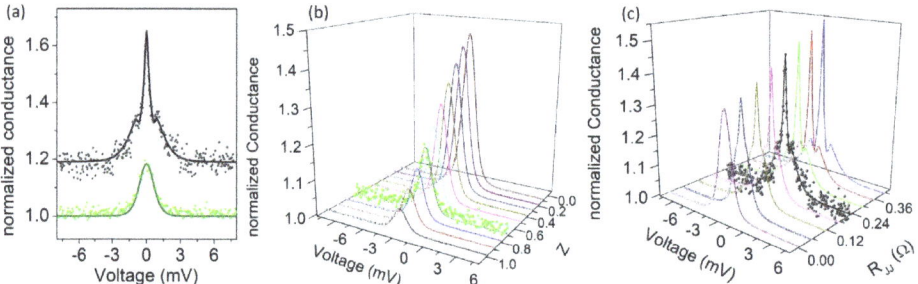

**Figure 5.** (**a**) Conductance spectra measured in a different location on the same superconducting sample: the lower (green) spectrum was measured soon after the tip approach on the surface. The upper spectrum was measured after increasing the tip pressure on the surface. The upper (black) spectrum was vertically shifted (+0.2) for clarity. Solid lines represent the numerical fits. (**b**) Evolution of conductance spectra (solid lines) calculated numerically for $\Delta = 0.55$ meV and $\alpha = 0.46$, and for $0 < Z < 1$. The scattered (green) points refer to experimental data of Figure 5a. (**c**) Evolution of conductance spectra (solid lines) calculated numerically for $\Delta = 0.55$ meV, $Z = 0.39$, $\alpha = 0.29$, and $0 < R_{JJ} < 0.42$ Ω. The scattered (black) points refer to experimental data of Figure 5a.

Another completely different shape is observed in the spectrum of Figure 4d, where a wide ZBCP is followed by several features that cannot be reproduced by simply applying the model discussed above. However, we need to take into account that the superconducting sample is a pellet formed by pressed powders. Consequently, the tip pressure on the surface can cause the formation of an inter-grain Josephson junction in series with the point contact junction as depicted in the inset of Figure 4d. The effect of such inter-grain effects in point contact measurements has already been observed in experiments on MgB$_2$ [61], MgCNi$_3$ [89], and Pr$_{1-x}$La$Ce_x$CuO$_{4-y}$ [57]. In this extended model, we need to take into account that the metallic tip (N electrode) forms a point contact junction on a superconducting grain, and this in turn forms a Josephson junction with another superconducting grain. Consequently, the total voltage drop $V$ (experimentally measured) is given by the sum of the point contact $V_{PC}$ and the Josephson junction $V_{JJ}$ contributions $V = V_{PC} + V_{JJ}$. If the flowing current $I$ is lower than $I_{JJ}$ there is no voltage drop at the inter-grain junction ($V_{JJ} = 0$). Otherwise, $V_{JJ}$ can be calculated according to Lee formula [90] as $V_{JJ} = R_{JJ}I_{JJ}\sqrt{(I/I_{JJ})^2 - 1}$, where $R_{JJ}$ and $I_{JJ}$ are the resistance and the critical current of the Josephson junction, respectively. If the flowing current $I$ is lower than $I_{JJ}$ there is no voltage drop at the inter-grain junction ($V_{JJ} = 0$). Then, the total conductance $G$ can be calculated from the condition $1/G = \left[\frac{dV_{PC}}{dI} + \frac{dV_{JJ}}{dI}\right]$. We succeeded in simulating the conductance spectrum reported in Figure 4d assuming $\Delta = 0.55$ meV, $Z = 0.54$ and $\alpha = 0.20$. The fitting parameters related to the Josephson junctions were $R_{JJ} = 0.1$ Ω and $I_{JJ} = 3.2$ mA. We notice that these parameters are not completely free, being necessarily $R_N = R_{PC} + R_{JJ}$ and $R_{JJ}I_{JJ} < \Delta$. We remark here that neglecting the existence of a Josephson junction in series with the point contact would result in an over-estimation of the superconducting energy gap, because the measured voltage at which the conductance features are observed is larger than the real voltage $V_{PC}$ applied to the point contact junction ($V = V_{PC} + V_{JJ}$). We observe that the superconducting energy gap values obtained from the numerical fittings of most of the experimental spectra are in the range 0.85–0.95 meV that correspond to a ratio $2\Delta/k_B T_C$ in the range 2.5–2.8, smaller than the BCS value (3.52). In the case of the conductance curve of Figure 4d, we estimate a superconducting energy even smaller ($\Delta = 0.55$ meV, i.e., $2\Delta/k_B T_C = 1.6$). This may be an indication of suppressed superconductivity on the probed surface, with the point contact experiments being sensitive to a thin surface layer of tens of nanometres. Consequently, the correct procedure for estimating the ratio $2\Delta/k_B T_C$ would be to use the local critical temperature, which should be estimated based on the temperature evolution of the conductance spectra (not available in this experiment); this local Tc could be lower than the bulk sample Tc, giving an increased $2\Delta/k_B T_C$ ratio. We note that in the case of d-wave symmetry, electrons injected along different directions may experience different pairing amplitudes. Consequently, the shape of the conductance curves does not depend only on the height Z of the potential barrier at the interface, but also on the direction of the current injection. In Figure 5a, we show conductance measurements performed in a different location of the sample. The two spectra are the result of two successive measurements, in which the second spectrum was measured after increasing the tip pressure on the surface to increase the barrier transparency. The lower spectrum shows a ZBCP with limited amplitude (about 1.2) and is reproduced by the extended BTK model by assuming $\Delta = 0.55$ meV, $Z = 0.71$ and $\alpha = 0.46$. However, the second spectrum (shifted for clarity) has a much higher and more narrow ZBCP with two relative maxima appearing at the side of the peak. To understand the evolution of the second conductance curve, we show in Figure 5b the expected behaviour of the spectra obtained by keeping fixed the parameters $\Delta = 0.55$ meV and $\alpha = 0.46$, varying the barrier strength Z in the range $0 < Z < 1$. We notice that in this scenario the main effect of the Z parameter is on the ZBCP height. The appearance of further conductance features is explained considering that the increased pressure of the tip on the surface has a double effect: it helps to obtain a more transparent barrier (lower Z), while it favours the formation of an inter-grain junction. Indeed, the numerical simulation of the experimental spectrum is obtained with good agreement by assuming $\Delta = 0.55$ meV, $Z = 0.39$, $\alpha = 0.29$ and $R_{JJ} = 0.22~\Omega$, $I_{JJ} = 0.24$ mA. In Figure 5c, we show the evolution of conductance spectra numerically calculated by fixing the parameters $\Delta = 0.55$ meV, $Z = 0.39$, $\alpha = 0.29$ and varying only $R_{JJ}$ in the range $0-0.42~\Omega$.

## 4. Conclusions

We investigated the superconducting properties of polycrystalline $Pr_{1-x}Ce_xPt_4Ge_{12}$ pellets, reporting the magnetic field phase diagram H-T for the Ce-doped compound with $x = 0.07$, as well as the point contact spectroscopy characterization of the parent compound $PrPt_4Ge_{12}$ ($x = 0$).

Interestingly, the irreversibility field line, found for $Pr_{0.93}Ce_{0.07}Pt_4Ge_{12}$, shows a scaling behaviour similar to high-temperature superconducting cuprates. The vortex activation energy was also evaluated at different applied magnetic fields. At magnetic fields lower than 0.4 T, the activation energy follows a power law of the type $H^{-\alpha}$, with the exponents $\alpha \approx 0.5$, which could indicate a collective pinning regime with a quasi-2D character.

For the compound with $x = 0$ ($PrPt_4Ge_{12}$), we realized normal metal/superconductor nano-junctions, with lateral dimensions of few nanometres, by pushing a gold tip onto the surface of polycrystalline sample. Several conductance spectra were measured at low temperatures, showing zero bias conductance peak with variable amplitude, height and width. All experimental data for the $PrPt_4Ge_{12}$ sample were consistently interpreted in the framework of extended BTK theory. A small energy gap was observed in the range 0.55 meV–0.95 meV, indicating the possible formation of inter-grain Josephson junctions in series with the point contact.

**Author Contributions:** Conceptualization, F.G. and P.R.; Data curation, F.A., A.L. and A.D.B.; Investigation, P.R., A.N., G.G., A.L. and F.G.; Resources, L.S. and J.Z.; Supervision, F.G.; Writing—original draft, F.G., P.R., A.L. and A.N.; Writing—review & editing, F.G., P.R., A.D.B. and A.N. All authors have read and agreed to the published version of the manuscript.

**Funding:** This research was funded by the National Research and Development Program of China, No. 2017YFA0303104, Shanghai Municipal Science and Technology Major Project (Grant No.~2019SHZDZX01).

**Conflicts of Interest:** The authors declare no conflict of interest.

## References

1. Bauer, E.D.; Frederick, N.A.; Ho, P.-C.; Zapf, V.S.; Maple, M.B. Superconductivity and heavy fermion behavior in PrOs4Sb12. *Phys. Rev. B* **2002**, *65*, 100506. [CrossRef]
2. MacLaughlin, D.E.; Sonier, J.E.; Heffner, R.H.; Bernal, O.O.; Young, B.-L.; Rose, M.S.; Morris, G.D.; Bauer, E.D.; Do, T.D.; Maple, M.B. Muon Spin Relaxation and Isotropic Pairing in Superconducting PrOs4Sb12. *Phys. Rev. Lett.* **2002**, *89*, 157001. [CrossRef] [PubMed]
3. Aoki, Y.; Tsuchiya, A.; Kanayama, T.; Saha, S.R.; Sugawara, H.; Sato, H.; Higemoto, W.; Koda, A.; Ohishi, K.; Nishiyama, K.; et al. Time-Reversal Symmetry-Breaking Superconductivity in Heavy-Fermion PrOs4Sb12 Detected by Muon-Spin Relaxation. *Phys. Rev. Lett.* **2003**, *91*, 067003. [CrossRef] [PubMed]
4. Sekine, C.; Uchiumi, T.; Shirotani, I.; Yagi, T. Metal-Insulator Transition in PrRu4P12 with Skutterudite Structure. *Phys. Rev. Lett.* **1997**, *79*, 3218–3221. [CrossRef]
5. Suderow, H.; Vieira, S.; Strand, J.D.; Bud'ko, S.; Canfield, P.C. Very-low-temperature tunneling spectroscopy in the heavy-fermion superconductor PrOs4Sb12. *Phys. Rev. B* **2004**, *69*, 060504. [CrossRef]
6. Zhang, J.L.; Pang, G.M.; Jiao, L.; Nicklas, M.; Chen, Y.; Weng, Z.F.; Smidman, M.; Schnelle, W.; Leithe-Jasper, A.; Maisuradze, A.; et al. Weak interband-coupling superconductivity in the filled skutterudite LaPt4Ge12. *Phys. Rev. B* **2015**, *92*, 220503. [CrossRef]
7. Raza, Z.; Errea, I.; Oganov, A.R.; Saitta, A.M. Novel superconducting skutterudite-type phosphorus nitride at high pressure from first-principles calculations. *Sci. Rep.* **2014**, *4*, 5889. [CrossRef]
8. Kawamura, Y.; Deminami, S.; Salamakha, L.; Sidorenko, A.; Heinrich, P.; Michor, H.; Bauer, E.; Sekine, C. Filled skutterudite superconductor CaOs4P12 prepared by high-pressure synthesis. *Phys. Rev. B* **2018**, *98*, 024513. [CrossRef]
9. Izawa, K.; Nakajima, Y.; Goryo, J.; Matsuda, Y.; Osaki, S.; Sugawara, H.; Sato, H.; Thalmeier, P.; Maki, K. Multiple Superconducting Phases in New Heavy Fermion Superconductor PrOs4Sb12. *Phys. Rev. Lett.* **2003**, *90*, 117001. [CrossRef]
10. Gumeniuk, R.; Schnelle, W.; Rosner, H.; Nicklas, M.; Leithe-Jasper, A.; Grin, Y. Superconductivity in the Platinum Germanides MPt4Ge12 (M=Rare-Earth or Alkaline-Earth Metal) with Filled Skutterudite Structure. *Phys. Rev. Lett.* **2008**, *100*, 017002. [CrossRef]
11. Toda, M.; Sugawara, H.; Magishi, K.; Saito, T.; Koyama, K.; Aoki, Y.; Sato, H. Electrical, Magnetic and NMR Studies of Ge-Based Filled Skutterudites RPt4Ge12 (R=La, Ce, Pr, Nd). *J. Phys. Soc. Jpn.* **2008**, *77*, 124702. [CrossRef]
12. Bauer, E.; Grytsiv, A.; Chen, X.-Q.; Melnychenko-Koblyuk, N.; Hilscher, G.; Kaldarar, H.; Michor, H.; Royanian, E.; Giester, G.; Rotter, M.; et al. Superconductivity in Novel Ge-Based Skutterudites: SrBaPt4Ge12. *Phys. Rev. Lett.* **2007**, *99*, 217001. [CrossRef] [PubMed]
13. Kanetake, F.; Mukuda, H.; Kitaoka, Y.; Magishi, K.; Sugawara, H.; M. Itoh, K.; E. Haller, E. Superconducting Characteristics of Filled Skutterudites LaPt4Ge12 and PrPt4Ge12: 73Ge-NQR/NMR Studies. *J. Phys. Soc. Jpn.* **2010**, *79*, 063702. [CrossRef]
14. Sharath Chandra, L.S.; Chattopadhyay, M.K.; Roy, S.B.; Pandey, S.K. Thermal properties and electronic structure of superconducting germanide skutterudites and: A multi-band perspective. *Philos. Mag.* **2016**, *96*, 2161–2175. [CrossRef]
15. Sharath Chandra, L.S.; Chattopadhyay, M.K.; Roy, S.B. Critical current density and vortex pinning in the two gap superconductor PrPt4Ge12. *Supercond. Sci. Technol.* **2012**, *25*, 105009. [CrossRef]
16. Wang, J.; Shi, Z.X.; Lv, H.; Tamegai, T. Effect of two-gap structure on flux pinning in MgB2. *Phys. C Supercond. Its Appl.* **2006**, *445–448*, 462–465. [CrossRef]
17. Giubileo, F.; Roditchev, D.; Sacks, W.; Lamy, R.; Thanh, D.X.; Klein, J.; Miraglia, S.; Fruchart, D.; Marcus, J.; Monod, P. Two-Gap State Density inMgB2: A True Bulk Property Or A Proximity Effect? *Phys. Rev. Lett.* **2001**, *87*, 177008. [CrossRef]
18. Nagamatsu, J.; Nakagawa, N.; Muranaka, T.; Zenitani, Y.; Akimitsu, J. Superconductivity at 39 K in magnesium diboride. *Nature* **2001**, *410*, 63–64. [CrossRef]
19. Kohen, A.; Giubileo, F.; Proslier, T.; Bobba, F.; Cucolo, A.M.; Sacks, W.; Noat, Y.; Troianovski, A.; Roditchev, D. Two regimes in the magnetic field response of superconducting MgB2. *Eur. Phys. J. B* **2007**, *57*, 21–25. [CrossRef]

20. Zhang, J.; MacLaughlin, D.E.; Hillier, A.D.; Ding, Z.F.; Huang, K.; Maple, M.B.; Shu, L. Broken time-reversal symmetry in superconducting Pr1-xCexPt4Ge12. *Phys. Rev. B* **2015**, *91*, 104523. [CrossRef]
21. Maisuradze, A.; Schnelle, W.; Khasanov, R.; Gumeniuk, R.; Nicklas, M.; Rosner, H.; Leithe-Jasper, A.; Grin, Y.; Amato, A.; Thalmeier, P. Evidence for time-reversal symmetry breaking in superconducting PrPt4Ge12. *Phys. Rev. B* **2010**, *82*, 024524. [CrossRef]
22. Zhang, J.; Ding, Z.F.; Huang, K.; Tan, C.; Hillier, A.D.; Biswas, P.K.; MacLaughlin, D.E.; Shu, L. Broken time-reversal symmetry in superconducting Pr1-xLaxPt4Ge12. *Phys. Rev. B* **2019**, *100*, 024508. [CrossRef]
23. Zang, J.-W.; Zhang, J.; Zhu, Z.-H.; Ding, Z.-F.; Huang, K.; Peng, X.-R.; Hillier, A.D.; Shu, L. Broken Time-Reversal Symmetry in Superconducting Partially Filled Skutterudite PrPt4Ge12. *Chin. Phys. Lett.* **2019**, *36*, 107402. [CrossRef]
24. Pfau, H.; Nicklas, M.; Stockert, U.; Gumeniuk, R.; Schnelle, W.; Leithe-Jasper, A.; Grin, Y.; Steglich, F. Superconducting gap structure of the skutterudite LaPt4Ge12 probed by specific heat and thermal transport. *Phys. Rev. B* **2016**, *94*, 054523. [CrossRef]
25. Bardeen, J.; Cooper, L.N.; Schrieffer, J.R. Theory of Superconductivity. *Phys. Rev.* **1957**, *108*, 1175–1204. [CrossRef]
26. Bergk, B.; Klotz, J.; Förster, T.; Gumeniuk, R.; Leithe-Jasper, A.; Lorenz, V.; Schnelle, W.; Nicklas, M.; Rosner, H.; Grin, Y.; et al. Fermi surface studies of the skutterudite superconductors LaPt4Ge12 and PrPt4Ge12. *Phys. Rev. B* **2019**, *99*, 245115. [CrossRef]
27. Huang, K.; Shu, L.; Lum, I.K.; White, B.D.; Janoschek, M.; Yazici, D.; Hamlin, J.J.; Zocco, D.A.; Ho, P.-C.; Baumbach, R.E.; et al. Probing the superconductivity of PrPt4Ge12 through Ce substitution. *Phys. Rev. B* **2014**, *89*, 035145. [CrossRef]
28. Tinkham, M. *Introduction to Superconductivity*, 2nd ed.; Dover Books on Physics; Dover Publications: Mineola, NY, USA, 2004; ISBN 978-0-486-43503-9.
29. Chandra, L.S.S.; Chattopadhyay, M.K. Magnetic properties in the vortex state of Pr1-xNdxPt4Ge12 and PrPt3.88Fe0.12Ge12 superconductors. *Phys. C Supercond. Its Appl.* **2018**, *546*, 50–54. [CrossRef]
30. Maisuradze, A.; Nicklas, M.; Gumeniuk, R.; Baines, C.; Schnelle, W.; Rosner, H.; Leithe-Jasper, A.; Grin, Y.; Khasanov, R. Superfluid Density and Energy Gap Function of Superconducting PrPt 4 Ge 12. *Phys. Rev. Lett.* **2009**, *103*, 147002. [CrossRef]
31. Singh, Y.P.; Adhikari, R.B.; Zhang, S.; Huang, K.; Yazici, D.; Jeon, I.; Maple, M.B.; Dzero, M.; Almasan, C.C. Multiband superconductivity in the correlated electron filled skutterudite system Pr(1-x)Ce{x}Pt4Ge. *Phys. Rev. B* **2016**, *94*, 144502. [CrossRef]
32. Romano, P.; Avitabile, F.; Shu, L.; Zhang, J.; Nigro, A.; Leo, A.; Grimaldi, G.; Giubileo, F. Low temperature point contact spectroscopy and transport measurements on filled skutterudite compounds. In *Proceedings of the 2019 IEEE 5th International Workshop on Metrology for AeroSpace (MetroAeroSpace)*; Torino, Italy, 19–21 June 2019, pp. 573–578.
33. Huang, K.; Yazici, D.; White, B.D.; Jeon, I.; Breindel, A.J.; Pouse, N.; Maple, M.B. Superconducting and normal state properties of the systems La{1-x}MxPt4Ge12 (M = Ce, Th). *Phys. Rev. B* **2016**, *94*, 094501. [CrossRef]
34. Jeon, I.; Huang, K.; Yazici, D.; Kanchanavatee, N.; White, B.D.; Ho, P.-C.; Jang, S.; Pouse, N.; Maple, M.B. Investigation of superconducting and normal-state properties of the filled-skutterudite system PrPt4Ge(12-x)Sb{x}. *Phys. Rev. B* **2016**, *93*, 104507. [CrossRef]
35. Helfand, E.; Werthamer, N.R. Temperature and Purity Dependence of the Superconducting Critical Field, H c 2. II. *Phys. Rev.* **1966**, *147*, 288–294. [CrossRef]
36. Helfand, E.; Werthamer, N.R. Temperature and Purity Dependence of the Superconducting Critical Field, H c 2. *Phys. Rev. Lett.* **1964**, *13*, 686–688. [CrossRef]
37. Caixeiro, E.S.; González, J.L.; de Mello, E.V.L. Upper critical field H c 2 calculations for the high critical temperature superconductors considering inhomogeneities. *Phys. Rev. B* **2004**, *69*, 024521. [CrossRef]
38. Ślebarski, A.; Zajdel, P.; Fijałkowski, M.; Maśka, M.M.; Witas, P.; Goraus, J.; Fang, Y.; Arnold, D.C.; Maple, M.B. The effective increase in atomic scale disorder by doping and superconductivity in Ca 3 Rh 4 Sn 13. *New J. Phys.* **2018**, *20*, 103020. [CrossRef]
39. Chandra, L.S.S.; Chattopadhyay, M.K.; Roy, S.B. Evidence for two superconducting gaps in the unconventional superconductor PrPt 4 Ge 12. *Philos. Mag.* **2012**, *92*, 3866–3881. [CrossRef]
40. Matsushita, T.; Fujiyoshi, T.; Toko, K.; Yamafuji, K. Flux creep and irreversibility line in high-temperature oxide superconductors. *Appl. Phys. Lett.* **1990**, *56*, 2039–2041. [CrossRef]

41. Yeshurun, Y.; Malozemoff, A.P. Giant Flux Creep and Irreversibility in an Y-Ba-Cu-O Crystal: An Alternative to the Superconducting-Glass Model. *Phys. Rev. Lett.* **1988**, *60*, 2202–2205. [CrossRef]
42. Prando, G.; Carretta, P.; De Renzi, R.; Sanna, S.; Palenzona, A.; Putti, M.; Tropeano, M. Vortex dynamics and irreversibility line in optimally doped $SmFeAsO_{0.8}F_{0.2}$ from ac susceptibility and magnetization measurements. *Phys. Rev. B* **2011**, *83*, 174514. [CrossRef]
43. Shen, B.; Cheng, P.; Wang, Z.; Fang, L.; Ren, C.; Shan, L.; Wen, H.-H. Flux dynamics and vortex phase diagram in $Ba(Fe_{1-x}Co_x)_2As_2$ single crystals revealed by magnetization and its relaxation. *Phys. Rev. B* **2010**, *81*, 014503. [CrossRef]
44. Ding, S.Y.; Wang, G.Q.; Yao, X.X.; Peng, H.T.; Peng, Q.Y.; Zhou, S.H. Magnetic relaxation and the flux diffusion barrier for $TlSr_2Ca_2Cu_3O_y$ doped with Pb and Ba determined by complex ac susceptibility measurements. *Phys. Rev. B* **1995**, *51*, 9107–9110. [CrossRef] [PubMed]
45. Gümbel, A.; Eckert, J.; Fuchs, G.; Nenkov, K.; Müller, K.-H.; Schultz, L. Improved superconducting properties in nanocrystalline bulk MgB2. *Appl. Phys. Lett.* **2002**, *80*, 2725–2727. [CrossRef]
46. Miura, M.; Maiorov, B.; Balakirev, F.F.; Kato, T.; Sato, M.; Takagi, Y.; Izumi, T.; Civale, L. Upward shift of the vortex solid phase in high-temperature-superconducting wires through high density nanoparticle addition. *Sci. Rep.* **2016**, *6*, 20436. [CrossRef] [PubMed]
47. Blatter, G.; Feigel'man, M.V.; Geshkenbein, V.B.; Larkin, A.I.; Vinokur, V.M. Vortices in high-temperature superconductors. *Rev. Mod. Phys.* **1994**, *66*, 1125–1388. [CrossRef]
48. Palstra, T.T.M.; Batlogg, B.; van Dover, R.B.; Schneemeyer, L.F.; Waszczak, J.V. Dissipative flux motion in high-temperature superconductors. *Phys. Rev. B* **1990**, *41*, 6621–6632. [CrossRef]
49. Cirillo, C.; Guarino, A.; Nigro, A.; Attanasio, C. Critical currents and pinning forces in $Nd_{2-x}Ce_xCuO_{4-\delta}$ thin films. *Phys. Rev. B* **2009**, *79*, 144524. [CrossRef]
50. Chin, C.C.; Morishita, T. The transport properties of YBa2Cu3O7−χ thin films. *Phys. C Supercond.* **1993**, *207*, 37–43. [CrossRef]
51. Guarino, A.; Leo, A.; Grimaldi, G.; Martucciello, N.; Dean, C.; Kunchur, M.N.; Pace, S.; Nigro, A. Pinning mechanism in electron-doped HTS NdCeCuO epitaxial films. *Supercond. Sci. Technol.* **2014**, *27*, 124011. [CrossRef]
52. Duif, A.M.; Jansen, A.G.M.; Wyder, P. Point-contact spectroscopy. *J. Phys. Condens. Matter* **1989**, *1*, 3157–3189. [CrossRef]
53. Goll, G. Point-Contact Spectroscopy on Conventional and Unconventional Superconductors. In *Advances in Solid State Physics*; Kramer, B., Ed.; Springer: Berlin/Heidelberg, Germany, 2006; pp. 213–225, ISBN 978-3-540-32430-0.
54. Giubileo, F.; Romeo, F.; Di Bartolomeo, A.; Mizuguchi, Y.; Romano, P. Probing unconventional pairing in LaO0.5F0.5BiS2 layered superconductor by point contact spectroscopy. *J. Phys. Chem. Solids* **2018**, *118*, 192–199. [CrossRef]
55. Zimmermann, U.; Dikin, D.; Kuhlmann, M.; Lamprecht, H.; Keck, K.; Wolf, T. Point—Contact spectroscopy on BSCCO—And YBCO—Break—Junctions. *Phys. B Condens. Matter* **1994**, *194–169*, 1707–1708. [CrossRef]
56. Deutscher, G. Point Contact Spectroscopy in the High Tc Oxides. In *Phase Separation in Cuprate Superconductors*; Sigmund, E., Müller, K.A., Eds.; Springer: Berlin/Heidelberg, Germany, 1994; pp. 26–36.
57. Giubileo, F.; Piano, S.; Scarfato, A.; Bobba, F.; Di Bartolomeo, A.; Cucolo, A.M. A tunneling spectroscopy study of the pairing symmetry in the electron-doped Pr1−xLaCexCuO4−y. *J. Phys. Condens. Matter* **2010**, *22*, 045702. [CrossRef]
58. Giubileo, F.; Piano, S.; Scarfato, A.; Bobba, F.; Di Bartolomeo, A.; Cucolo, A.M. Study of the pairing symmetry in the electron-doped cuprate Pr1-xLaCexCuO4-y by tunneling spectroscopy. *Phys. C Supercond.* **2010**, *470*, 922–925. [CrossRef]
59. Mass, N.; Ilzycer, D.; Deutscher, G.; Desgardin, G.; Monot, I.; Weger, M. Sharp gap edge and determination of the fermi velocity in Y1Ba2Cu3O7−δ by point contact spectroscopy. *J. Supercond.* **1992**, *5*, 191–194. [CrossRef]
60. Bugoslavsky, Y.; Miyoshi, Y.; Perkins, G.K.; Berenov, A.V.; Lockman, Z.; MacManus-Driscoll, J.L.; Cohen, L.F.; Caplin, A.D.; Zhai, H.Y.; Paranthaman, M.P.; et al. Structure of the superconducting gap in MgB2 from point-contact spectroscopy. *Supercond. Sci. Technol.* **2002**, *15*, 526–532. [CrossRef]
61. Giubileo, F.; Aprili, M.; Bobba, F.; Piano, S.; Scarfato, A.; Cucolo, A.M. Subharmonic gap structures and Josephson effect in MgB2/Nb microconstrictions. *Phys. Rev. B* **2005**, *72*, 174518. [CrossRef]

62. Gonnelli, R.S.; Daghero, D.; Calzolari, A.; Ummarino, G.A.; Dellarocca, V.; Stepanov, V.A.; Kazakov, S.M.; Karpinski, J.; Portesi, C.; Monticone, E.; et al. Point-contact spectroscopy in MgB2: From fundamental physics to thin-film characterization. *Supercond. Sci. Technol.* **2004**, *17*, S93. [CrossRef]
63. Giubileo, F.; Bobba, F.; Scarfato, A.; Piano, S.; Aprili, M.; Cucolo, A.M. Temperature evolution of subharmonic gap structures in MgB2/Nb point-contacts. *Phys. C Supercond. Its Appl.* **2007**, *460–462*, 587–588. [CrossRef]
64. Szabó, P.; Samuely, P.; Pribulová, Z.; Angst, M.; Bud'ko, S.; Canfield, P.C.; Marcus, J. Point-contact spectroscopy of Al- and C-doped MgB2: Superconducting energy gaps and scattering studies. *Phys. Rev. B* **2007**, *75*, 144507. [CrossRef]
65. Piano, S.; Bobba, F.; Giubileo, F.; Cucolo, A.M.; Gombos, M.; Vecchione, A. Pairing state in the ruthenocuprate superconductor RuSr2GdCu2O8: A point-contact Andreev reflection spectroscopy study. *Phys. Rev. B* **2006**, *73*, 064514. [CrossRef]
66. Daghero, D.; Gonnelli, R.S. Probing multiband superconductivity by point-contact spectroscopy. *Supercond. Sci. Technol.* **2010**, *23*, 043001. [CrossRef]
67. Fogelström, M.; Park, W.K.; Greene, L.H.; Goll, G.; Graf, M.J. Point-contact spectroscopy in heavy-fermion superconductors. *Phys. Rev. B* **2010**, *82*, 014527. [CrossRef]
68. Parab, P.; Singh, D.; Haram, S.; Singh, R.P.; Bose, S. Point contact Andreev reflection studies of a non-centro symmetric superconductor Re6Zr. *Sci. Rep.* **2019**, *9*, 2498. [CrossRef] [PubMed]
69. Yonezawa, S. Nematic Superconductivity in Doped Bi2Se3 Topological Superconductors. *Condens. Matter* **2018**, *4*, 2. [CrossRef]
70. Soulen, R.J.; Byers, J.M.; Osofsky, M.S.; Nadgorny, B.; Ambrose, T.; Cheng, S.F.; Broussard, P.R.; Tanaka, C.T.; Nowak, J.; Moodera, J.S.; et al. Measuring the Spin Polarization of a Metal with a Superconducting Point Contact. *Science* **1998**, *282*, 85. [CrossRef]
71. Romeo, F.; Giubileo, F.; Citro, R.; Di Bartolomeo, A.; Attanasio, C.; Cirillo, C.; Polcari, A.; Romano, P. Resonant Andreev Spectroscopy in normal-Metal/thin-Ferromagnet/Superconductor Device: Theory and Application. *Sci. Rep.* **2015**, *5*, 17544. [CrossRef]
72. de Jong, M.J.M.; Beenakker, C.W.J. Andreev Reflection in Ferromagnet-Superconductor Junctions. *Phys. Rev. Lett.* **1995**, *74*, 1657–1660. [CrossRef]
73. Giubileo, F.; Romeo, F.; Citro, R.; Di Bartolomeo, A.; Attanasio, C.; Cirillo, C.; Polcari, A.; Romano, P. Point contact Andreev reflection spectroscopy on ferromagnet/superconductor bilayers. *Phys. C Supercond. Its Appl.* **2014**, *503*, 158–161. [CrossRef]
74. Upadhyay, S.K.; Palanisami, A.; Louie, R.N.; Buhrman, R.A. Probing Ferromagnets with Andreev Reflection. *Phys. Rev. Lett.* **1998**, *81*, 3247–3250. [CrossRef]
75. Catapano, M.; Romeo, F.; Citro, R.; Giubileo, F. Generalized Blonder-Tinkham-Klapwijk theory and conductance spectra with particle-hole mixing interface potential. *Eur. Phys. J. B* **2015**, *88*, 329. [CrossRef]
76. Andreev, A.F. The Thermal Conductivity of the Intermediate State in Superconductors. *J. Exp. Theor. Phys.* **1964**, *19*, 1228.
77. Deutscher, G. Andreev–Saint-James reflections: A probe of cuprate superconductors. *Rev. Mod. Phys.* **2005**, *77*, 109–135. [CrossRef]
78. Blonder, G.E.; Tinkham, M.; Klapwijk, T.M. Transition from metallic to tunneling regimes in superconducting microconstrictions: Excess current, charge imbalance, and supercurrent conversion. *Phys. Rev. B* **1982**, *25*, 4515–4532. [CrossRef]
79. Kashiwaya, S.; Tanaka, Y. Tunnelling effects on surface bound states in unconventional superconductors. *Rep. Prog. Phys.* **2000**, *63*, 1641–1724. [CrossRef]
80. Hu, C.-R. Midgap surface states as a novel signature for d-wave superconductivity. *Phys. Rev. Lett.* **1994**, *72*, 1526–1529. [CrossRef]
81. Liu, C.S.; Wu, W.C. Theory of point-contact spectroscopy in electron-doped cuprate superconductors. *Phys. Rev. B* **2007**, *76*, 220504. [CrossRef]
82. Piano, S.; Bobba, F.; Giubileo, F.; Vecchione, A.; Cucolo, A.M. Point-contact spectroscopy on RuSr2GdCu2O8. *J. Phys. Chem. Solids* **2006**, *67*, 384–386. [CrossRef]
83. Giubileo, F.; Jossa, A.; Bobba, F.; Akimenko, A.I.; Cucolo, A.M. Temperature dependence of the YBa2Cu3O7 energy gap in differently oriented tunnel junctions. *Eur. Phys. J. B* **2001**, *24*, 305–308. [CrossRef]

84. Giubileo, F.; Jossa, A.; Bobba, F.; Akimenko, A.I.; Malandrino, G.; Perdicaro, L.M.S.; Fragala, I.L.; Cucolo, A.M. Study of Andreev reflections in Tl2Ba2CaCu2O8/Ag interfaces. *Phys. C Supercond.* **2002**, *367*, 170–173. [CrossRef]
85. Giubileo, F.; Akimenko, A.I.; Bobba, F.; Cucolo, A.M. Tunneling spectroscopy and surface states in YBa2Cu3O7 and Tl2Ba2CaCu2O8 break junctions. *Phys. C Supercond. Its Appl.* **2001**, *364–365*, 626–628. [CrossRef]
86. Wysokiński, M.M. Thermoelectric Effect in the Normal Conductor-Superconductor Junction: A BTK Approach. *Acta Phys. Pol. A* **2012**, *122*, 758–764. [CrossRef]
87. Zhang, J.L.; Chen, Y.; Jiao, L.; Gumeniuk, R.; Nicklas, M.; Chen, Y.H.; Yang, L.; Fu, B.H.; Schnelle, W.; Rosner, H.; et al. Multiband superconductivity in PrPt4Ge12 single crystals. *Phys. Rev. B* **2013**, *87*, 064502. [CrossRef]
88. Dynes, R.C.; Narayanamurti, V.; Garno, J.P. Direct Measurement of Quasiparticle-Lifetime Broadening in a Strong-Coupled Superconductor. *Phys. Rev. Lett.* **1978**, *41*, 1509–1512. [CrossRef]
89. Shan, L.; Tao, H.J.; Gao, H.; Li, Z.Z.; Ren, Z.A.; Che, G.C.; Wen, H.H. s-wave pairing in MgCNi$_3$ revealed by point contact tunneling. *Phys. Rev. B* **2003**, *68*, 144510. [CrossRef]
90. Lee, P.A. Effect of Noise on the Current-Voltage Characteristics of a Josephson Junction. *J. Appl. Phys.* **1971**, *42*, 325–334. [CrossRef]

© 2020 by the authors. Licensee MDPI, Basel, Switzerland. This article is an open access article distributed under the terms and conditions of the Creative Commons Attribution (CC BY) license (http://creativecommons.org/licenses/by/4.0/).

Article

# Current-Resistance Effects Inducing Nonlinear Fluctuation Mechanisms in Granular Aluminum Oxide Nanowires

Carlo Barone [1,2,3,*], Hannes Rotzinger [4,5], Jan Nicolas Voss [4], Costantino Mauro [1], Yannick Schön [4], Alexey V. Ustinov [4,6,7] and Sergio Pagano [1,2,3]

1. Dipartimento di Fisica "E.R. Caianiello", Università degli Studi di Salerno, I-84084 Fisciano, Salerno, Italy; cmauro@unisa.it (C.M.); spagano@unisa.it (S.P.)
2. CNR-SPIN Salerno, c/o Università degli Studi di Salerno, I-84084 Fisciano, Salerno, Italy
3. INFN Gruppo Collegato di Salerno, c/o Università degli Studi di Salerno, I-84084 Fisciano, Salerno, Italy
4. Physikalisches Institut, Karlsruher Institut für Technologie, 76131 Karlsruhe, Germany; rotzinger@kit.edu (H.R.); jan.voss@kit.edu (J.N.V.); y.schoen@kit.edu (Y.S.); alexey.ustinov@kit.edu (A.V.U.)
5. Institut für Quantenmaterialien und Technologien (IQMT), Karlsruher Institut für Technologie, 76131 Karlsruhe, Germany
6. National University of Science and Technology MISIS, 119049 Moscow, Russia
7. Russian Quantum Center, Skolkovo, 143025 Moscow, Russia
* Correspondence: cbarone@unisa.it; Tel.: +39-089-968212

Received: 17 February 2020; Accepted: 11 March 2020; Published: 14 March 2020

**Abstract:** The unusual superconducting properties of granular aluminum oxide have been recently investigated for application in quantum circuits. However, the intrinsic irregular structure of this material requires a good understanding of the transport mechanisms and, in particular, the effect of disorder, especially when patterned at the nanoscale level. In view of these aspects, electric transport and voltage fluctuations have been investigated on thin-film based granular aluminum oxide nanowires, in the normal state and at temperatures between 8 and 300 K. The nonlinear resistivity and two-level tunneling fluctuators have been observed. Regarding the nature of the noise processes, the experimental findings give a clear indication in favor of a dynamic random resistor network model, rather than the possible existence of a local ordering of magnetic origin. The identification of the charge carrier fluctuations in the normal state of granular aluminum oxide nanowires is very useful for improving the fabrication process and, therefore, reducing the possible sources of decoherence in the superconducting state, where quantum technologies that are based on these nanostructures should work.

**Keywords:** quantum electronics; noise spectroscopy; granular aluminum oxide; superconducting nanowires; current-resistance effects

## 1. Introduction

Granular superconductors have attracted great interest for their rich phase diagram and for practical advantages, such as increased critical field [1], critical temperature [2,3], and kinetic inductance [4]. In particular, granular aluminum oxide ($AlO_x$) has recently proven to play a prominent role in quantum electronics and in quantum bit (qubit) design due to its low electric loss and high kinetic inductance [5]. As a matter of fact, the kinetic inductance of an $AlO_x$ wire is proportional to its normal state resistance and, therefore, can be orders of magnitude higher than its geometric inductance [6]. Such a super-inductance could be very useful for the realization of a novel type of superconducting quantum circuit with an impedance above the vacuum impedance, and it could easily be constructed from $AlO_x$ wires [5,7]. The robustness of the material and the simplicity of fabrication make them a promising candidate to replace conventional Josephson tunnel junction arrays. The main differences with Josephson junctions are observed when AlO$_x$ is patterned in the form of a nanowire. The nanoscale structure can be advantageous in terms of electric loss, and in the limit of a short constriction can even be used as a non-linear element for quantum circuit design [8].

Although granular aluminum seems to be a very promising alternative material for qubit architecture, it has a disordered nature, due to a large amount of amorphous aluminum oxide. Previous published structural and morphological studies suggest that the granularity on the size of grains, connectedness, and the intergrain spacing depend on the preparation method [9], which results in films with a disorder distributed on a scale that ranged from few units to few tens of nanometers [10,11]. These types of granular films have different electric transport mechanisms, whose understanding is important, especially for systems realized at the nanoscale level. In this respect, noise spectroscopy has already been used for the sensitive investigation of low-dimensional superconducting films [12] and two-dimensional (2D) oxide interfaces [13,14], allowing for a better understanding of the charge carriers kinetic processes. Moreover, from a technological point of view, the integration of nanowire-based elements with standard circuit processing can be seriously limited by the increase of the 1/f electric noise. Therefore, such a noise component has to be carefully studied in order to have a deep comprehension of the nature of fluctuation mechanisms.

In view of all these considerations, DC electric and magneto-transport measurements, as well as voltage-noise investigations, have been performed on AlO$_x$ nanowires. The observed phenomenology, although related to the normal state, deserves to be understood in details, since it could also have an impact on the superconducting state, where qubit-based technology operates.

## 2. Materials and Methods

All of the investigated wires, as well as the surrounding structures, were made from a single layer of oxidized aluminum. As a first step, a 20 nm thick layer of disordered oxidized (granular) aluminum was grown by reactive sputter deposition on a c-plane sapphire substrate in a controlled oxygen atmosphere, thus allowing for a wide range of sheet resistances. The mean sheet resistance of the AlO$_x$ film was determined to be about 2.2 kΩ. However, the sheet resistance can vary up to 50% for different film areas across a 20 mm by 20 mm chip due to inhomogeneities that are related to the sputtering process.

An electron beam lithography process was used to define the wire structures, while using a bilayer of hydrogen silsesquioxane (HSQ) and polymethylmethacrylate (PMMA) resist. Here, the high resolution of the HSQ and the ability to use an organic solvent to lift off the PMMA are beneficial for a clean interface and also to contact the AlO$_x$ structures. The PMMA serves as a sacrificial layer, it, however, also influences (limits) the achievable nanowire resolution. Two anisotropic dry etch (RIE) steps were performed to transfer the structures into the AlO$_x$ layer after the resist definition: oxygen RIE for the PMMA, and argon/chlorine RIE for the AlO$_x$.

The left panel of Figure 1 shows a typical scanning electron microscope image of another nanowire sample that was fabricated with similar process conditions. Here, the wires have a thickness of 20 nm and a width of few tens of nanometers, in the order of 60 nm. It has been found that small variations in the process parameters can lead to a significant spread in the wire width and resolution of the above described bilayer process. We suspect that the limited temperature stability of the PMMA resist might be responsible for this and, however, further optimizations may be necessary for a better reproducibility of the nanowire shape. Several devices were measured, each of them made by two 150 µm × 150 µm contact pads connected by a narrow stripline, as shown in the right panel of Figure 1. Nanowires of different lengths are fabricated in the middle of each stripline. Devices, named "a", "b", "g", and "h" are the nanowires of length ($W_L$) 250, 500, 750, and 1000 nm, respectively. Devices named "i", instead, are microstrips 5 µm-long and, nominally, 100 nm-wide.

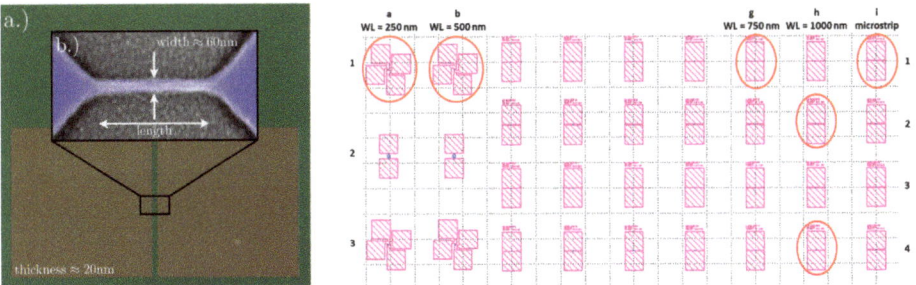

**Figure 1.** (Left panel) Colorized optical picture of a device investigated. The colorized scanning electron microscope image of a typical nanowire is shown in the enlargement. The wire is 20 nm thick and it has a typical width up to 60 nm. (Right panel) Layout of the chip. The measured nanowire samples are evidenced by the circles. The contacts are made by 50 µm thick with aluminum wire by ultrasonic bonding.

A simple two-probe measurement method was employed, since all of the measured resistances were much higher than that of the contact wires to investigate the samples transport and noise properties. Additionally, the wires and contacts contribution to the overall electric noise was verified to be negligible [15]. The value of resistance measured involves the whole stripline, not only the submicron part. This implies that, for devices "a", "b", "g", and "h", there are additionally 10 squares contributions to consider for the total resistance. Electric transport measurements were performed in a temperature stabilized closed-cycle refrigerator, between 300 and 8 K. A dipole electromagnet, type 3470 from GMW Associates, generated an external magnetic field (maximum value of 1500 Gauss). The field is applied in the plane of the sample and parallel to the nanowire length which coincides with the bias current direction. Low-noise DC and AC electronic bias and readout have been used [15,16], thus giving very low statistical errors on the experimental data points (in the following plots, the error bars are usually smaller than the points dimension). The range of explored bias currents depends on the sample resistance, being limited by the overall voltage drop that is available at the current source (100 V).

## 3. Results

### 3.1. DC Electrical Transport Measurements

Figure 2 shows the temperature dependence of the resistance of all the investigated devices. Differently from the previously analyzed case of AlO$_x$ thin films [17], the nanowires are characterized by a monotonic resistivity decrease by increasing the temperature between 8 and 300 K. This decreasing behavior, which is not unusual in high resistive samples, seems to be more pronounced at low temperatures, although the resistance value does not scale with the wire length, probably due to differences of the average wire width and resistivity across the nanowire devices. By using the microstrip (nominally 100 nm-wide) as a reference, it is possible to estimate the room-temperature resistivity of the nanowires $\rho_{RT} \approx 5.2 \times 10^3$ µΩ cm. For these values of $\rho_{RT}$ (higher than $4 \times 10^3$ µΩ cm), the granular aluminum specimens are characterized by a resistance that rises monotonically as the temperature is reduced, confirming the experimental behavior shown in Figure 2, as reported in literature [18,19]. Conversely, for $\rho_{RT}$ values between $1 \times 10^3$ and $4 \times 10^3$ µΩ cm there is an intermediate regime in which the resistance changes very little with temperature and it shows a logarithmic increase at low temperatures (Kondo regime). This is the case of the previously analyzed AlO$_x$ thin films [17], which, therefore, have a resistivity temperature dependence different from the nanowires studied here. It is also important to underline that the strictly metallic regime is usually characterized by values of $\rho_{RT}$ that are lower than $10^3$ µΩ cm [20].

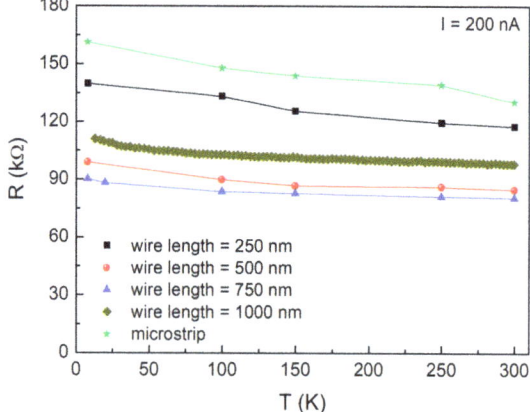

**Figure 2.** Resistance versus temperature plots. The data refer to five investigated devices. The solid lines are obtained by interpolating the experimental points and they are guides for the eyes.

All of the devices exhibit almost linear current voltage characteristics, with a small curvature that can be observed for bias current above few µA. By analyzing in detail the bias current dependence of the static resistance $R$, defined as the ratio $V/I$, the wire resistance shows a tendency to decrease for increasing bias. The repeatability of this effect has been verified in all of the nanostructures analyzed, by performing several current cycles from 0 to 80 µA. Consequently, the reversible resistance change is independently present from the temperature, but is more pronounced at low temperatures, as shown in Figure 3. This has been also observed on manganite compounds and it is known as the negative current-resistance (CR) effect [21–24]. Several mechanisms could be considered to explain the experimental evidence of reversible CR effects in $AlO_x$ nanowires. In analogy with the case of magnetic multilayered structures [25,26], the CR effect could be attributed to a local ordering that is produced by a current-induced local magnetic field. Alternatively, the CR effect could be ascribed to a percolative process between metallic $AlO_x$ clusters that are separated by an insulating matrix [27,28]. In this framework, an important role is played by the tunneling barrier between conducting grains and by the shape of such a barrier, which the applied current can change.

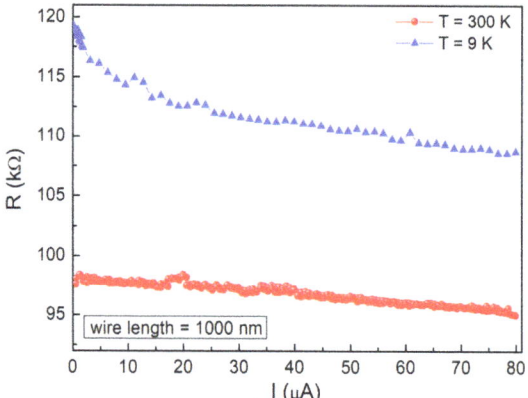

**Figure 3.** Static resistance versus bias current at different temperatures. The data refer to the nanowires 1000 nm-long at $T = 300$ K (red dots) and at $T = 9$ K (blue triangles). The small jumps visible in the traces are reproducible and are, most probably, due to different current paths in the sample.

Overall, DC measurements alone are not able to distinguish the possible mechanism that is responsible for the CR effect. Therefore, more sensitive investigations, such as electric noise spectroscopy, have been performed, in order to acquire additional information.

*3.2. Voltage-Noise Spectral Density Measurements*

The first indication on the nature of the fluctuation processes is obtained by analyzing the frequency composition of the voltage-noise spectral density $S_V$. In Figure 4, typical noise spectral traces are reported for the four nanowires under test at different bias current values and temperatures. The peaks are due to external sources and they should not be considered. The relevant information is in the background curves. $S_V$ is characterized by a frequency dependence that varies on temperature. In particular, the presence of a $1/f$ noise component followed by a constant amplitude spectrum is observed at temperatures down to 150 K (Figure 4a,b). Conversely, below 150 K, Lorentzian components, with a $1/f^2$ dependence of $S_V$, are clearly visible (Figure 4c,d). This behavior is typically associated with physical fluctuation mechanisms that are ascribed to two-level tunneling fluctuators (TLTFs) [29,30]. According to this interpretation, groups of atoms can occupy two configurations; therefore, their energy can be represented in the form of two potential wells that are separated by a barrier. In general, the wells are asymmetric and the atoms can tunnel from one well to the other with a transition rate that is strongly temperature-dependent. By indicating with $\tau$ the minimum relaxation time of such processes, for frequencies $f \ll 1/2\pi\tau$ the main contribution to $S_V$ is given by the $1/f$ noise, while, for frequencies $f \gg 1/2\pi\tau$, the spectral density is dominated by Lorentzian noise. By lowering the temperature, $\tau$ increases and the cut-off frequency, above which the $1/f^2$ noise component dominates, decreases, being visible inside the frequency bandwidth of acquisition (see, for details, all of the low-temperature spectra in Figure 4).

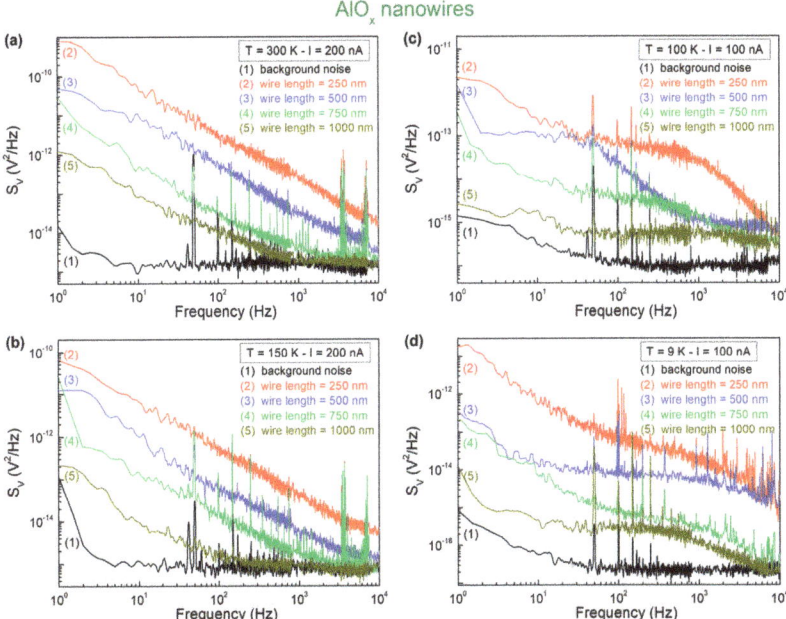

**Figure 4.** Voltage-noise spectra. The frequency dependence of $S_V$ is shown for all of the investigated nanodevices for two bias currents and four different temperatures: 300 K (**a**), 150 K (**b**), 100 K (**c**), and 9 K (**d**). The black trace, which is the lowest spectral trace for each temperature, shows the unbiased noise, which is composed by the instrumental, the external, and the sample Johnson noise.

Spontaneous transitions between the levels of the TLTFs can lead to fluctuations of macroscopic quantities, such as resistance [29]. In the ohmic region, where resistance does not depend on the bias current, resistance fluctuations are characterized by a $S_V$ versus $I^2$ dependence. This means that the overall noise level, being defined as:

$$\text{Noise Level} = \frac{1}{V^2} \int_{f_{min}}^{f_{max}} S_V(f) df, \qquad (1)$$

with $[f_{min}; f_{max}]$ as the frequency bandwidth, should be constant as a function of the bias current. A confirmation of this behavior is found in the plots of Figure 5, where the current dependence of the noise level is shown for three devices at different temperatures, for low levels of the applied bias. In Figure 5, it is also evident a noise level increase when the temperature is reduced below 150 K. This is due to the activation of additional low-temperature noise sources, being identified in the framework of the TLTFs model and evidenced in the spectral traces as Lorentzian components (see Figure 4c,d, for details).

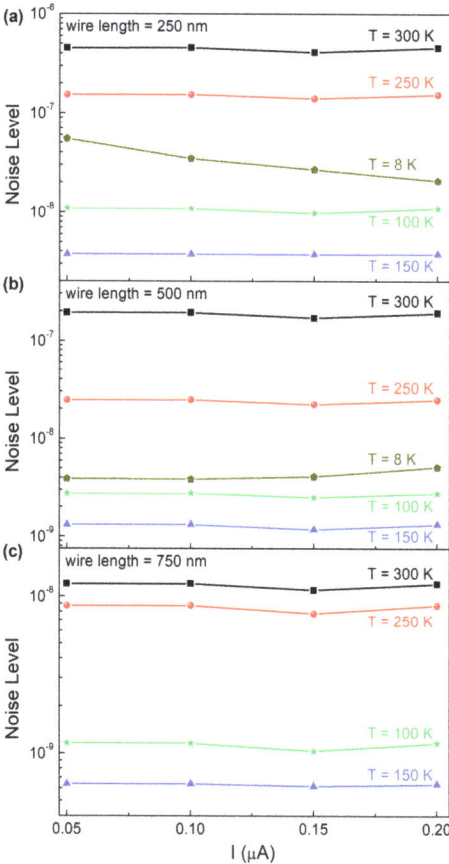

**Figure 5.** Current dependence of the nanodevices noise level in the low-bias region. The noise level dependence on the bias current, as evaluated from Equation (1), is shown for currents up to 200 nA and for devices of different lengths: 250 nm (**a**), 500 nm (**b**), and 750 nm (**c**). The investigated temperature range is from 8 to 300 K.

However, for bias currents where CR effects are present, the noise level also changes. In particular, the data in Figure 6 show a noise level reduction at large levels of the applied bias. This behavior, which is evident both at room temperature and at 9 K (black squares and magenta diamonds in Figure 6, respectively), indicates, therefore, that the local ordering that is attributed to CR effects gives origin to a decrease of noise fluctuators. The decrease of the noise level, both for decreasing temperature and for increasing DC bias current, seems to be incompatible with a Joule heating effect. In fact, Joule heating would imply an increase of the nanowire temperature with the bias current, and this should also result in an increased noise level, since it is enhanced by temperature. Instead, Figure 6 shows clearly that the noise level decreases at larger bias currents.

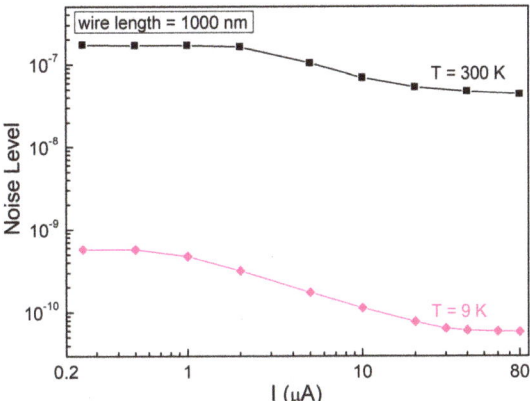

**Figure 6.** Current dependence of the nanodevices noise level in the full-bias region. The overall noise level, as evaluated with Equation (1), is shown as a function of the bias current for the nanowire 1000 nm-long. The temperatures of 300 and 9 K are reported.

The nature of the noise decrease and, consequently, the nature of reversible-type CR phenomena is at this stage unclear, but a better insight could be obtained by looking at its dependence on external parameters, such as external magnetic field or electric field.

## 4. Discussion

As said before, in other materials, it has been found that possible mechanisms producing the current-resistance effects and, at the same time, the noise level reduction could be of magnetic origin or could be due to the percolative process. Whether one of these models can be associated to granular $AlO_x$ nanowires has to be investigated.

Magnetic resistance fluctuations are usually characterized by a noise level increase in the low-temperature region. This type of fluctuation process, which is already found for granular aluminum oxide thin films, is ascribed to Kondo-like conductivity when the noise level, especially at low temperatures, decreases with an external magnetic field of the order of one thousand Gauss [17,31]. In the case of $AlO_x$ nanowires, no magnetic dependence is observed in both DC and AC measurements, even if a noise enhancement is evident by lowering the temperature (for details, see Figure 7). By applying an external magnetic field $H = 1000$ Gauss, the magnitude of the CR effect is unaltered (Figure 7a). Moreover, the normalized $1/f$ noise power ($f \cdot S_V$) does not change with $H$ for all of the bias currents used (Figure 7b). This experimental finding indicates that, contrarily to what observed for the films, in $AlO_x$ nanowires, a local ordering of magnetic origin does not produce the noise reduction and, therefore, does not seem to be responsible of the measured CR effect. The different behavior that was observed between granular aluminum film and nanowires could be related to differences in morphology and grain structure in the two cases, which also show different resistivity, as discussed above.

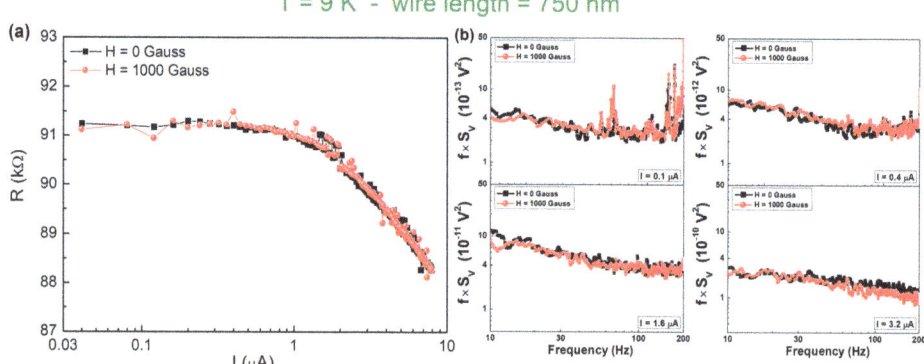

**Figure 7.** Magnetic field behavior of DC and AC data at 9 K. The current dependence of (a) the resistance and of (b) the normalized 1/f noise component of device 750 nm-long is plotted in absence and in presence of a magnetic field of 1000 Gauss (black and red curves, respectively).

Alternative to the magnetic effect, a nonlinear transport regime can also result from a random resistor network (RRN) model and, consequently, percolation processes [32–34]. These conduction mechanisms have been already considered in granular films that are similar to the ones investigated here [9], being realized by reactive sputter deposition and with a grain size in the order of 3–4 nm [5]. In particular, a reasonable description of nonlinear conduction is given by the dynamic random resistor network (DRRN) model, which considers a network that consists of conducting and insulating bonds [35]. For sufficiently low applied electric field across the network, the current flows only through the backbone of the percolating system, so that the conduction is linear. As the applied bias is increased, some of the insulating bonds of the network will experience an electric field exceeding a critical field ($E_c$), above which they become conducting [35]. The macroscopic conduction becomes nonlinear when insulating bonds start to be conducting. This is similar to what is shown in Figure 8a, where the nanowire resistance is plotted versus the local electric field $E$, being computed as the voltage difference divided by the nanowire length. In this framework, the conducting clusters forming the network backbone are separated by insulating regions of very small widths. Through such regions, it is expected that tunneling or hopping conduction will take place, thus providing extra paths for electrons. The appearance of extra parallel conduction channels with the increase in bias, which add to an existing network, does lead to a decrease in the total noise of the network, which is consistent with that observed in Figure 8b.

The noise reduction above the onset of nonlinearity has been already observed in conductor-insulator mixtures, such as the carbon-wax system, and, in terms of the DRRN model, has been explained as due to an increase in the total number of fluctuators or, equivalently, in the system size from the fluctuation point of view [36]. A better display of the nonlinear transport in $AlO_x$ nanowires can be made by computing the negative reversible CR effect, as:

$$CR\ effect\ (\%) = \frac{R(E) - R_0}{R_0}, \qquad (2)$$

where $R(E)$ is the resistance at a fixed electric field and $R_0$ is the resistance value in the linear region. The quantity that is defined with Equation (2) is plotted in Figure 8c as a function of $E$ for three nanodevices of different length at the temperature of 9 K. Here, it is possible to identify a nonlinearity threshold at a critical electric field $E_c \approx 7.2 \times 10^4$ V m$^{-1}$. Similarly, the noise reduction in percentage can be computed as:

$$NR\,(\%) = \frac{NL(E) - NL_0}{NL_0},\qquad(3)$$

where $NL(E)$ is the noise level value at a fixed electric field and $NL_0$ is the noise level value in the linear region. $NR$ is shown in Figure 8d for the same nanodevices of Figure 8c and it confirms the existence of a threshold field. This effect has been well documented at 9 K, and is present also at higher temperatures, see Figure S1 (Supplementary Materials). However, further analysis of the temperature dependence of the high current behavior of the nanowires has not been performed, being beyond the scope of this work, as the main applications of AlO$_x$ nanowires are at cryogenic temperatures. The noise reduction effect is much more evident than the CR effect, revealing a greater sensitivity of the noise spectroscopy with respect to the resistivity measurements. Moreover, the evidence of a saturated noise level at high bias values finds strict analogy with the saturated transport properties that were observed in carbon-wax composites and described in terms of the DRRN theoretical approach [36]. This gives a further indication on the applicability of this model to explain the reversible nonlinear transport regime in AlO$_x$ nanowires.

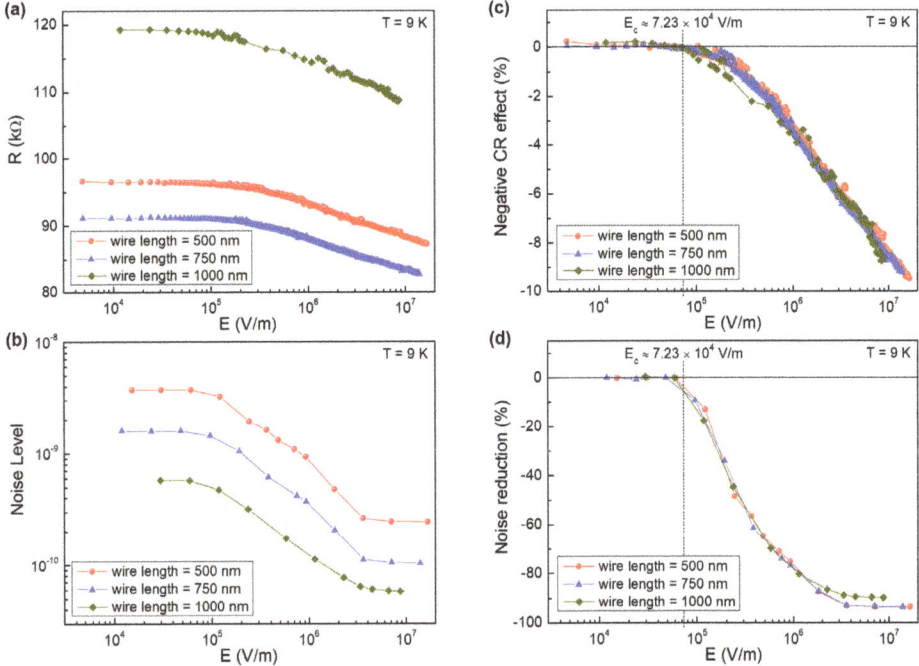

**Figure 8.** Electric field behavior of DC and AC data at 9 K. For the nanowires 500 nm-long (red circles), 750 nm-long (blue triangles), and 1000 nm-long (yellow diamonds), it is shown the electric field dependence of the: (**a**) static resistance, (**b**) noise level evaluated with Equation (1), (**c**) current-resistance effect evaluated with Equation (2), and (**d**) noise reduction evaluated with Equation (3).

Although a nonlinear conducting behavior is expected for metal-dielectric composite nanostructures falling around the percolation threshold [37,38], the strong effect on the magnitude of voltage-noise is a peculiar feature of AlO$_x$ nanowires, not being observed in common nonlinear composites dielectrics. This property of the charge carriers fluctuation mechanisms has a direct impact on the normal state conductance and, as a consequence, on the kinetic inductance of granular aluminum nanodevices, a key requirement for their use in superconducting quantum circuits.

## 5. Conclusions

The electric transport and voltage-noise properties of granular aluminum oxide nanowires have been investigated for nanodevices of different width and length and in a temperature range from 8 to 300 K. Differently from thin films, which show a linear ohmic regime, nanowires are characterized by a resistivity reduction with increasing bias. In cycled devices, the negative resistance change is reversible. In this regime, above a critical electric field, the nonlinear current-voltage characteristics are also associated with a strong noise level reduction, whose amplitude exceeds that observed on DC resistance of more than one order of magnitude. This nonlinear electric transport behavior of the nanowires does not seem to have a magnetic origin. Moreover, the magnetic field does not affect the noise amplitude, contrarily to what found in thin films with lower resistivity and at low temperatures. The nonlinear resistance could be explained, instead, in terms of a dynamic random resistor network model, usually considered as a variant of the standard random percolation mechanism. If a DRRN model describes the physics of the $AlO_x$ nanowires, then it is expected that noise sources can be activated whenever there is an electric field in the material higher than a threshold critical value, and large enough fields can suppress it. In the superconducting state, one could expect that $E$ field is zero inside the nanowire and no noise sources are activated. However, in the presence of RF fields, this is no longer true and the noise sources could play an important role in the dynamics of the circuit attached to these devices. Therefore, the identification and reduction of the charge carrier fluctuations in the normal state, by e.g. improving the fabrication process, could be important for reducing the possible sources of decoherence in the superconducting state.

**Supplementary Materials:** The following are available online at http://www.mdpi.com/2079-4991/10/3/524/s1, Figure S1: Electric field behavior of resistance and noise data at different temperatures.

**Author Contributions:** C.B., H.R., A.V.U. and S.P. conceived and designed the experiments; C.B., C.M. and S.P. performed the experiments; C.B., H.R. and J.N.V. analyzed the data; J.N.V., C.M., Y.S. and A.V.U. contributed materials/analysis tools; C.B., H.R. and S.P. wrote the paper. All authors have read and agreed to the published version of the manuscript.

**Funding:** This research received no external funding.

**Acknowledgments:** The authors would like to thank S. Abate of CNR-SPIN Salerno (Italy) for his technical support. A.V.U. acknowledges partial support from the Ministry of Education and Science of the Russian Federation in the framework of Increase Competitiveness Program of the National University of Science and Technology MISIS (Contract No. K2-2017-081). C.B. and S.P. acknowledge partial support from University of Salerno through grants FARB17PAGAN and FARB18CAVAL, and from INFN through experiment FEEL.

**Conflicts of Interest:** The authors declare no conflict of interest.

## References

1. Abeles, B.; Cohen, R.W.; Stowell, W.R. Critical Magnetic Fields of Granular Superconductors. *Phys. Rev. Lett.* **1967**, *18*, 902–905. [CrossRef]
2. Cohen, R.W.; Abeles, B. Superconductivity in Granular Aluminum Films. *Phys. Rev.* **1968**, *168*, 444–450. [CrossRef]
3. Deutscher, G.; Fenichel, H.; Gershenson, M.; Grünbaum, M.; Ovadyahu, Z. Transition to Zero Dimensionality in Granular Aluminum Superconducting Films. *J. Low Temp. Phys.* **1973**, *10*, 231–243. [CrossRef]
4. Maleeva, N.; Grünhaupt, L.; Klein, T.; Levy-Bertrand, F.; Dupre, O.; Calvo, M.; Valenti, F.; Winkel, P.; Friedrich, F.; Wernsdorfer, W.; et al. Circuit quantum electrodynamics of granular aluminum resonators. *Nat. Commun.* **2018**, *9*, 3889. [CrossRef] [PubMed]
5. Grünhaupt, L.; Spiecker, M.; Gusenkova, D.; Maleeva, N.; Skacel, S.T.; Takmakov, I.; Valenti, F.; Winkel, P.; Rotzinger, H.; Wernsdorfer, W.; et al. Granular aluminium as a superconducting material for high-impedance quantum circuits. *Nat. Mater.* **2019**, *18*, 816–819. [CrossRef] [PubMed]

6. Rotzinger, H.; Skacel, S.T.; Pfirrmann, M.; Voss, J.N.; Münzberg, J.; Probst, S.; Bushev, P.; Weides, M.P.; Ustinov, A.V.; Mooij, J.E. Aluminium-oxide wires for superconducting high kinetic inductance circuits. *Supercond. Sci. Technol.* **2016**, *30*, 25002. [CrossRef]
7. Grünhaupt, L.; Maleeva, N.; Skacel, S.T.; Calvo, M.; Levy-Bertrand, F.; Ustinov, A.V.; Rotzinger, H.; Monfardini, A.; Catelani, G.; Pop, I.M. Loss Mechanisms and Quasiparticle Dynamics in Superconducting Microwave Resonators Made of Thin-Film Granular Aluminum. *Phys. Rev. Lett.* **2018**, *121*, 117001. [CrossRef]
8. Schön, Y.; Voss, J.N.; Wildermuth, M.; Schneider, A.; Skacel, S.T.; Weides, M.P.; Cole, J.H.; Rotzinger, H.; Ustinov, A.V. Rabi oscillations in a superconducting nanowire circuit. *arXiv* **2019**, arXiv:1907.04107. [CrossRef]
9. Yamada, K.; Shinozaki, B.; Kawaguti, T. Weak localization and magnetoconductance in percolative superconducting aluminum films. *Phys. Rev. B* **2004**, *70*, 144503. [CrossRef]
10. Frydman, A.; Naaman, O.; Dynes, R.C. Universal transport in two-dimensional granular superconductors. *Phys. Rev. B* **2002**, *66*, 052509. [CrossRef]
11. Yamada, K.; Shinozaki, B.; Kawaguti, T. Percolation and weak localization in thin discontinuous aluminum films. *Phys. E Low Dimens. Syst. Nanostruct.* **2003**, *18*, 286–287. [CrossRef]
12. Barone, C.; Romeo, F.; Pagano, S.; Adamo, M.; Nappi, C.; Sarnelli, E.; Kurth, F.; Iida, K. Probing transport mechanisms of $BaFe_2As_2$ superconducting films and grain boundary junctions by noise spectroscopy. *Sci. Rep.* **2014**, *4*, 6163. [CrossRef] [PubMed]
13. Barone, C.; Romeo, F.; Pagano, S.; Di Gennaro, E.; Miletto Granozio, F.; Pallecchi, I.; Marrè, D.; Scotti di Uccio, U. Carrier-number fluctuations in the 2-dimensional electron gas at the $LaAlO_3/SrTiO_3$ interface. *Appl. Phys. Lett.* **2013**, *103*, 231601. [CrossRef]
14. Barone, C.; Mauro, C.; Sambri, A.; Scotti di Uccio, U.; Pagano, S. Conductivity response of amorphous oxide interfaces to pulsed light illumination. *Nanotechnology* **2019**, *30*, 254005. [CrossRef]
15. Barone, C.; Galdi, A.; Pagano, S.; Quaranta, O.; Méchin, L.; Routoure, J.-M.; Perna, P. Experimental technique for reducing contact and background noise in voltage spectral density measurements. *Rev. Sci. Instrum.* **2007**, *78*, 093905. [CrossRef]
16. Routoure, J.; Wu, S.; Barone, C.; Méchin, L.; Guillet, B. A Low-Noise and Quasi-Ideal DC Current Source Dedicated to Four-Probe Low-Frequency Noise Measurements. *IEEE Trans. Instrum. Meas.* **2020**, *69*, 194–200. [CrossRef]
17. Barone, C.; Rotzinger, H.; Mauro, C.; Dorer, D.; Münzberg, J.; Ustinov, A.V.; Pagano, S. Kondo-like transport and magnetic field effect of charge carrier fluctuations in granular aluminum oxide thin films. *Sci. Rep.* **2018**, *8*, 13892. [CrossRef]
18. Deutscher, G.; Bandyopadhyay, B.; Chui, T.; Lindenfeld, P.; McLean, W.L.; Worthington, T. Transition to Localization in Granular Aluminum Films. *Phys. Rev. Lett.* **1980**, *44*, 1150–1153. [CrossRef]
19. Chui, T.; Lindenfeld, P.; McLean, W.L.; Mui, K. Localization and Electron-Interaction Effects in the Magnetoresistance of Granular Aluminum. *Phys. Rev. Lett.* **1981**, *47*, 1617–1620. [CrossRef]
20. Bachar, N.; Lerer, S.; Hacohen-Gourgy, S.; Almog, B.; Deutscher, G. Kondo-like behavior near the metal-to-insulator transition of nanoscale granular aluminum. *Phys. Rev. B* **2013**, *87*, 214512. [CrossRef]
21. Gao, J.; Shen, S.Q.; Li, T.K.; Sun, J.R. Current-induced effect on the resistivity of epitaxial thin films of $La_{0.7}Ca_{0.3}MnO_3$ and $La_{0.85}Ba_{0.15}MnO_3$. *Appl. Phys. Lett.* **2003**, *82*, 4732–4734. [CrossRef]
22. Hu, F.X.; Gao, J. Unusual current-induced electroresistance in epitaxial thin films of $La_{0.8}Ca_{0.2}MnO_3$. *Phys. Rev. B* **2004**, *69*, 212413. [CrossRef]
23. Gao, J.; Hu, F.X. Current-sensitive electroresistance and the response to a magnetic field in $La_{0.8}Ca_{0.2}MnO_3$ epitaxial thin films. *J. Appl. Phys.* **2005**, *97*, 10H706. [CrossRef]
24. Barone, C.; Adamo, C.; Galdi, A.; Orgiani, P.; Petrov, A.Y.; Quaranta, O.; Maritato, L.; Pagano, S. Unusual dependence of resistance and voltage noise on current in $La_{1-x}Sr_xMnO_3$ ultrathin films. *Phys. Rev. B* **2007**, *75*, 174431. [CrossRef]
25. Slonczewski, J.C. Current-driven excitation of magnetic multilayers. *J. Magn. Magn. Mater.* **1996**, *159*, L1–L7. [CrossRef]
26. Berger, L. New origin for spin current and current-induced spin precession in magnetic multilayers. *J. Appl. Phys.* **2001**, *89*, 5521–5525. [CrossRef]
27. Wu, T.; Ogale, S.B.; Garrison, J.E.; Nagaraj, B.; Biswas, A.; Chen, Z.; Greene, R.L.; Ramesh, R.; Venkatesan, T.; Millis, A.J. Electroresistance and Electronic Phase Separation in Mixed-Valent Manganites. *Phys. Rev. Lett.* **2001**, *86*, 5998–6001. [CrossRef]

28. Markovich, V.; Rozenberg, E.; Yuzhelevski, Y.; Jung, G.; Gorodetsky, G.; Shulyatev, D.A.; Mukovskii, Y.M. Correlation between electroresistance and magnetoresistance in La$_{0.82}$Ca$_{0.18}$MnO$_3$ single crystal. *Appl. Phys. Lett.* **2001**, *78*, 3499–3501. [CrossRef]
29. Kogan, S. *Electronic Noise and Fluctuations in Solids*; Cambridge University Press: Cambridge, UK, 1996; ISBN 9780521460347.
30. Dolgin, B.; Lorite, I.; Kumar, Y.; Esquinazi, P.; Jung, G.; Straube, B.; de Heluani, S.P. Conductivity fluctuations in proton-implanted ZnO microwires. *Nanotechnology* **2016**, *27*, 305702. [CrossRef]
31. Barone, C.; Rotzinger, H.; Mauro, C.; Dorer, D.; Ustinov, A.V.; Pagano, S. Unconventional magnetic field effect on noise properties of AlO$_x$ thin films in Kondo-like transport regime. *Eur. Phys. J. Spec. Top.* **2019**, *228*, 697–702. [CrossRef]
32. Chen, C.C.; Chou, Y.C. Electrical-Conductivity Fluctuations near the Percolation Threshold. *Phys. Rev. Lett.* **1985**, *54*, 2529–2532. [CrossRef] [PubMed]
33. Rudman, D.A.; Calabrese, J.J.; Garland, J.C. Noise spectra of three-dimensional random metal-insulator composites. *Phys. Rev. B* **1986**, *33*, 1456–1459. [CrossRef] [PubMed]
34. Barone, C.; Pagano, S.; Neitzert, H.C. Transport and noise spectroscopy of MWCNT/HDPE composites with different nanotube concentrations. *J. Appl. Phys.* **2011**, *110*, 113716. [CrossRef]
35. Gefen, Y.; Shih, W.-H.; Laibowitz, R.B.; Viggiano, J.M. Nonlinear Behavior near the Percolation Metal-Insulator Transition. *Phys. Rev. Lett.* **1986**, *57*, 3097–3100. [CrossRef] [PubMed]
36. Nandi, U.N.; Mukherjee, C.D.; Bardhan, K.K. 1/f noise in nonlinear inhomogeneous systems. *Phys. Rev. B* **1996**, *54*, 12903–12914. [CrossRef] [PubMed]
37. Christen, T.; Donzel, L.; Greuter, F. Nonlinear resistive electric field grading part 1: Theory and simulation. *IEEE Electr. Insul. Mag.* **2010**, *26*, 47–59. [CrossRef]
38. Yang, X.; Hu, J.; Chen, S.; He, J. Understanding the Percolation Characteristics of Nonlinear Composite Dielectrics. *Sci. Rep.* **2016**, *6*, 30597. [CrossRef]

© 2020 by the authors. Licensee MDPI, Basel, Switzerland. This article is an open access article distributed under the terms and conditions of the Creative Commons Attribution (CC BY) license (http://creativecommons.org/licenses/by/4.0/).

*Article*

# Iron-Based Superconducting Nanowires: Electric Transport and Voltage-Noise Properties

Sergio Pagano [1,2,3,*], Nadia Martucciello [2,3], Emanuele Enrico [4], Eugenio Monticone [4], Kazumasa Iida [5] and Carlo Barone [1,2,3]

1. Dipartimento di Fisica "E.R. Caianiello", Università degli Studi di Salerno, I-84084 Fisciano, Salerno, Italy; cbarone@unisa.it
2. CNR-SPIN Salerno, c/o Università degli Studi di Salerno, I-84084 Fisciano, Salerno, Italy; nadia.martucciello@spin.cnr.it
3. INFN Gruppo Collegato di Salerno, c/o Università degli Studi di Salerno, I-84084 Fisciano, Salerno, Italy
4. Istituto Nazionale di Ricerca Metrologica, I-10135 Torino, Italy; e.enrico@inrim.it (E.E.); e.monticone@inrim.it (E.M.)
5. Department of Materials Physics, Nagoya University, Nagoya 464-8603, Japan; iida@mp.pse.nagoya-u.ac.jp
* Correspondence: spagano@unisa.it; Tel.: +39-089-968210

Received: 26 March 2020; Accepted: 20 April 2020; Published: 30 April 2020

**Abstract:** The discovery of iron-based superconductors paved the way for advanced possible applications, mostly in high magnetic fields, but also in electronics. Among superconductive devices, nanowire detectors have raised a large interest in recent years, due to their ability to detect a single photon in the visible and infrared (IR) spectral region. Although not yet optimal for single-photon detection, iron-based superconducting nanowire detectors would bring clear advantages due to their high operating temperature, also possibly profiting of other peculiar material properties. However, there are several challenges yet to be overcome, regarding mainly: fabrication of ultra-thin films, appropriate passivation techniques, optimization of nano-patterning, and high-quality electrical contacts. Test nanowire structures, made by ultra-thin films of Co-doped $BaFe_2As_2$, have been fabricated and characterized in their transport and intrinsic noise properties. The results on the realized nanostructures show good properties in terms of material resistivity and critical current. Details on the fabrication and low temperature characterization of the realized nanodevices are presented, together with a study of possible degradation phenomena induced by ageing effects.

**Keywords:** iron-based superconductors; nanowires; single-photon detectors

## 1. Introduction

Most widespread applications of superconducting nanowires regard their use as single-photon detectors, due to their ability in detecting single photons in the visible and IR spectral region [1,2]. Moreover, their peculiar physics has brought to the development of novel electronic cryodevices, such as pulse discriminators [3,4], logic gates [5], and also memory elements [6].

The interest in superconducting nanowires has also recently increased, due to their possible application in quantum technologies, including quantum sensing and computing. This has been highlighted in the case of $YBa_2Cu_3O_{7-x}$ (YBCO) nanowires with phase-slip dynamics, where evidence of energy-level quantization in the nanowires has been reported [7]. Moreover, it has also been shown that the absorption of a single photon changes the quantum state of the nanowire, an important result for the development of single-photon detectors with high operating temperature and superior temporal resolution [7].

Although traditional superconducting nanowire single-photon detectors (SNSPDs) have the advantage of offering single-photon sensitivity, combined with low dark count rates [8], low jitter [9], short recovery times, and free-running operation [2], one drawback is their low operating temperature. This is essentially due to the fact that current SNSPDs are fabricated using mostly conventional low-temperature superconductors, such as NbN and WSi [10,11], in order to achieve high sensitivity and to simplify nanofabrication processes. Several efforts have been made to realize nanowires with high critical temperature ($T_c$) materials, including $MgB_2$ and cuprate superconductors [12–15]. The recently discovered iron-based superconductors have attracted great interest to explore their potentialities in the field of large-scale current transport [16,17] and in microelectronics or nanoelectronics applications [18,19]. These compounds could pave a new way to the fabrication of superconducting nanowires, also profiting of intrinsic material properties to improve detection performances (in particular, speed and efficiency). In this respect some preliminary results are reported in [20]. However, there are several issues to be taken into account that are mainly related to the occurrence of non-hysteretic current-voltage characteristics (no switching), to the difficulty in fabricating ultra-thin films (dead layer problem of high-$T_c$ compounds), and to the easy surface degradation.

In order to overcome these difficulties and address these challenges, we have realized and tested a number of nanowires made of iron-based superconductors. A detailed investigation of their electric transport properties is reported in this work. In addition, a study of the charge carrier fluctuation effects, in a wide temperature range, has been carried out, in order to get useful information on the physics of the nanowires for the optimization of nanopatterning processes and for the realization of high-quality electrical contacts. To our knowledge, there are no other noise measurements on iron-based nanowires reported in the scientific literature. By means of noise spectroscopy, moreover, a deeper understanding of physical mechanisms and of ageing-induced degradation effects can be obtained, as already demonstrated for graphene [21,22], for iron-chalcogenide [23], and for the same Co-doped $BaFe_2As_2$ superconductors [24] used here. The reported experimental results, together with theoretical interpretations, may be useful in view of the fabrication of more performant and usable nanodevices.

## 2. Materials and Methods

A necessary starting point to realize a nanowire detector is a very thin superconducting film, ideally with a thickness of the order of the material coherence length, in order to maintain the superconductive state and maximize the photon energy sensitivity. However, the growth mechanism of high-$T_c$ superconductors is complex and often results in a "dead" layer at the interface with the substrate. Therefore, a compromise between thickness and film quality has to be achieved. In this respect, Co-doped $BaFe_2As_2$ superconducting thin films, with a thickness of about 20 nm, were grown, by using a pulsed laser deposition (PLD) technique, on 0.5-mm-thick $CaF_2$ (001) substrates. The choice of the Co doping level is done in order to optimize the superconducting transition temperature of the material [25]. This resulted in a nominal composition of the PLD target of Ba:Fe:Co:As = 1:1.84:0.16:2. The fabrication parameters, such as laser repetition frequency (7 Hz) and growth temperature (700 °C) [26], together with the choice of $CaF_2$ substrate, were selected in order to optimize the $T_c$ of the films, as well as other material properties [27]. The high phase purity of the target material and of the samples was observed with X-ray diffraction (Malvern Panalytical Ltd., Malvern, UK) and by using transmission electron microscopy (JEOL Ltd., Tokyo, Japan) the absence of appreciable defects was also verified [26]. Moreover, to reduce possible degradation effects due to ageing, an in-situ passivation process was employed, by depositing a thin layer of magnesium aluminate ($MgAl_2O_4$) spinel (MAS). Its high resistance against chemical attack, high thermal shock resistance and compatibility with a large variety of metals are important properties that make MAS very advantageous as a protective cap layer [28].

Subsequently, the superconducting films were patterned in the shape of several nanowires using a combination of optical and e-beam lithography and ion beam etching. The design used for the geometry definition, shown in Figure 1a, consists of a series of nanowires with a nominal width and length of 500 nm and 5 μm, respectively, each connected to 1 mm × 0.5 mm bonding pads. A 100 nm thick resist layer, type ma-N 2401, was used for reproducing the design on the samples (Figure 1b).

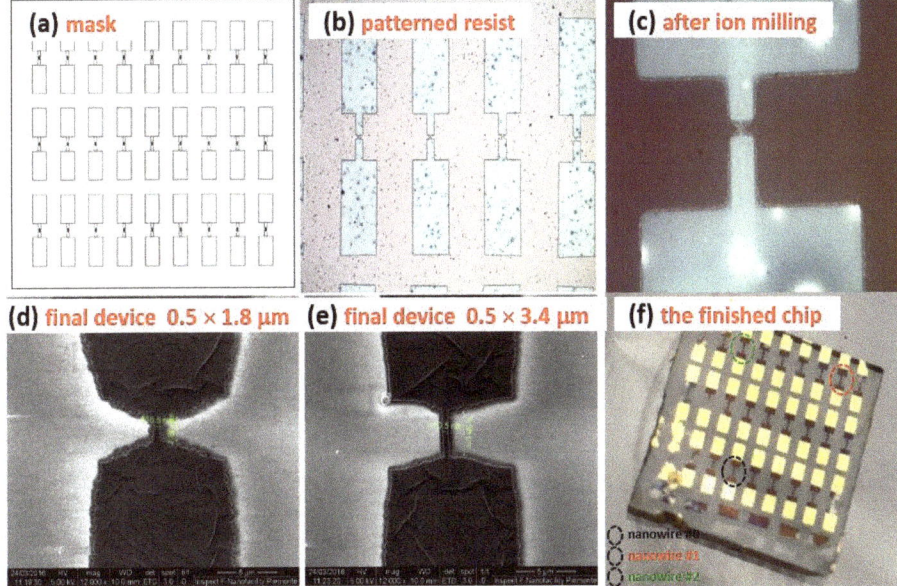

**Figure 1.** Microphotographs and images representing the different steps of the nanowires fabrication process: from the used mask design (**a**) to the finished 1 cm² chip, after electronic and optical lithography (**b–f**). The devices, whose experimental results are here reported and discussed, are evidenced with colorized circles.

A subsequent ion milling process (Figure 1c) defined the nanowire geometry. After etching, due to nanolithography process imperfections, the final devices realized showed different lengths, ranging from 1.8 (Figure 1d) to 3.4 µm (Figure 1e), while keeping the same width. Finally, to reduce the contact resistance, a thin layer of Ti/Au (5/50 nm) was deposited after Ar ion cleaning, on the contact pads area, obtaining the finished chip consisting of 27 separated devices. Among these, the ones here investigated are evidenced with circles of different colors and refer to pristine (black circle) and to two years-aged (red and green circles) nanostructures (see Figure 1f, for details).

All the electrical characterizations were performed in a closed cryocooler system, characterized by an operation temperature range from 8 to 325 K, with a temperature stabilization better than 0.2 K. Low-noise DC bias, and DC and AC readout electronics were used to record the sample electrical response, as shown Figure 2 [29]. In particular, the measurements were performed by using a two-probe technique (green box of Figure 2). A low-pass passive filter was inserted at the input of the bias current source, with a user variable series resistance $R_S$, much larger than the sample resistance $R_M$, and a cutoff frequency of few Hz (blue box of Figure 2). The output AC voltage was amplified by a low-noise instrumentation amplifier, model AD8429 having 1 nV/$\sqrt{Hz}$ noise level, (red box of Figure 2), and its spectral analysis was done by a dynamic signal analyzer model HP35670A. The DC voltage was amplified by a low noise instrumentation amplifier, model AD8221, and recorded by a digital voltmeter. The absence of unwanted contact noise contribution was verified by resorting to a specific procedure [30], whose validity has been already tested in the case of superconductors [31], innovative carbon nanotube and photovoltaic devices [32,33], and magnetic compounds [34,35]. The lowest noise level measured, corresponding to the instrumental background, was $1.71 \times 10^{-18}$ V²/Hz.

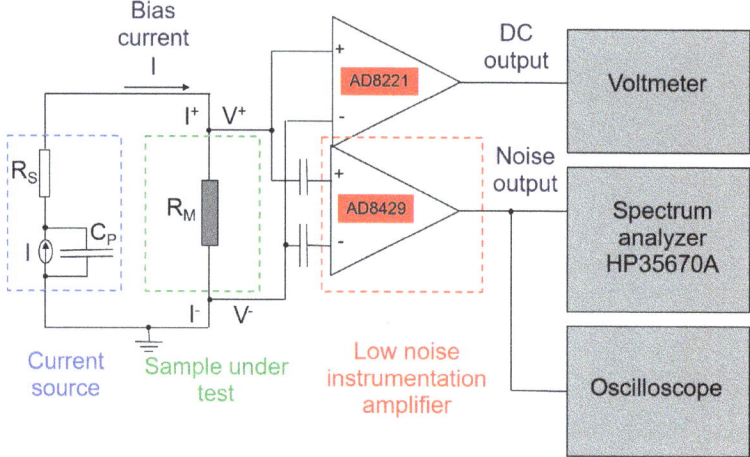

**Figure 2.** Schematic of the bias and readout electronics. The colored dashed boxes enclose the bias circuit (blue), the device under test (green), and the instrumentation amplifier (red). See text for details.

## 3. Results

*3.1. DC Electrical Transport Measurements*

The temperature dependence of the resistance of Co-doped BaFe$_2$As$_2$ nanowires was very similar to what already found for thin films [27]. In particular, the data in Figure 3a show a metallic behavior for temperatures higher than 100 K, both for the thin film (blue circles) and for a nanowire (black squares). A minimum of the resistivity was observed around 100 K, with an upturn down to the onset of superconductivity ($T_c^{onset}$), which was about 30 K for the thin film and 24 K for the nanowire. The difference in critical temperature was due to different film thickness, much larger in the case of the thin film. The resistance increase, observed by decreasing the temperature from 100 K to $T_c^{onset}$, can be attributed to the occurrence of localization effects [36]. In this respect, a detailed analysis, reported in [37], limits to variable-range hopping (VRH) or to weak-localization (WL) effects the possible explanation of the resistivity behavior. The DC measurements alone were not able to distinguish between the two mechanisms and, therefore, additional experimental investigations, such as noise spectroscopy, are necessary.

The results obtained by studying the fluctuation processes are shown in the following and will be useful to clarify this issue. The most evident difference between thin films and nanowires concerns the value of $T_c$. More in details, for the single nanowire the superconducting transition, defined at 50% of the normal-state resistance $R_N$, occurred at around 16 K and was significantly lower than that of the thin film. This fact, as already discussed above, was due to the choice of fabricating a very thin film for the nanowire sample, in order to boost the device sensitivity. The observed low $T_c$ was, however, larger than that of standard NbN nanowires (about 11 K). Moreover, as shown in Figure 3b, where the normalized resistance was reported in the superconducting transition region, after two years of ageing the nanodevices maintained comparable critical temperatures. This finding gives the important indication that iron-based nanowires, realized with the passivation process described above, do not show degradation of their superconducting properties after up to two years of storage at room temperature and normal atmosphere. This result might be very useful in technological applications requiring long-time operation and stable performances, as also strengthened by an evident homogeneous distribution of the critical temperatures all over the chip area. Such a feature is confirmed by the experimental data of Figure 3b, which refer to differently positioned nanowires.

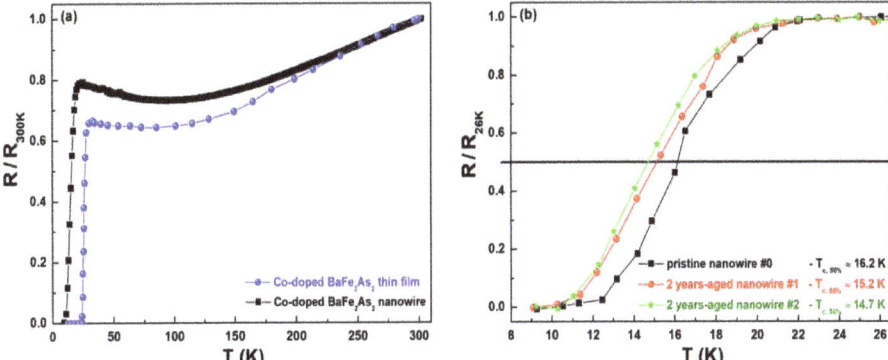

**Figure 3.** Resistance versus temperature plots. (**a**) The data refer to the resistance of thin films (blue circles) and of nanowires (black squares), normalized to their room temperature values. (**b**) An enlargement of the superconducting transition region is shown, where the resistances, normalized to their normal state values at $T = 26$ K, are reported for pristine and two years-aged nanostructures.

All the realized nanowires have non-hysteretic current–voltage (I–V) curves down to a temperature of 8 K, as shown in Figure 4a. Although the absence of degradation is a positive feature, the absence of hysteresis in I–V curves in the superconducting state is, instead, a negative point, when aiming at developing SNSPDs. It cannot be excluded that, by further lowering the temperature, a hysteretic I–V curve could be observed. However, as our aim was to realize high operating temperature nanowires, this is not of interest for this work. A critical current $I_c$ of the order of 10 µA is measured at 8 K, as shown in the inset of Figure 4a. A non-hysteretic behavior was also reported in [20] for iron-based superconductors and in [38,39] in the case of YBCO. Some hysteresis was observed for a YBCO microbridge (not a nanowire) at $T = 4$ K [40]. Compared to the reported results, the nanowires presented here have, however, the advantage of showing higher resistance values, similar to that of the low-$T_c$ nanowires. Figure 4b shows the DC current dependence of the nanowire differential resistance $R_D$ for various temperatures. A gradual change of $R_D$ can be observed in the temperature range across the superconducting transition up to the normal resistance value, of about 1200 Ω. In the inset are clearly visible abrupt changes in $R_D$ occurring at bias current of about 0.6–0.7 mA, both for positive and negative values. These are most probably due to the transition to the normal state of the large area structures (see Figure 1b). Overall, it is evident that iron-based nanowires do not yet show characteristics optimal for light detection. In order to get more information on the transport processes, noise measurement have been employed.

### 3.2. Voltage–Noise Spectral Density Measurements

The basic properties of random data in the time domain, known as noise or fluctuations, are described by the autocorrelation function. In the frequency domain, information on the noise mechanisms in action are obtained by the spectral density function $S_x$, which is the Fourier transform of the autocorrelation function, as derived from the Wiener–Khintchine theorem [41]. In condensed matter physics, the noise quantity usually measured is the spectral density of voltage fluctuations, whose frequency composition $S_V(f)$ gives indications on the different electric noise contributions. In particular, the most common types of low-frequency noises are: (I) Johnson or thermal noise, that is generated by the thermal agitation of the charge carriers inside an electrical conductor at equilibrium and is defined as $S_V = 4k_B TR$ (with $k_B$ the Boltzmann constant, $T$ the temperature, and $R$ the electrical resistance); (II) the shot noise, that is originated from the discrete nature of the electric charge and is defined as $S_V = 2eIR^2$ (with $e$ the electron charge, and $I$ the bias current); and (III) the $1/f$ or flicker noise, that is related to the ensemble average of thermally activated two levels random resistance fluctuations, due to intrinsic material aspects, such as grain boundaries, defects, etc. [41]. The noise of type (I) and (II) has frequency-independent spectral density amplitude ("white noise"), while noise type (III) has a clear frequency dependence ("colored noise").

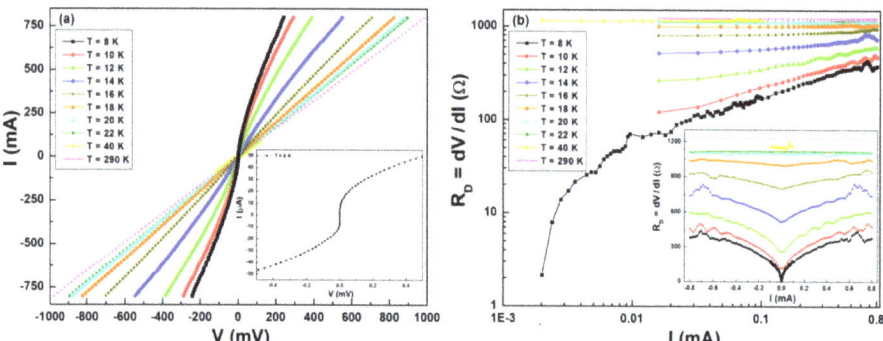

**Figure 4.** Current–voltage (I–V) characteristics. (**a**) The different curves refer to temperatures from 8 to 290 K. An enlargement of the I–V curve at the temperature of 8 K is shown in the inset. (**b**) The DC current dependence of the differential resistance $R_D$ is reported at different temperatures in the log-scale. In the inset, the full current range, spanning from negative to positive values, is shown using a linear-scale.

Both white and 1/f noise components were evident in the frequency dependence of $S_V$ for the iron-based nanowires investigated here, as shown in Figure 5 for two devices (nanowire #1 and nanowire #2 indicated in Figure 1f) and at the temperature of 290 K. More in details, the overall experimental noise spectral density can be modeled as:

$$S_V(I,T) = \frac{K(I,T)}{f} + S_0 + S_B \tag{1}$$

where $K(I,T)$ is the 1/f noise amplitude, dependent on bias current and temperature; $S_0$ is the "white noise" amplitude, which also may be bias and temperature dependent; $S_B$ is the instrumental background noise amplitude, in our case estimated to be a constant value of $1.71 \times 10^{-18}$ V$^2$/Hz (see Section 2). All the physical information on the transport processes resides in $K$ and $S_0$, whose analysis in temperature and in bias current can be very useful for understanding the dynamic processes of the charge carriers. It is worth noting that a similar approach has been used to study nanowires made of granular aluminum oxide [42].

The experimental data can be interpreted in terms of the model described in Equation (1) to obtain the temperature and bias current dependence of $K$ and $S_0$. In Figure 6a,b are shown the DC current dependencies of the 1/f and "white noise" amplitudes, respectively, at various temperatures near $T_c$. Figure 6a shows a noise peak occurring at both low temperatures and DC currents, with a characteristic slope of two, and a noise growth occurring at high temperatures and currents, with a characteristic slope of 1.4. Figure 6b shows a large noise peak at low currents and temperatures, in correspondence of the superconducting transition of the nanowire, and a noise increase at larger temperatures, almost current independent.

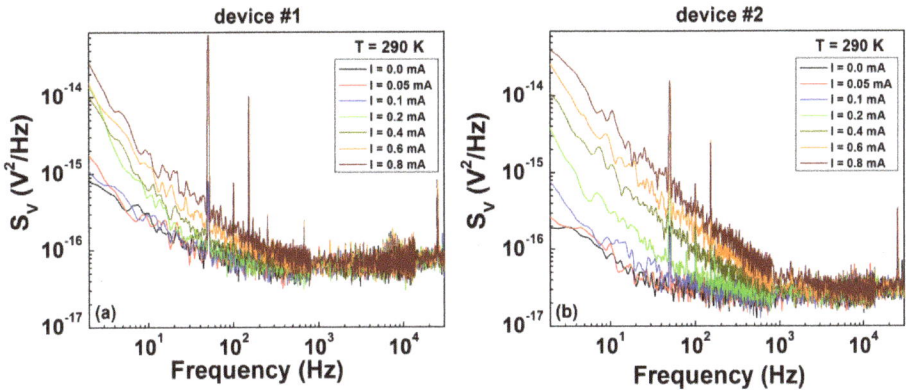

**Figure 5.** Voltage-spectral density traces. The frequency dependence of $S_V$ is shown for two different devices of the same chip, device #1 (**a**) and device #2 (**b**), at room temperature (290 K) and for bias currents ranging from 0 to 0.8 mA.

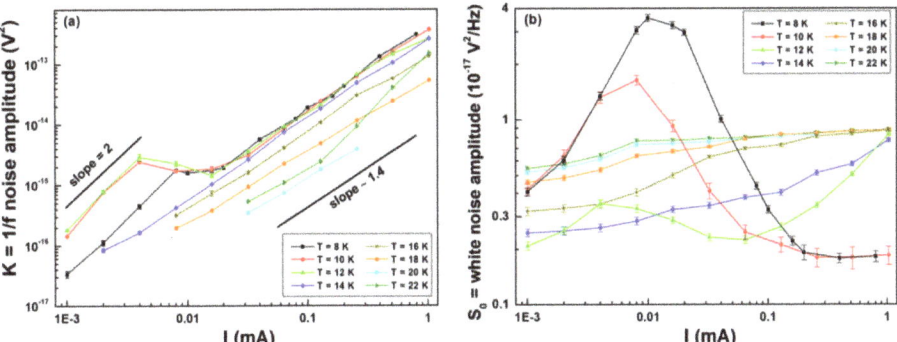

**Figure 6.** Electric noise amplitudes behavior. The dependencies on bias current, and at several temperatures, are shown for the $1/f$ (**a**) and for the "white" (**b**) noise components, respectively.

To better appreciate the dependence of the noise on temperature and bias current, the experimental data can be shown in three-dimensional (3D) plots. In Figure 7a the $1/f$ noise amplitude $K$ is plotted, with a linear temperature and bias current scale, and three noise peaks, evidenced by arrows, are clearly visible. The peaks indicated by the green and red arrows are expected and are due to percolation fluctuations occurring in the transition region of the nanowire (red arrow) and of the large area region (green arrow), respectively, where the superconductor is a mixture of normal metallic and superconducting phases [41,43,44]. On the contrary, the strong increase of the $1/f$ noise at low temperatures and high currents (blue arrow in Figure 7a) cannot be explained by reported theoretical interpretations and deserves more investigation in the next future.

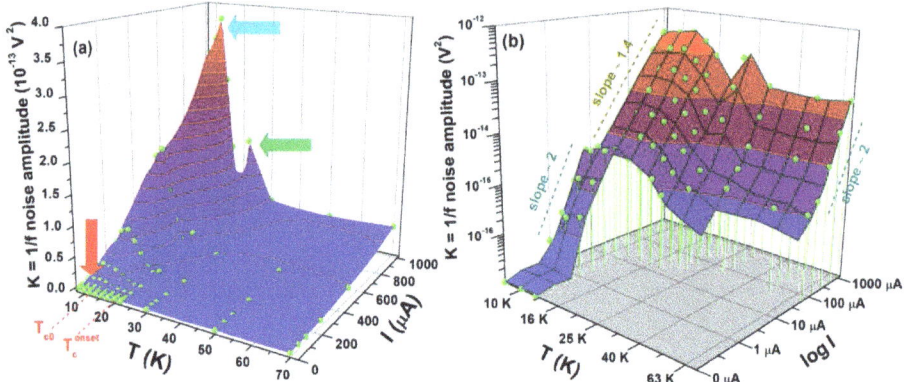

**Figure 7.** Amplitude of the 1/f noise component. The temperature and bias current dependencies of the 1/f noise are shown by using linear-axes scales (**a**) and logarithmic-axes scales (**b**) for the noise amplitude and for the bias current. The 1/f noise peaks at different temperatures are indicated with colorized arrows in panel (**a**). The bias current slopes are explicitly reported in panel (**b**).

The same behavior of the 1/f noise amplitude is shown in Figure 7b by using a linear temperature x-scale and a logarithmic bias current and noise scale. This choice allows evidencing the power law dependence of the noise amplitude on bias current. The figure shows a (standard) quadratic dependence at low temperatures and below $I_c$. This is expected according to a simple percolation model describing the full superconducting regime [41,43,44]. Unexpectedly, a current slope of 1.4 is observed for temperatures up to $T_c^{onset}$ and for higher currents than $I_c$. This unusual finding may be connected with the unusual 1/f noise peak and could reveal the activation of additional noise sources that occurs in a region where the nanowire is already in the normal state but the thin-film part is still superconducting. This "intermediate" regime is characterized by a strong non-uniform conductivity, which could be responsible for both the high noise level and its non-standard bias current dependence. Additionally, the graph of Figure 7b shows that, at temperatures above $T_c^{onset}$, where the nanowire normal resistivity is characterized by a metal-insulator behavior, the current slope of the 1/f noise is again quadratic. This finding excludes the presence of WL effects, which appear as a linear current dependence of the 1/f noise component [45,46], while indicates the occurrence of VRH conductivity in the insulating regime and of resistance fluctuation processes in the metallic region [37,41].

The temperature and bias current dependence of the "white noise" $S_0$ amplitude, shown in Figure 8, has a peculiar behavior. $S_0$ has a maximum at low currents (centered near $I_c$) and low temperatures (when the nanowire is superconducting), and seems to peak when the bias current reaches the critical one of the nanowire. Moreover, $S_0$ has a smaller peak near $T_c^{onset}$, where the large area regions start their superconducting transition. At larger current and higher temperature, the "white noise" amplitude tends to become current independent and to approach the standard Johnson noise value. These experimental findings are new and, to our knowledge, not been reported in literature.

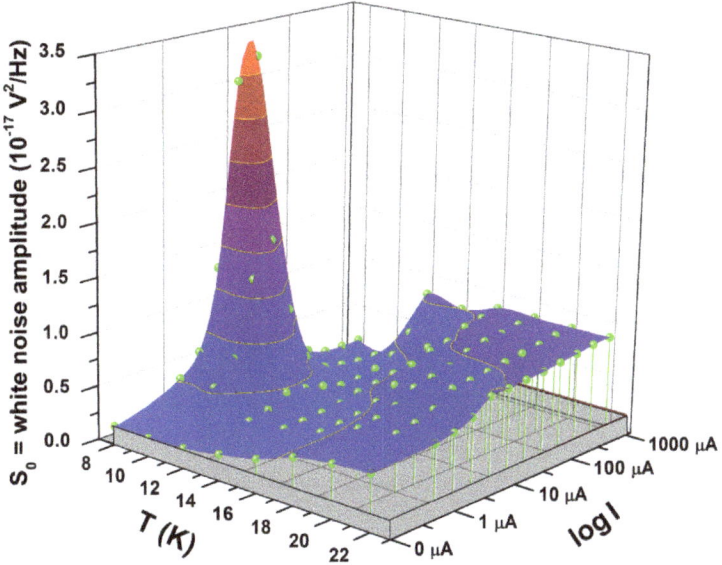

**Figure 8.** Amplitude of the "white noise" component. The temperature and bias current dependencies of the "white noise" are shown by using linear-axes scales for the noise amplitude and for the temperature, and logarithmic-axis scale for the bias current. The instrumental background noise is also shown as a gray floor.

## 4. Conclusions

Nanowire structures were realized using ultra-thin films of Co-doped $BaFe_2As_2$. The sample fabrication and nanolithography techniques were optimized to preserve the superconducting properties of the material. The resulting critical temperature, about 16 K, was reduced of only 1 K after two years of room temperature and ambient atmosphere storage, showing that degradation effects due to ageing were not relevant. Due to their high superconducting transition temperature, iron-based nanowires represent an interesting alternative to NbN-based nanowires, whose critical temperature was about 10 K in ultra-thin film devices, for application as single-photon detectors. However, additional improvements in the fabrication technology are needed in order to achieve hysteretic $I$–$V$ characteristic, a necessary ingredient for SSPD device. In this respect, a deep investigation of the transport mechanism in these devices is important, and it has been shown that noise spectroscopy can provide useful information. The study of the noise sources and their effect on dark counts, combined with the photo-response analysis, is currently in progress with the aim of developing useful single photon detectors operating at temperature above 10 K.

**Author Contributions:** S.P., N.M. and C.B. conceived and designed the experiments; S.P. and C.B. performed the experiments; S.P., N.M., K.I. and C.B. analyzed the data; E.E., E.M. and K.I. contributed materials/analysis tools; S.P. and C.B. wrote the paper. All authors have read and agreed to the published version of the manuscript.

**Funding:** This research received no external funding.

**Acknowledgments:** The authors would like to thank S. Abate of CNR-SPIN Salerno (Italy) for his technical support. The nanowires patterning has been performed at NanoFacility Piemonte, INRiM, a laboratory supported by Compagnia di San Paolo. S.P., N.M. and C.B. acknowledge partial support from University of Salerno through grants FARB17PAGAN and FARB18CAVAL, and from INFN through experiment FEEL.

**Conflicts of Interest:** The authors declare no conflict of interest.

## References

1. Gol'tsman, G.N.; Okunev, O.; Chulkova, G.; Lipatov, A.; Semenov, A.; Smirnov, K.; Voronov, B.; Dzardanov, A.; Williams, C.; Sobolewski, R. Picosecond superconducting single-photon optical detector. *Appl. Phys. Lett.* **2001**, *79*, 705–707. [CrossRef]
2. Natarajan, C.M.; Tanner, M.G.; Hadfield, R.H. Superconducting nanowire single-photon detectors: Physics and applications. *Supercond. Sci. Technol.* **2012**, *25*, 063001. [CrossRef]
3. Quaranta, O.; Marchetti, S.; Martucciello, N.; Pagano, S.; Ejrnaes, M.; Cristiano, R.; Nappi, C. Superconductive Three-Terminal Amplifier/Discriminator. *IEEE Trans. Appl. Supercond.* **2009**, *19*, 367–370. [CrossRef]
4. Ejrnaes, M.; Casaburi, A.; Cristiano, R.; Martucciello, N.; Mattioli, F.; Gaggero, A.; Leoni, R.; Villégier, J.-C.; Pagano, S. Characterization of superconducting pulse discriminators based on parallel NbN nanostriplines. *Supercond. Sci. Technol.* **2011**, *24*, 035018. [CrossRef]
5. Zhao, Q.-Y.; Toomey, E.A.; Butters, B.A.; McCaughan, A.N.; Dane, A.E.; Nam, S.-W.; Berggren, K.K. A compact superconducting nanowire memory element operated by nanowire cryotrons. *Supercond. Sci. Technol.* **2018**, *31*, 035009. [CrossRef]
6. Pagano, S.; Martucciello, N.; Bobba, F.; Carapella, G.; Attanasio, C.; Cirillo, C.; Cristiano, R.; Lisitskiy, M.; Ejrnaes, M.; Pepe, G.P.; et al. Proposal for a Nanoscale Superconductive Memory. *IEEE Trans. Appl. Supercond.* **2017**, *27*, 1801004. [CrossRef]
7. Lyatti, M.; Wolff, M.A.; Gundareva, I.; Kruth, M.; Ferrari, S.; Dunin-Borkowski, R.E.; Schuck, C. Energy-level quantization and single-photon control of phase slips in $YBa_2Cu_3O_{7-x}$ nanowires. *Nat. Commun.* **2020**, *11*, 763. [CrossRef]
8. Ejrnaes, M.; Casaburi, A.; Cristiano, R.; Quaranta, O.; Marchetti, S.; Pagano, S. Maximum count rate of large area superconducting single photon detectors. *J. Mod. Opt.* **2009**, *56*, 390–394. [CrossRef]
9. Ejrnaes, M.; Casaburi, A.; Cristiano, R.; Quaranta, O.; Marchetti, S.; Martucciello, N.; Pagano, S.; Gaggero, A.; Mattioli, F.; Leoni, R.; et al. Timing jitter of cascade switch superconducting nanowire single photon detectors. *Appl. Phys. Lett.* **2009**, *95*, 132503. [CrossRef]
10. Leoni, R.; Mattioli, F.; Castellano, M.G.; Cibella, S.; Carelli, P.; Pagano, S.; Perez de Lara, D.; Ejrnaes, M.; Lisitskyi, M.P.; Esposito, E.; et al. Fabrication and test of Superconducting Single Photon Detectors. *Nucl. Instrum. Methods Phys. Res. A* **2006**, *559*, 564–566. [CrossRef]
11. Pagano, S.; Martucciello, N.; Cristiano, R.; Ejrnaes, M.; Casaburi, A.; Leoni, R.; Gaggero, A.; Mattioli, F.; Villegier, J.C.; Cavalier, P. Nano-Strip Three-Terminal Superconducting Device for Cryogenic Detector Readout. *IEEE Trans. Appl. Supercond.* **2011**, *21*, 717–720. [CrossRef]
12. Shibata, H.; Takesue, H.; Honjo, T.; Akazaki, T.; Tokura, Y. Single-photon detection using magnesium diboride superconducting nanowires. *Appl. Phys. Lett.* **2010**, *97*, 212504. [CrossRef]
13. Zhang, C.; Wang, D.; Liu, Z.-H.; Zhang, Y.; Ma, P.; Feng, Q.-R.; Wang, Y.; Gan, Z.-Z. Fabrication of superconducting nanowires from ultrathin $MgB_2$ films via focused ion beam milling. *AIP Adv.* **2015**, *5*, 027139. [CrossRef]
14. Shibata, H.; Kirigane, N.; Fukao, K.; Sakai, D.; Karimoto, S.; Yamamoto, H. Photoresponse of a $La_{1.85}Sr_{0.15}CuO_4$ nanostrip. *Supercond. Sci. Technol.* **2017**, *30*, 074001. [CrossRef]
15. Arpaia, R.; Golubev, D.; Baghdadi, R.; Ciancio, R.; Dražić, G.; Orgiani, P.; Montemurro, D.; Bauch, T.; Lombardi, F. Transport properties of ultrathin $YBa_2Cu_3O_{7-\delta}$ nanowires: A route to single-photon detection. *Phys. Rev. B* **2017**, *96*, 064525. [CrossRef]
16. Ma, Y. Progress in wire fabrication of iron-based superconductors. *Supercond. Sci. Technol.* **2012**, *25*, 113001. [CrossRef]
17. Ma, Y. Development of high-performance iron-based superconducting wires and tapes. *Phys. C Supercond. Appl.* **2015**, *516*, 17–26. [CrossRef]
18. Hiramatsu, H.; Katase, T.; Kamiya, T.; Hosono, H. Thin Film Growth and Device Fabrication of Iron-Based Superconductors. *J. Phys. Soc. Jpn.* **2011**, *81*, 011011. [CrossRef]
19. Seidel, P. Josephson effects in iron based superconductors. *Supercond. Sci. Technol.* **2011**, *24*, 043001. [CrossRef]
20. Yuan, P.; Xu, Z.; Li, C.; Quan, B.; Li, J.; Gu, C.; Ma, Y. Transport properties of ultrathin $BaFe_{1.84}Co_{0.16}As_2$ superconducting nanowires. *Supercond. Sci. Technol.* **2018**, *31*, 025002. [CrossRef]
21. DiCarlo, L.; Williams, J.R.; Zhang, Y.; McClure, D.T.; Marcus, C.M. Shot Noise in Graphene. *Phys. Rev. Lett.* **2008**, *100*, 156801. [CrossRef] [PubMed]

22. Laitinen, A.; Paraoanu, G.S.; Oksanen, M.; Craciun, M.F.; Russo, S.; Sonin, E.; Hakonen, P. Contact doping, Klein tunneling, and asymmetry of shot noise in suspended graphene. *Phys. Rev. B* **2016**, *93*, 115413. [CrossRef]
23. Mauro, C.; Barone, C.; Pagano, S.; Imai, Y.; Nabeshima, F.; Maeda, A. Noise Spectroscopy Investigation of Aging-Induced Degradation in Iron-Chalcogenide Superconductors. *IEEE Trans. Appl. Supercond.* **2017**, *27*, 7300804. [CrossRef]
24. Barone, C.; Romeo, F.; Pagano, S.; Adamo, M.; Nappi, C.; Sarnelli, E.; Kurth, F.; Iida, K. Probing transport mechanisms of BaFe$_2$As$_2$ superconducting films and grain boundary junctions by noise spectroscopy. *Sci. Rep.* **2014**, *4*, 6163. [CrossRef] [PubMed]
25. Kurth, F.; Iida, K.; Trommler, S.; Hänisch, J.; Nenkov, K.; Engelmann, J.; Oswald, S.; Werner, J.; Schultz, L.; Holzapfel, B.; et al. Electronic phase diagram of disordered Co doped BaFe$_2$As$_{2-\delta}$. *Supercond. Sci. Technol.* **2013**, *26*, 025014. [CrossRef]
26. Kurth, F.; Reich, E.; Hänisch, J.; Ichinose, A.; Tsukada, I.; Hühne, R.; Trommler, S.; Engelmann, J.; Schultz, L.; Holzapfel, B.; et al. Versatile fluoride substrates for Fe-based superconducting thin films. *Appl. Phys. Lett.* **2013**, *102*, 142601. [CrossRef]
27. Ichinose, A.; Tsukada, I.; Nabeshima, F.; Imai, Y.; Maeda, A.; Kurth, F.; Holzapfel, B.; Iida, K.; Ueda, S.; Naito, M. Induced lattice strain in epitaxial Fe-based superconducting films on CaF$_2$ substrates: A comparative study of the microstructures of SmFeAs(O,F), Ba(Fe,Co)$_2$As$_2$, and FeTe$_{0.5}$Se$_{0.5}$. *Appl. Phys. Lett.* **2014**, *104*, 122603. [CrossRef]
28. Ganesh, I. A review on magnesium aluminate (MgAl$_2$O$_4$) spinel: Synthesis, processing and applications. *Int. Mater. Rev.* **2013**, *58*, 63–112. [CrossRef]
29. Routoure, J.; Wu, S.; Barone, C.; Méchin, L.; Guillet, B. A Low-Noise and Quasi-Ideal DC Current Source Dedicated to Four-Probe Low-Frequency Noise Measurements. *IEEE Trans. Instrum. Meas.* **2020**, *69*, 194–200. [CrossRef]
30. Barone, C.; Galdi, A.; Pagano, S.; Quaranta, O.; Méchin, L.; Routoure, J.-M.; Perna, P. Experimental technique for reducing contact and background noise in voltage spectral density measurements. *Rev. Sci. Instrum.* **2007**, *78*, 093905. [CrossRef]
31. Barone, C.; Pagano, S.; Pallecchi, I.; Bellingeri, E.; Putti, M.; Ferdeghini, C. Thermal and voltage activated excess 1/f noise in FeTe$_{0.5}$Se$_{0.5}$ epitaxial thin films. *Phys. Rev. B* **2011**, *83*, 134523. [CrossRef]
32. Barone, C.; Landi, G.; Mauro, C.; Neitzert, H.C.; Pagano, S. Universal crossover of the charge carrier fluctuation mechanism in different polymer/carbon nanotubes composites. *Appl. Phys. Lett.* **2015**, *107*, 143106. [CrossRef]
33. Landi, G.; Barone, C.; Mauro, C.; Neitzert, H.C.; Pagano, S. A noise model for the evaluation of defect states in solar cells. *Sci. Rep.* **2016**, *6*, 29685. [CrossRef] [PubMed]
34. Barone, C.; Galdi, A.; Lampis, N.; Maritato, L.; Granozio, F.M.; Pagano, S.; Perna, P.; Radovic, M.; Scotti Di Uccio, U. Charge density waves enhance the electronic noise of manganites. *Phys. Rev. B Condens. Matter Mater. Phys.* **2009**, *80*, 115128. [CrossRef]
35. Asa, M.; Autieri, C.; Barone, C.; Mauro, C.; Picozzi, S.; Pagano, S.; Cantoni, M. Detecting antiferromagnetism in tetragonal Cr$_2$O$_3$ by electrical measurements. *Phys. Rev. B* **2019**, *100*, 174423. [CrossRef]
36. Lee, P.A.; Ramakrishnan, T.V. Disordered electronic systems. *Rev. Mod. Phys.* **1985**, *57*, 287–337. [CrossRef]
37. Pagano, S.; Barone, C.; Martucciello, N.; Enrico, E.; Croin, L.; Monticone, E.; Iida, K.; Kurth, F. Co-Doped BaFe$_2$As$_2$ Superconducting Nanowires for Detector Applications. *IEEE Trans. Appl. Supercond.* **2018**, *28*, 2200204. [CrossRef]
38. Papari, G.; Carillo, F.; Stornaiuolo, D.; Massarotti, D.; Longobardi, L.; Beltram, F.; Tafuri, F. Dynamics of vortex matter in YBCO sub-micron bridges. *Phys. C* **2014**, *506*, 188–194. [CrossRef]
39. Arpaia, R.; Ejrnaes, M.; Parlato, L.; Cristiano, R.; Arzeo, M.; Bauch, T.; Nawaz, S.; Tafuri, F.; Pepe, G.P.; Lombardi, F. Highly homogeneous YBCO/LSMO nanowires for photoresponse experiments. *Supercond. Sci. Technol.* **2014**, *27*, 044027. [CrossRef]
40. Ejrnaes, M.; Parlato, L.; Arpaia, R.; Bauch, T.; Lombardi, F.; Cristiano, R.; Tafuri, F.; Pepe, G.P. Observation of dark pulses in 10 nm thick YBCO nanostrips presenting hysteretic current voltage characteristics. *Supercond. Sci. Technol.* **2017**, *30*, 12LT02. [CrossRef]
41. Kogan, S. *Electronic Noise and Fluctuations in Solids*; Cambridge University Press: Cambridge, UK, 1996; ISBN 9780521460347.

42. Barone, C.; Rotzinger, H.; Voss, N.J.; Mauro, C.; Schön, Y.; Ustinov, V.A.; Pagano, S. Current-Resistance Effects Inducing Nonlinear Fluctuation Mechanisms in Granular Aluminum Oxide Nanowires. *Nanomaterials* **2020**, *10*, 524. [CrossRef] [PubMed]
43. Testa, J.A.; Song, Y.; Chen, X.D.; Golben, J.; Lee, S.-I.; Patton, B.R.; Gaines, J.R. 1/f-noise-power measurements of copper oxide superconductors in the normal and superconducting states. *Phys. Rev. B* **1988**, *38*, 2922–2925. [CrossRef] [PubMed]
44. Kiss, L.B.; Svedlindh, P. New Noise Exponents in Random Conductor-Superconductor and Conductor-Insulator Mixtures. *Phys. Rev. Lett.* **1993**, *71*, 2817–2820. [CrossRef] [PubMed]
45. Barone, C.; Romeo, F.; Galdi, A.; Orgiani, P.; Maritato, L.; Guarino, A.; Nigro, A.; Pagano, S. Universal origin of unconventional 1/f noise in the weak-localization regime. *Phys. Rev. B* **2013**, *87*, 245113. [CrossRef]
46. Barone, C.; Romeo, F.; Pagano, S.; Attanasio, C.; Carapella, G.; Cirillo, C.; Galdi, A.; Grimaldi, G.; Guarino, A.; Leo, A.; et al. Nonequilibrium fluctuations as a distinctive feature of weak localization. *Sci. Rep.* **2015**, *5*, 10705. [CrossRef]

© 2020 by the authors. Licensee MDPI, Basel, Switzerland. This article is an open access article distributed under the terms and conditions of the Creative Commons Attribution (CC BY) license (http://creativecommons.org/licenses/by/4.0/).

MDPI
St. Alban-Anlage 66
4052 Basel
Switzerland
Tel. +41 61 683 77 34
Fax +41 61 302 89 18
www.mdpi.com

*Nanomaterials* Editorial Office
E-mail: nanomaterials@mdpi.com
www.mdpi.com/journal/nanomaterials

www.ingramcontent.com/pod-product-compliance
Lightning Source LLC
LaVergne TN
LVHW070044120526
838202LV00101B/431